TWENTY FIVE MILK RUNS

(And a few others)

To Hell's Angels and back

Richard Riley Johnson

Printed in Victoria, Canada

Note for Librarians: a cataloguing record for this book that includes Dewey Classification and US Library of Congress numbers is available from the National Library of Canada. The complete cataloguing record can be obtained from the National Library's online database at: www.nlc-bnc.ca/amicus/index-e.html
ISBN 1-4120-2501-X

TRAFFORD

This book was published *on-demand* in cooperation with Trafford Publishing.
On-demand publishing is a unique process and service of making a book available for retail sale to the public taking advantage of on-demand manufacturing and Internet marketing. **On-demand publishing** includes promotions, retail sales, manufacturing, order fulfilment, accounting and collecting royalties on behalf of the author.

Suite 6E, 2333 Government St., Victoria, B.C. V8T 4P4, CANADA

Phone	250-383-6864	Toll-free	1-888-232-4444 (Canada & US)
Fax	250-383-6804	E-mail	sales@trafford.com
Web site	www.trafford.com		

TRAFFORD PUBLISHING IS A DIVISION OF TRAFFORD HOLDINGS LTD.
Trafford Catalogue #04-0329   www.trafford.com/robots/04-0329.html

10   9   8   7   6   5   4   3   2   1

The combat narrative in this book is dedicated to my buddies who did not return from the most dangerous place one could be in world war two: The skies over Europe.

To my wife, Majorie who has tolerated me for more than fifty years. And our children, Carl, Leslie and Brenda who bugged me to write this memoir.

TABLE OF CONTENTS

Chapter 1

INTRODUCTION: How it all began.

It may seem a little unusual that a former sharecropper, migrant farm worker with only a high school education could one day be pilot of a large four-engine bomber. But this is the way it happened.

My parents moved about the mid-west and south during the Great Depression, looking for a better life, but seldom finding anything to better themselves. Unfortunately, they chose an area of the country that was in the worst possible location for jobs and security during a major depression.

I was born at 231 West Water St. in Piqua, Ohio on Friday, March 10, 1922, at 7:45 PM. Mom was attended by mid-wife, Edith Popp, and later by Dr. J. T. Beachler. It seems that I was an accident caused by ignorance. My folks believed that a woman couldn't get pregnant while nursing another child. It was when my brother, Harold, started getting sick that they discovered that Mom was pregnant again. At this time Dad was working at a pool hall-restaurant owned by Dick Shepard. He told Dad that if I was a boy and they named me after him, he would buy me my first pair of long pants.

So my first name became Richard. My middle name, Riley, was for my paternal grandfather. Unfortunately for Dick Shepard, he never got to buy me those long pants, as his girl friend did him in with a handgun when I was about four years old.

Harold had been born on December 13, 1920 while my folks were living in Naylor, Missouri, where they had met a year earlier, near Poplar Bluff.

Before I was born, Dad took a job with Huntzinger's Photography doing all kinds of photo work. He did photos of the dirigible "Shenandoah" after it crashed near Caldwell, Ohio on the early morning hours of September 3rd, 1925. It was the first U. S. built

1

dirigible that was helium filled, instead of the highly combustible hydrogen. It was the weather related crash of this dirigible that caused General Billy Mitchell to go off the deep end with his insubordinate statements about Dirigible vulnerability to the army, causing his famous court-martial.

Dad traveled as far as Florida, doing layouts for school pictures. He also managed the Huntzinger baseball team, which played the local circuits. One of the earliest photos of me is in the back of a Model T Ford touring car with Mom and Harold. We are in the background of the team photo during the start of the 1922-baseball season. A year and eight months after I was born, my younger brother, Lora Lewis Johnson, Jr. was born. Lora was a girl's name bestowed on Dad by his father. Grandpa liked the name so much that he said his next child would have that name, whether girl or boy. It reminds one of the song; " A Boy Named Sue."

Sadly, at age four, Lora Jr. contracted rheumatic fever and died.

We moved about Piqua quite a bit, and when I started kindergarten in 1927 at Bennett School, which taught classes through eighth grade, future air ace Don S. Gentile was in the first grade there. I easily remember my first day at kindergarten when the teacher gave us some modeling clay to play with. I remember making two small wheels on an axle and rolling them down the desk. I had never seen modeling clay before.

Also, four of the later to be famous Mills Brothers attended the upper grades there at Bennett. These four teens were a regular sight in downtown Piqua, singing on street corners. They were extremely good, and managed to get a few donations. They later became world famous as a black quartet, singing soft rhythm songs. The Bennett school was integrated, as were all schools in Ohio, and during a talent contest held on the stage at Bennett, the Mills Brothers were easy winners, which may have been their start in the commercial world of music.

While we lived near the corner of Main and Wayne Streets, Don Gentile lived with his parents near Wayne and South Streets about a block away. Having gotten really muddy one day, we saw his mother in the yard hosing him down before he could go into the house.

Don went into combat early in 1943 and by April 5, 1944 was

the top ace, having scored 27 kills. He was sent back to the states on a recruiting and bond tour, leaving the door open for Gabby Grabowski to exceed his record. Don had only been back in the States a short time when on May 20th, 1944, he met his future wife, and childhood friend, Isabella Masdea, and they fell in love almost at first sight. Don received a hero's welcome in Piqua, and the entire town turned out to greet their hometown hero.

Before he went into the service, Don had flown his small private Aero Sport single-seat Biplane under the "Iron" Bridge, known locally as the "Oatmeal" Bridge, and over the "Shawnee" bridge. Both Bridges are about thirty feet or less over the Miami River that runs through the heart of Piqua. He received a reprimand for this stunt, but he was unfazed by such a minor thing.

After World War Two, Don was assigned to the P-80, Shooting Star and its trainer version, T-33, out of Andrews Air Force Base in Washington DC He was killed in a disabled T-33 while trying to avoid a built-up area near Morningside, just outside Andrews Field on January 28, 1951. A ground crewman had asked Don to take him for a ride in the T-33, which is a two-seat trainer version of the P-80, Shooting star.

According to the radio monitor, Don had told the enlisted man to bail out when the plane malfunctioned, but he had not done so because of fear or panic. Don had no choice but to try to bring the disabled plane to Andrews Field, but if fell short and crashed, killing both men. After six years of marriage and three children, Isabella was a widow. Don had earned almost every combat medal, and was almost awarded the Medal of Honor. Eight years after Don's death, Isabella married Air Force Colonel Jesse Beitman, and they still live in a suburb of Columbus, Ohio.

When Don's parents emigrated from Italy, they Americanized their last name to Gen-tile. As he grew up, Don preferred the European, Gen-tilly, or Gen-tilee, as it would have been in Italy. A distant cousin of Don's, Joe Gentile, is a spokesman for the Washington DC Police department who still uses the Americanized version. At any rate, the Gentile family was well off financially and Don's father learned to fly during the First World War. He was building a plane in his back yard when my family left Piqua.

Don learned to fly as a teenager and soon bought an early Aero Sports biplane One day, according to stories, (which later turned out to be an exaggeration), he landed the little plane in the back yard of his girl friend, Marji Dill. After a visit, he found that there was not enough room for take off, and he had to remove the wings and tow it back to the airport. This story must have been told as a joke. Perhaps it came about because of an emergency landing Don made in a cornfield shortly after he bought the plane. He destroyed several rows of corn in a field about midway between the Greenville airport and the town of Covington, Ohio. The farmer was quite upset about it and I never heard if Don paid for the damage to the corn. Don did buzz Marji's house on occasion as well as the home of Betty Levering.

Don's father had bought a Lincoln V-12 Coupe that Don drove around Piqua just before he joined the Royal Canadian Air Force in 1940.

(The following is from a letter from Don's widow, dated June 2, 1997)

"After graduation from high school Don's parents wanted him to go to college, but with the impending war, Don wanted to join the Army Air Corps. To do that, he needed two years of college so he decided to join the Royal Canadian Air Force. Don enlisted in the RAF in September 1940 and got his wings a year later. He was commissioned a Pilot Officer in the RAF on November 11, 1941. After getting his wings in Canada Don was sent to the Eagle Squadron in England."

"During Operation Jubilee, Don got his first victory: A German Junkers 88 and a Folke-Wolfe 190 over Dieppe."
"When America got into the war, Don transferred over to the 8th Air Force and on April 2, 1943 they went from the Spitfire to the P-47 Thunderbolt."

"On April 6, 1944 Don got his 27th plane destroyed and was the first one to break Eddie Rickenbacher's record of 26. Don's record was 30 planes destroyed. He did receive just about every decoration except the Medal of Honor. His commander put him in for it but when he crashed his plane on his last mission, the commander was so upset that he withdrew the commendation."

(Signed) Isabella Gentile Beitman (Don's widow, in her own words)

Piqua is also the home of the Hartzell Propeller factory, where Mom's brother, Charles worked. At that time, in the early 1920s the plant made industrial fans and gunstocks of American Black Walnut lumber. The gunstocks were made of stumps because of the beautiful grain. Uncle Charles almost lost his life there in later years. A machine that ground up waste wood sometimes became clogged, and needed to be cleared away. His rule was to always turn off the machine for this purpose. Except one day. He decided that it was a minor clog, and so stuck a crow bar into the blades a little too far. A blade caught the end of the crow bar and rammed it down, thus causing the hooked end to catch under his jaw, ripping away a large portion of his lower jaw and severing his carotid artery. Quick action by a fellow worker saved his life. He carried a terrible scar the rest of his life. It impressed me first hand, how a moment's inattention can destroy one's life.

What kid hasn't licked an icicle? One night we had a freezing rain, and with the sun shining brightly next morning, I went to kindergarten with the whole world glistening in ice. The temperature had gotten much colder, but the swing set looked so nice, I decided to lick it. Big mistake! I was instantly frozen to the pipe and couldn't get loose. A teacher finally rescued me by removing his gloves and clasping the pipe with his bare hands until it warmed enough for me to get loose without ripping off half my tongue. This was one of the many dumb things I have done in my life.

Soon thereafter, I did another dumb thing. We were living over Jake Fess's grocery store on Main St. with our front door set back about ten feet from the front of the store. The grocer had placed baskets of apples in front of the store to attract customers. My brother Harold, and I, wanted an apple, but had no money to buy one. So we walked back and forth in front of the store a few times to case the joint. Not seeing the grocer on one of our trips past the apples, we each squatted for a split second and grabbed an apple, walked around the corner and hid them in the flowerbed. We then went up and sat on the porch. Almost instantly, Jake Fess walked around the corner and said, "All right, where are they?" In a panic I just pointed to the flowerbed. Without another word Jake picked up the apples and returned them to the basket. I learned at that moment that I was too nervous for a criminal career.

It was in Piqua that I remember hearing radio for the first time. Uncle Charles had bought a crystal radio that had to have earphones since it had no speaker. I remember my father and uncles listening and laughing, so I naturally wanted to listen, too. After a bit of begging I was allowed to listen for about fifteen seconds. This brief session so impressed me that I can still remember it to this day.

It was also in Piqua that I saw my first talking picture. We had been seeing a few silent films with Mom reading the captions to Harold, Junior and me. A lady sat at a piano at the foot of the stage and played music to match the mood of the film. I was truly amazed when Tarzan, played by Elmo Lincoln, swung through the trees doing his famous yell, sounding like he was right in the theater. This all occurred late in 1926, and is among the first of my life-long memories. We were living in an apartment over Ralph Meyers' store at the time. Ralph had a nickelodeon with fake monkeys that played all kinds of instruments for a nickel. He sold fireworks and all kinds of goodies.

One of our later moves was to the Hem Road, near an abandoned stone quarry, now full of water, owned by Acton, "Ack" Hall. "Ack" was one of the earlier aviators in the Piqua area, and it was not unusual to see him flying across town in an inverted position.

Mom's father, Charles Edwin Burt lived at the corner of Hem Road and the Dixie Highway, Route 25. This was also Main St. that ran through Piqua, along the Miami River. Mom's younger sister, Wanda lived with her family on Hem road just around the corner from Grandpa and Grandma. It was almost like a Burt compound. This was where my father's father and stepmother were also living just down Hem road near the quarry. They were living upstairs in the abandoned Tom Kaiser gristmill there. Both of my grandmothers died before I was born. I don't remember when Grandpa and Grandma Johnson went back to Naylor, Missouri, but there seemed to be a lot of wandering in both sides of the family. The Burt side of the family was mostly Scotch, and probably came to America during the potato famine of the 1840's or before.

It was Grandpa Burt's grandfather or uncle, Henry M. Burt who established a small newspaper at the top of Mt. Washington in New Hampshire in 1877. He sold copies to tourists after they rode the cog-rail train to the top. There was quite a tourist rush up that windy mountain in those days. His paper was called "Among the Clouds," and was printed in that forbidding place above the tree line for several years. In 1934 a gust of wind hit 231 MPH on that 6200-foot peak. That is the strongest sustained wind ever recorded anywhere on the surface of the earth.

In Piqua, two of Mom's sisters lived next to each other near Grandpa Burt. Aunt Bernice lived two doors away and Aunt Lucille just past that. Aunt Lucille was the youngest of Mom's siblings, being only four years older than I was. She and her older brother, James, and sister Wanda sometimes went with my brothers and I down Hem Road to pick apples off the ground from the Hem farm. Grandma Burt fussed about us gathering apples without being "invited," but she made apple pies out of them anyhow. We were one big happy family in those days, but it didn't last.

In those days there were a lot of horse drawn delivery wagons and chain driven trucks on the streets of Piqua. One day while walking home from school, my brother Harold and a couple of other kids decided to hop on the back of one of the wagons that was going their way. Unfortunately, Harold slipped and his leg went through the spokes, and the turning wheel broke his leg. Harold fell onto the street, and the man driving the wagon never knew about it. Harold was not in much pain, but said that every time he tried to take a step, it felt like he was stepping into a "Big Black hole." Harold spent several days in the hospital, and wore a cast to school for several weeks.

When I was age 6, my parents moved to Hazel Park, near Royal Oak, Michigan, a suburb of Detroit, at the urging of my father's brother-in-law, Frank Childers who worked on the railroad for the Ford Motor Company. Uncle Frank was married to Dad's sister Daisy, and they had two children, Frank Jr. and Dorothy. My father was unable to get work, and so obtained an open huckster's wagon and in that first spring, my mother and father with my older brother, Harold and I, sold produce along the streets of Detroit. I still remember my first sale of a large bag of green beans to a nice lady who came to the second door I knocked on. At age seven I received fifteen cents for my first sale. We were selling produce one day when we had to wait for a train. On the last car was a little old man that Dad said was Henry Ford. Another time we saw him alone in a brand new Model A Ford fitted with train wheels, speeding down the tracks. He was busy reading a newspaper, paying no attention to his driving.

That fall (1929) I went to first grade at Hazel Park Grammar school and soon became a favorite of the teacher, as I was one of the best readers in the class. I had learned to read during Kindergarten in Piqua's Bennett School the previous year. The wonderful stories the teacher was able to get from printed words fascinated me, and I was determined to learn how to do the same thing. And Mom read to us quite a bit.

However, I was quite shy and dreaded what the first grade teacher had in store for me. Since I was one of the best readers, the teacher often had me come to the front of the room to read to the other first graders. On one occasion when I had this dubious honor, the teacher started me reading, and then left the room. I read for awhile, but needed to go to the bathroom really bad. When the teacher finally returned, I was still standing in front of the class reading, although by then I was standing in a large puddle. The teacher was very nice about it and called the janitor, who brought a mop. She asked me if I needed to go to the bathroom to which I replied in the negative. I was grateful that none of the other children laughed at me. This shyness was to haunt me for many years, even into my tour of duty in the Great War.

We had arrived in Detroit during a bitterly cold spell of weather, and my first recollection of that area was the cars that were completely covered with snow from the snowplows. Seeing people digging their cars from the snow made quite an impression.

At the end of the huckstering season, My parents decided that Houston, Texas probably had a friendlier climate. My Uncle Frank and Aunt Daisy decided that they would go there with us, so Uncle Frank got a leave from his job and treated the adventure as a vacation, and if it didn't work out he could return to his work in Detroit.

The weather was already turning cold when we left Detroit. Mom and Dad with my brother and I got together with uncle Frank and Aunt Daisy and their two children, Frank Junior, and Dorothy. We piled into two cars and headed south, and since motels didn't exist in 1929, we stayed in abandoned houses along the way. We stopped in Piedmont, Missouri on the day before my mother's grandfather and grandmother Gustin were celebrating their sixtieth wedding anniversary. These were my great grandparents that we had just seen the year before at the Gustin Family Reunion, near Piqua.

They had been expecting us, since Mom had written to them before we left Detroit. Great Grandma Elizabeth Gustin was busy baking bread the next morning when my mother told her,

"Grandma, I hope that when I am your age I can bake bread as well as you do."

"Well, Esther, dear," she replied, "If you have any trouble, you just call me, and I'll help you again." Mom was 29 years old and Great Grandma was past 80.

Great Grandpa John Gustin gave me a little fuzzy black chick to take to Texas. Dad said that I could call it "Fuzzy Nut," which I did. Dad and Great Grandpa got quite a laugh out of this, but after we were on the road the next day, Dad said that I should give it a different name. After some discussion, I decided that I would name the chick after the dog "Bingo" in the "Our Gang" comedies of that era. The color of the chick was just as black as the ring around the movie dog's eye. Except that Bingo wasn't the dog's name.

We never saw my great grandparents again, as Great Grandma died several years later, after the sixtieth wedding anniversary. And Great Grandpa died two years after her. They were both in their upper eighties. I am privileged to have the tintype photo taken at their wedding. I also have a "Brownie" snapshot made on the day of their sixtieth wedding anniversary. Great grandma had a twin sister, Della, who was in the wedding picture and also in the 60th anniversary picture as they were inseparable throughout life. Great Grandpa Gustin was born in 1850 and died in 1937. Great Grandma was born in 1852 and died in 1935. Great Grandpa Gustin was the Great Grandson of John Augustine who was born on the French Isle of Jersey in 1647. His name became Gustine and later Gustin when he moved to Massachusetts.

There were few paved roads and no motels in 1930, so traveling was a slow process. The first abandoned house we stayed in after leaving Piedmont had most of the windows broken out and it was quite cold, so Dad and uncle Frank filled some buckets with sand, poured kerosene into the sand and lighted it. The result was a lot of black smoke and a little bit of heat.

Somehow we survived the trip and found ourselves in a slum section of Houston. We moved into a house that didn't seem to have an owner, and that night, My father and a neighbor climbed the electric pole out in front of the house and hooked up the electricity. We were never allowed to turn lights on at night for fear the electric company would get wise, but they never did catch us.

The little black chick that Grandpa Gustin gave me became a part of our family for some time. I handled it so much that I could pick it up anywhere it happened to be. It was sort of like a kitten, but stayed outdoors most of the time. As it grew up I never did know if it was a boy or a girl until one day it came through a big hole in our screen door, hopped up into a chair and laid an egg. This became a daily ritual and Bingo would cackle every time she laid an egg. When she got to be about six months old she disappeared one day and I figure that she being so gentle, a dog must have gotten her. Or perhaps we had her for dinner without my being notified.

Harold and I went to elementary school nearby and the first cold snap brought a snow shower that whitened the landscape with about two inches of snow early one afternoon. It was the first snow that many of the children had ever seen and they let school out so we could go out and play in it. The kids made a big snowman and had a snowball fight. Of course this was sort of Ho Hum to Harold and me since we had spent the previous winter in Detroit. I still remember my favorite teacher's name. It was Miss Seabaugh who taught us about good hygiene and she was very good at it.

One family living near us in Houston was named Soap. They had two teen-age boys. One was named Ivory and we called the other "Pal" as in Palmolive. I have never come across another family named Soap.

We were down to one car by this time, having sold one to make expenses. Mom took in washing and Dad did odd jobs. Uncle Frank and his family had moved into another house down the street that was a little better. Uncle Frank had more money than we did, since he had a job before moving, and thus could afford to pay rent.

One morning we woke up to find that Uncle Frank had taken his family and our one car and, without a word headed back to Detroit. We hadn't been there but a month or so, and he left us stranded with no money. There were no auto title laws in 1929, so whoever owned the keys owned the car. Instead of a title, cars were sold by bill of sale, much as farm machinery is sold to this day.

Chapter 2

Share cropping

Somehow Mom and Dad managed to get a little money together, bought a used car, and we headed out into the country to try our hand at sharecropping. We settled upon a large farm that had been abandoned by its original owner and who had left it to a grocery store. The owner, Mr. Harris, took it in payment of a debt. The farm was about two miles off the main road, state route 1725. An old logging trail led us back through a Magnolia swamp to the farm, which was in the San Jacinto, Sam Houston National forest.

Mr. Harris agreed to furnish seed and a mule, and all we had to supply was labor. We were to receive fifty percent of the profits from crops that we raised. We moved into the old house that was there and went to work. Unfortunately, a big thunderstorm arrived on about the third day, and the roof leaked so bad that we decided to move into the barn which didn't leak. It had been a barn for live stock and had a wide walkway of wood planks between the hay bins. My mother scrubbed this walkway until the wood was white. We lived there the entire remainder of our Texas odyssey.

But first the land had to be cleared. The forty acres had lain fallow for ten or fifteen years, and was overgrown with ten-year-old pine saplings. It took our family nearly a month to get the land ready for corn and peas. We also planted a large garden and an acre of white potatoes. We had a problem with deer eating our corn, but we could never get in gun range to have one for food.

We also decided to raise a few rows of sweet potatoes so dad bought a couple bushels of sweet potatoes and we buried them in a hot frame to grow sprouts. Each potato would grow five or six sprouts, which we pulled off after they were about a foot long. These we planted every two feet, pushing them into the ground with a forked stick. When they grew, they covered the entire area. Before we were able to raise any edible produce we ran short of food so Dad dug up the spent sweet potatoes and we made several meals out of them. I often worried about us not having any money and very little food. I remember many nights hearing Mom and Dad talking about it.

Mom and Dad ran out of coffee one week and having no money, Dad tried making his own. He spread wheat onto a flat pan and baked it until the wheat turned dark brown. He then ground it up in an old coffee mill and made ersatz coffee, which tasted just like Postum that was later made by the Post Cereal Company.

The owner of the farm, Mr. Harris, allowed us to charge our groceries at his store until the crop was harvested. The year didn't turn out to be very good for corn, but was good for potatoes. We had been supplementing our diet with wild game, mostly by my father's night hunting with a neighbor and his dogs. This was my first meal of raccoon, opossum and armadillo. We ate large numbers of armadillo. After cleaning the shell, My parents would bring the tail of the animal into its mouth and pin it there, thus making a basket. Mom sold about three of these for a quarter each, and the other ten or so hung on a rack near our outside entrance. When we abandoned Texas, we also abandoned most of these critter baskets. We didn't know that armadillos sometimes harbored leprosy, but we lucked out since none of us got it.

At this age, I was obsessively curious about everything in nature. I could watch ants or tumblebugs (dung beetles) work for hours. Texas had some king-sized millipedes, which I knew were harmless, so I often picked them up to count their legs. I was never able to get a good count, since they wiggled their legs constantly. One day I saw a large one at a crack near our back step, so I picked it up. Only it wasn't a millipede, but a rather large scorpion. The only part I had seen was its tail and fortunately I had picked it up in such a position that it couldn't sting me. Needless to say I didn't play with it very long

Another time I was watching some small beetles and decided to touch one. It made a little "Spit" noise and shot a little pink mist from its back end. I had never seen anything like this before, and didn't know what they were. I finally named them "Spitfires," because the mist burned my finger. I later learned that they were called "Bombardier" beetles. Strange that I would be involved with big "Spitfires" and "Bombardiers" in less than fifteen years!

Another time I was walking home from school and happened to see a skink on a fence post with his tail on the side next to me. These little lizards are as quick as double-geared lightening and I had never been able to catch one before. With their iridescent stripes, the urge to catch one got the better part of my judgment. I quietly sneaked over to the post and pressed my index finger against its tail. The lizard immediately whipped around and grabbed my middle finger in his mouth and started making chewing motions. Of course I let his tail go but he didn't let my finger go. We had a standoff for about ten seconds at which time I yanked my finger away, slinging the skink about twenty feet. Skinks don't have enough teeth to hurt anyone, but this one certainly intimidated me.

At harvest time Mr. Harris came with a tractor to dig the late fall potatoes that we had raised. We had already hand picked and shucked the corn. Mr. Harris dug the potatoes with a potato plow and we picked them off the ground for him. Our grocery bill had gotten to forty dollars and some cents, so Mr. Harris took the entire crop and said that we still owed him a few more dollars that we could make up next season.

After he left, we picked up a few bushels of potatoes that we had "accidentally" overlooked, gathered up our few chickens and other "valuable" belongings, piled them on the flivver that Dad had acquired, and headed north without a word to Mr. Harris.

After a couple of day's travel, trading produce for gas, we went through Texarkana and made a wrong turn. We had a flat tire, which Dad fixed since the spare tire had already been used the day before. We no sooner got going again, than another tire suffered a major blow out. The tire patch equipment that we carried was no match for the hole in the tire, so Dad made a "boot" out of a magazine. Our destination was Naylor, Missouri, but we ran out of gas, food and tires in the little town of Ozone, Arkansas. Someone in the local grocery store told us of an abandoned house that wasn't being lived in, just out of town. The car wheezed us out the last two miles to that house, and we moved in just before the magazine boot wore out. The roof didn't leak much, but there were no unbroken windows. It wasn't as warm there as in southern Texas, but spring, 1930 was fast approaching. This house was situated on the very top of one of the highest Ozark Mountains in the area. The first thunderstorm of the spring was a doozie, and rain came in one window and flew out the other, so the next morning Dad boarded up the worst windows with scrap lumber and fixed the worst leaks in the roof.

For one dollar, Dad bought two hundred chicks from the grocery store, and we planted a garden that covered the entire flat top of the mountain. The one dirt road came up one side of the ridge and continued down the other side. We found that we had to walk to a neighbor, who lived a quarter mile down that road past our house, to get water from his spring. This was for all our cooking, washing, and bathing. To take a bath, we had to heat water on a wood-burning cook stove and pour it into a galvanized washtub on the floor of the kitchen. All four of us had to share this same water, with the dirtiest one having the last turn. I was usually last, but I always said that it was because I was the youngest. And Harold might say; "I only peed in it a little bit." My brother and I got to know that path to the spring very well over the next few months.

Ozone was the first place that I tasted woodchuck or groundhog. It was as good as rabbit or squirrel and it seems that we ate every-thing that walked, swam or flew. One night Dad and the neighbor caught a groundhog that was so big that I thought it was a small bear. It was so tough that we couldn't eat it, and Dad later joked that it was so tough that you couldn't even cut the gravy.

One day in mid-summer a small herd of cattle wandered up the roadway and decided to eat our crops. The mountaintop had a twenty-foot steatite cliff around the three sides away from the house. Harold and I had the chore of driving the cattle out of our garden. One yearling steer seemed a little reluctant to follow the others and ran through the thicket that grew all around the edge of the mountain and fell to his death. I ran and told my parents, but they thought I was putting them on, so I said nothing more. A few days later, as buzzards were circling the spot, my father realized that we had lost a good supply of meat. I felt guilty about the whole incident for a long time.

It was in Ozone that I was involved with another apple incident. In the early fall as Harold and I walked to and from school, we noticed a very large apple on a tree about a hundred feet off the path. We never met anyone on this path, and every day that big apple beckoned to me. One day while walking home, the temptation became too great, so I decided I would try another "Great Apple Caper." I dashed out to the tree, grabbed the apple and ran back to the path.

Lo and behold, the owner of the orchard appeared as if by magic walking toward us. I quickly thrust the apple under my left arm and put my right hand over it. The man was very friendly, and wanted to talk, but I left Harold there to cover for me. As I walked on. I kept telling Harold to come on, as we had chores to do. Finally, Harold caught up with me and said,

"Do you know that the apple is so big that it stuck out behind your arm?"

"What did he say?" I asked in a near panic.

"Nothing," Harold replied, "he just grinned." As I mentioned in the "Piqua Apple Incident," I was too nervous to steal.

Downstream from the spring that furnished our water was a small creek that was fed by other springs. In its steep descent down the mountain the creek had eroded grooves in the steatite rock that made it look much like a water slide of modern times. The grooves were covered with moss with the water flowing over them, giving the illusion of a man-made slide. At the bottom of one course the stream fell over a small waterfall into a clear plunge pool a couple of feet deep.

It was so inviting that Harold and I with a friend, Rodney Asher, tried sliding down without our bathing suits. After several twists and turns we plopped into the pool.

However, there was quite a bit of sand and grit in the moss, which soon wore out our backsides, so we tried it with swim suits which wore holes in them. We tried bringing a large piece of cardboard to sit on, but were not able to maintain a good grip on the edges. We had a lot of fun, and it made a lifetime memory.

Mom and Dad took us one Sunday to explore the stream farther down the mountain and we walked for several hours until we heard a waterfall in the distance. As we got closer we realized that there was a house near the creek. As we approached, we could see that the creek, much larger now, was going over a twenty or thirty foot high cliff and doing a free fall into a very large pool that appeared to be quite deep. The couple from the house came out to talk to us and told us that they had been living there for many years. He said that he was planning to place a generator in the falling water so that he could have electricity. It seemed such a Utopian place that I'll wager that there is now a resort of some sort there by that plunge pool.

Before winter set in, we moved to a strawberry farm near Clarksville, Arkansas belonging to "Froggy" Shreeves who raised about forty-five acres of strawberries. We were to be part of the migrant force of farm workers. There were no houses available that didn't cost rent money, so we moved into a tent near "Froggy's" barn. Nearby was a spring from which we got our drinking water, which was better than walking up and down the mountain at Ozone. Dad took a part time job driving a truck for Froggy, while Mom did all the cooking and washing out in front of the tent in a large iron pot which sat on stones. We built a fire under the pot for washing and cooking, using the same pot.

Strawberry picking time required a large number of people to pick berries for two cents per quart. After the berries were picked, my father drove them to Clarksville, or Little Rock, and sold them at the market.

Our tent was about eight by ten feet in size and Harold slept across the back, while I slept along the side with our heads almost touching at the corner. Mom and Dad slept near the front flap. Our beds were of dried corn shucks stuffed into a large cotton sack, which was noisy, but quite comfortable. While lying in this bed of corn duff, I could reach the underside of the tent, even though we slept on the ground. During a thunderstorm I found that the tent would leak if I touched the underside of it. I got into trouble over that. Anyhow, the next day, Dad and Froggy coated the outside of the tent with paraffin oil, which cured the leaking problem.

The tent was pretty rotten though, and one night Froggy brought some liquor over to sit and drink with Dad. Harold and I were in bed at the back end of the tent, when Mrs. Shreeves stuck her head out the farmhouse door and yelled for Froggy. He jumped up, and not wanting her to see him come out the front flap of the tent, he ran back and stepped over Harold, and tried to go under the edge of the tent. Instead of raising up, the tent just ripped about four feet, and Froggy made his escape. Mom sewed it up the next morning using a baseball stitch.

After berry picking time was over, we helped at the farm, which consisted of three patches. One patch was one year old, one was two, and the other was three years old. After picking the berries, the three-year old patch was plowed under, and new plants were taken from runners of the two-year old patch. These were planted three feet apart in a checkerboard design. Cultivation was done all fall in two directions on the checkerboard. At the final cultivation, the runners had grown a couple of feet long and were left in the direction of the other two patches where they were allowed to take root. The new patch was never picked the first year.

Strawberries are raised a little differently these days, being planted in raised rows only 18 inches apart and not usually cultivated as in old days. Thus, twice as many berries can be raised in the same space. Sets are taken from runners and planted directly in the raised rows, which usually are sided with black plastic. This keeps the rows virtually weed free and retains moisture.

At two cents per quart, I got sick of picking strawberries. Being ten years old, I could never pick more than twenty quarts per day, and probably ate a quart. But we managed to accumulate a little money, and at the end of the season we decided to move on to the next area. Migrant farm work was not our bag, so Dad wrote to his father in Naylor, Missouri and asked him to loan us ten dollars to help with gas which cost about fifteen cents per gallon in those days.

Grandpa sent us a ten-dollar bill in the mail, but complained that it had almost wiped him out. Dad acquired a small, unlighted trailer, loaded it with produce to sell or trade along the way, and we headed toward Missouri. The very first night on the road, as Harold and I slept in the back seat, we drove through a bad thunderstorm and it was pitch dark. Thunderstorms had a way of telling us that we weren't the chosen of the Earth, because another car traveling behind us rammed into the unlighted trailer and scattered produce all over the highway. Some of it even flew forty or fifty feet ahead of the car. No one was injured, there was no visible damage, and the man was very nice, giving us two dollars to cover the damage. During the constant rain and flashes of lightening we gathered up most of the spilled produce and went on our way.

Fifteen or twenty miles further on, Mom discovered that her purse was missing, including Grandpa's ten dollars and the newly acquired two dollars. She had remembered placing her purse on the running board of the car while we gathered up produce and now it was gone. We were all devastated, knowing that it was gone forever, maybe even stolen by the other driver. Dad turned back anyhow, and after looking along the right edge of the road near the accident scene, we spotted the purse lying just off the roadway with nothing missing. It was a great trauma averted, but the incident was burned into my memory forever.

In Missouri share cropping
Mom, dad, brother & me - Harold

Mom, Esther Johnson, next to our shanty in mo' 33
Dad peeking around the corner next to our flivver

Chapter 3

Naylor, Missouri

We finally arrived in Naylor, Missouri, where my Grandfather Johnson had three houses that he had built, he being a carpenter. No one seemed to be renting houses, so Mr. Tutterow lived in one house rent-free, and we moved into the one next door. Mr. Tutterow was the preacher for the General Baptist Church where my grand parents were members. Grandpa said that we could live in the three-room house with "path" until he found a renter.

We lived there in Naylor until early spring that year, which was 1933. In March, just after my 11th birthday, Grandpa said that he had found someone who would pay ten dollars a month for the house, and that Charley Penney was looking for a tenant that could do some share cropping raising cotton and sorghum, a type of sugar cane. So we moved nearly three miles out into the country to Mr. Penney's farm and moved into one of his tenant shanties. This was a three-room shack, with "Path," that was built "Missouri style," having vertical boards with narrower boards nailed over the cracks.

The weather was still cold at times, and the wind came in one side of the house and carried our meager heat out the other side. While waiting for planting time, Mom made curtains of feed sacks and Dad pasted newspapers over the entire inside of the house with flour and water paste. I got to know Andy Gump, Maggie and Jiggs, and Smokey Stover of The Toonerville Trolley from the comic strips throughout the house. The newspapers didn't insulate the house, but they kept the wind from blowing the covers off the bed. We had a small airtight stove that burned wood. It had a flat top for cooking. A small tin-box oven sat on top of it for baking.

We planted cotton and sorghum cane in the early spring and had some good times. Mom's brothers and sisters could now visit us from Piqua, Ohio, and we all went fishing and frog hunting nearly every weekend when they were there. It seems that we ate just about everything that Nature could provide.

We attended the little General Baptist Church in Naylor, where Mr. Tutterow preached, and every Sunday we walked there in time for Sunday School Mr. Tutterow was a lay preacher and was reluctant to accept money for his preaching, being employed outside the church. He was a "Hell fire and brimstone" preacher. I still have the small Bible that was awarded to me for good attendance from the Jr. Endeavor. It is dated November 19, 1933. I was not yet twelve years old. That winter I vowed to read it cover-to-cover, and did. It was an onerous task and took me all winter. There are some Jim-Dandy stories in there. Many are quite raunchy.

One summer day while Mom, Harold, and I were walking the two plus, miles home after church, a thunderstorm came up. We walked a little faster until lightening struck a tree along the road just about fifty feet away. Bark from the exploded tree very nearly struck us and we were instantly in full stride needless to say. Thunderstorms seemed to have a way of seeking us out.

A few days later, Mr. Penney's daughter, Charlene, gave us a puppy that looked exactly like Little Orphan Annie's dog Sandy, so that became his name. Sandy became part of our family for several years.

I hadn't had a pet since I raised Bingo, the chicken to adulthood in the Houston slum. It had disappeared one day after having laid many eggs in our living room chair. I always thought that someone or something (perhaps even us) had eaten Bingo. After the chicken, I had raised a young armadillo to adulthood while we were farming for Mr. Harris out in the Texas country. After following me around for several months it too disappeared. I often wondered if Dad had served up my pets at our table without telling me. I kept telling myself that the armadillo must have grown up and felt the call of the wild, or the call of companionship. I never knew if it was a boy or girl.

Cotton is a beautiful crop, with blossoms that come out a yellowish white. They turn pink and then almost red before forming the boll. But it requires a great deal of work to get it to the picking stage.

First, we plowed the land, then disked and then harrowed. The cottonseeds were planted with a mule drawn machine similar to a corn drill. After the plants were a few inches high, the rows had to be cultivated three or four times throughout the summer. A day or so after each cultivation, we had to walk down each row with a hoe to cut weeds between the plants. This was known as "Choppin' Cotton."

We lived in the Pig Ankle section of Butler County Missouri, and Harold and I attended Pig Ankle Grammar School. When the cotton ripened, the school closed for about two months, so that the children could help with the harvest. In the ten or so schools that I had attended to this point, I had never run across such a system. I don't know how general that system was, but we were out from the end of September to the first of December, just "Pickin' cotton." Amazingly, I never failed a grade in my life even after attending at least nine schools before I even started high school.

To pick cotton, you throw a long sack over your shoulder that is attached to a strap. You drag this sack down the row of cotton, plucking the cotton from the open boll with both hands and stuffing it into the sack. After getting to the end of the row, you turn back in the next un-picked row. By the time you return to your starting point the sack is getting heavy with about twenty pounds of picked cotton. At that point the sack is weighed on a balance-beam scale, and the weight recorded. At the end of the day I found that I usually had picked about seventy or eighty pounds. I thought that was pretty good, since we were being paid one cent per pound. Mom and Dad could manage about two hundred pounds each and Harold could pick about a hundred twenty pounds. This made us about six dollars a day, which was better money than we had ever made as a family. A six day week netted us about thirty five dollars.

But we still envied the black family that lived near us. They were so good at their job that they could pick four hundred pounds each. They told us that we, too, could pick that much, if we didn't stop to straighten the kinks from our backs so often. One day, I decided that I would pick a hundred pounds of cotton and make a whole dollar. I worked as hard as I could, trying not to un-kink my back too often.

At the end of the day I had picked ninety-eight pounds. One of life's little two-cent disappointments.

One problem to overcome was trash picked with the cotton. Dead leaves often contaminated the cotton, and if too much was in your bag, you were docked. The object was to pick only the long staple cotton the first couple of times in order to get the best price at the cotton gin. Picking cotton was done with both hands, trying to get the cotton out of the boll without making your knuckles bleed on the sharp points surrounding the boll. After the long staple cotton was about picked over, the entire boll was snapped off for poorer quality cotton. Some cotton didn't mature because of frost, and this was picked for use in paper making, and such. This was called "stripping," and in our time was done by hand. Before we left Missouri in 1934, I saw stripping done by a machine.

The picked cotton was always dumped in a high, wire sided wagon, compacted by Mr. Penney walking it down. We then drove the horse-drawn wagon to the cotton gin in Naylor where it was sucked out of the wagon by a large hose. It was sort of like a giant vacuum cleaner. One day while Dad was operating the suction end in the wagon his hat fell off and was immediately sucked up with the cotton. I thought that it was gone forever, but the man on the discharge end of the hose tossed it back out to the wagon, little the worse for having gone through the big fan that supplied the suction. We all had a good laugh, and Dad said that he was glad his head wasn't in the hat.

Dad always seemed to have a good sense of humor, but sometimes it got a little out of hand. He told us of the time he was a pre-teen in Missouri trying to help his grandfather, Zopher Alexander Johnson dig a well. His grandfather was down about fifteen feet while Dad pulled the dirt (and grandpa Zan) up in a bucket, using a block and tackle. Then Grandpa "Zan" told Dad to go to the house for drinking water while he filled the bucket with dirt.

Up near the house was "Maude," a blind horse that belonged to Grandpa "Zan." Maude wore a cowbell so that they could keep track of her in the dark. As a whim, Dad removed Maude's bell and slowly walked back toward the well, tinkling the bell, as he went. At the bottom of the well Grandpa "Zan" yelled for Maude to get back, but Dad said he got closer and closer, still tinkling the bell. Grandpa yelled for Dad and kept yelling for Maude to go away.

Finally Dad told that he got almost to the edge of the well and kicked in a few small clods of dirt. At this point Grandpa Zan fell to his knees and started praying.

Dad said that this made him feel so bad that he reversed his course with the bell and went back to the house and returned quickly with the drinking water.

Grandpa Zan was a preacher, as was his father and his grand-father before him, but he never mentioned that Maude had almost fallen into the well with him, and Dad said that he was not about to say anything about it either. Grandpa Zan's great grandfather, also named Zopher, was a soldier in the Revolutionary war from Greenville, Tennessee. He fought in the battle of Yorktown in the Gilkerson Company with Washington and he acquired a hundred acres of land in Greenville when the war was over.

During the Civil war Zan and his father Christopher had joined the Union Army on the same day and Zopher was wounded at Shiloh which damaged his health.

I have since come to suspect that this tale of the well and blind horse is one that my father, Lora, "borrowed" from his own father, Riley, as Grandpa Riley helped his own father, Zopher, who died before Dad was born.

On another occasion in Ohio, during Prohibition when I was a small child, an Irish friend of Dad's died, and a bunch of his friends and family gave an Irish Wake. They kept their contraband liquor hidden between sticks of firewood that was stacked for winter.

During the course of the evening they drank a number of toasts to their departed friend, and one participant got so drunk and obnoxious that they tossed him out. He wanted to come back in and drink with them, but they would have none of it.

Things finally got so out of hand that they took the departed friend out of the casket and leaned him in the corner of the room and put a drink in his hand. Meanwhile, the obnoxious one hid outside until somebody came to the woodpile to get a drink of the illegal moonshine stashed there. As soon as the obnoxious one found the hiding place, he removed the bottle and drank all he wanted of it, then peed in the bottle, returning it to its hiding place.

A few days later he was bragging to a friend about it and was overheard. It got him a couple of black eyes.

After hearing all of Dad's stories, it's a wonder that I didn't become a juvenile delinquent.

Late in the Missouri fall we had to strip the sorghum cane before cutting and stacking it. This was an onerous job, since it was still hot and the cane leaves cut like corn leaves, similar to a paper cut. At any rate we finally stripped and cut several acres of this cane and hauled it to the mill. The mill consisted of a tin shed and a large set of corrugated, mule powered, rollers that the cane was fed through to extract the juice which was very sweet. The juice was directed into a large metal vat that was cooking the juice to boil out the water, leaving the thick sorghum molasses. This molasses became a staple for our breakfast for the coming winter. It was quite good over biscuits when you didn't have much else. When there was an abundance of sorghum it was mixed with bran and fed to cattle as a supplement to their diet. I remember that we kept a barrel of molasses on the porch and during cold weather Mom would wind up a big ball of the stiff molasses on a wooden spoon and carry it into the kitchen to warm for breakfast.

While we lived in Charley Penny's tenant shanty we often went fishing in a nearby creek. Aunt Bernice and Uncle "Zip" Williams came from Piqua with Uncle Clarence Burt and Aunt Jane late in the second summer for a two-week visit. We all slept in the little three-room shanty and a trailer they had brought; ate together and played together for that time. We went frog hunting at night in this nearby creek and a few small lakes in the area. There were many of these sinkhole lakes left over from the great earthquake of New Madrid, Missouri in 1811. We used a carbide miners lamp to make the frog's eyes shine in the dark, at which time one of the grown-ups would gig him. We ate quite a few frog legs and fish during these visits.

One day in late summer of 1934 the creek was almost dry and

the fish were concentrated in pools in the creek bed. One pool had some rather large carp and the men decided to catch them by hand. The water was only about two feet deep, but the carp refused to lie quietly and be caught by our Indian style "hogging."

Dad, Uncle "Zip," Uncle Charles and Uncle Clarence decided to find the fish and surround them in the murky water. My brother Harold and I with our cousin Eddie Cook, Aunt Bernice's son by an earlier marriage, stayed on shore to point where the fish were headed. The men were all wearing bib overalls and when things got to splashing around, an especially large carp went dashing past Dad, and Uncle Charles made a dive for it. Suddenly Uncle Charles jumped up yelling,

"I got him, I got him!" The fish had swam into his bib overalls and when he stood up all we could see was a four inch wide fish tail slapping Uncle Charles in the face.

We ate a lot of carp in those days. While not a prize delicacy, they were abundant, especially during a spring flood when Dad speared several with a pitchfork when they swam into the knee-deep water in our cornfield.

The men were a bad influence on us kids some of the time. They were all very good shots with a 22-caliber rifle and practiced nearly every day. They had contests to see who could make the most out-landish scores, often tossing small targets in the air. Once, Uncle Charles tossed a quarter in the air and Dad hit it. We were a little while finding it, as it flew off some distance and it had a large dent in it.

Then Uncle Charles held a two-inch piece of watermelon be-tween his left thumb and forefinger and Dad shot it to pieces without injuring Uncle Charles. Mom came out at this point and made them all quit such foolishness. Besides, she said that breakfast was ready. But they were not done! Mom had country bacon with biscuits and gravy and sorghum molasses. Unfortunately, with all the shooting going on outside, she had forgotten to put baking powder in the biscuits and they didn't rise during the baking process. In just a little while some of these small, hard biscuits became targets on top of the kitchen doorframe. After the men each exploded a few of them while sitting at the table, laughing uproariously, Mom suddenly ran out of the house crying. This put an end to the target practice for that day.

Later in the fall we did a return visit to Piqua and stayed with Aunt Bernice and Uncle "Zip." Aunt Bernice, knowing my love of apples told me not to pull any apples off her tree, as she was going to make apple sauce. Time for another great apple caper!

Later that evening I was outside by myself and noticed that her apple tree had some ripe apples hanging within my reach. So I ate one without pulling it off the tree. Then another and another until I had about five apple cores hanging from the tree, right next to the path to the outhouse. I knew that she would see the evidence in the morning.

The next morning Aunt Bernice awakened me.

"Dick Johnson, you turd." she said. "I told you not to pull any of my apples, but I guess I'll have to be more specific."

"I didn't pull any apples." I protested, in mock indignation.

"I know you didn't pull them, but I know it was you who ate them anyhow," she said. She had to admit that it was sort of funny. This was the least traumatic of my apple capers, and it was the kind of joke that a twelve-year-old could understand.

Aunt Bernice and Uncle "Zip" lived near an active stone quarry, that every few days did blasting. They stopped traffic in the area and blew a big whistle to warn residents to stay indoors. For good reason, as their house was often struck with small stones. The company paid for any damage done to nearby houses.

One day we all visited the quarry where the chief of the blasting crew had some time off. He was to be my Aunt Lucille's future father in law. We asked Mr. Lynn about the nitroglycerin that they blasted with. We were at the top of the quarry rim, so Mr. Lynn said that he would show us how sensitive Nitroglycerin was. He took a small leather bottle from his pouch and opened it. He poured a few drops from the bottle into a small swatch of cotton, which he then wrapped around a small rock. He pitched the rock over the side of the quarry rim and when it struck the bottom it exploded with a resounding bang like a shotgun blast.

I think that this is the reason that in my later High School days

I decided not to follow through with the Nitroglycerin that Orland Johnson and I started to make in chemistry class. We had gotten some cellulose and glycerin and were about to add the nitric acid when we chickened out. It's just as well as there might be a large lake there now instead of a high school.

The entire Student Body of Accommodation School - 8 grades
Author is 2nd from left in 2nd row (smiling)

Chapter 4

Southern Illinois – Macedonia

After two years of sharecropping for Charley Penny in Naylor, we decided to leave the area. Dad and most of his brothers and sisters were born in the Naylor area, and there were nine of them, but Grandpa had been born in Macedonia, Illinois on July 13, 1873, to Zopher Alexander Johnson and Sarah Boster, just after the civil war ended. He had three brothers living in Southern Illinois, so he decided to sell out and go back with us to return to his roots. His father was almost killed in the Civil War and only had four children, all boys, before he died from being in poor health because of those wounds.

Dad, Grandpa and Grandma, packed Grandpa's car and went ahead to make living arrangements. Grandpa had sold his properties for a pittance, since renters weren't around. This was a time of abandonment in the south and mid-west, and he was lucky to get anything.

After being in Macedonia for two weeks, Dad sent for the rest of us, so Mom got us all together in one car with me, one brother, one dog, and all the rest of our worldly goods and drove the hundred miles or so, to our new share-cropping odyssey.

Macedonia is a small farming village astride the line between Hamilton and Franklin Counties in Southern Illinois. Down the hill, across the Little Muddy River, about a mile is Johnson's Corner. It consisted of a small gas station and a general store on State Route 34, belonging to Edd Johnson, my grandfather's brother. The station and store were in Hamilton County, while Great Uncle Edd lived across the street in Franklin County. Great Uncle Edd's daughter, Nellie Johnson Fowler and her husband, Bruce Fowler, ran the store. Nellie's brother, Wilford Johnson, ran the station.

Wilford owned a sizable farm with an old house across the street, in Franklin County, the farm being in Hamilton County. He planned for us to sharecrop some forty acres, with him furnishing the seed, and us doing the labor. We planted about ten acres in cow-peas, which taste exactly like black-eyed peas. The rest we planted in corn.

While waiting for the crops to mature, Dad took a job with the WPA, making two dollars per day, while Harold and I did the cultivating in the cornfield. We used a one-row cultivator that was designed to be pulled by a horse, but not having a horse, Dad had built a homemade tractor from an old model A Ford truck with the help of his cousin Everett. This is what we used instead of a horse. The cultivator had spring-loaded blades, so that hard ground or roots would make them kick backward. The ground was so hard that I soon became tired of lifting the beam with my foot to release the blade. One blade flipped back and I lifted it with my right hand instead of my foot, but as the blade released it sprang forward, and the set screw trapped my right middle finger at the first knuckle, severing the ligament. I never went to a doctor and I still carry this scar to remind me of my share cropping days. I was thirteen years old at that time.

Harold and I often went hunting with "Cousin Bruce." Bruce Fowler had an English Setter bird dog named Rex. One day after returning from a fruitless hunt, Bruce had his shotgun, still loaded, but with the hammer down so that it wouldn't fire. Except, as he rested the butt of the gun on the edge of the store's porch, it slipped off the edge and the hammer struck the floorboard causing the gun to fire. The pellets of the 12-gauge shotgun took all the flesh off his chest wall in a groove over an inch wide and more than a foot long, just grazing the ribs. The pellets missed his right ear by less than a half inch and he carried this odd scar for the rest of his life.

There was a drought that year and the corn didn't do well, so Dad borrowed forty dollars from the Farm Improvement Association, which was part of the Department of Agriculture. With this forty dollars he bought a fine Jersey cow that was with calf, due to deliver in six weeks. We would have milk, and a start of our own herd of cattle.

But, it was not to be. Three weeks after Dad bought "Bossy," as we called her, Thor paid us another visit in the night when a small thunderstorm developed. It contained not one drop of much needed rain, and with its only bolt of lightening, killed "Bossy" and our dreams of becoming cattle barons. "Bossy" and her unborn calf were inedible, and so the forty dollars was a total loss. The Federal Government billed us every month for two years before finally giving up. I always felt a little guilty about that. Harold took a job in the CCC or Civilian Conservation Corps during that summer, but I was too young to be accepted.

When things got rough that fall, Mom took a job at the dress factory in the County Seat of McLeansboro. I was attending seventh grade at Macedonia Elementary School at the time while Harold was at McLeansboro Township High School where I would graduate in 1940.

Meanwhile we had given up on sharecropping, since each year the drought seemed worse than the year before. Dad did some paper hanging and painting and hung around the pool hall, where he made a little money gambling. He was quite a pool shark, and I suppose he made enough to pay for his cigarettes. He smoked two packs a day all his adult life. My Brother had gotten into smoking by then, although I had gotten out of it.

While living in Naylor, Missouri, Harold and I and some other kids had gotten to smoking dried corn silk, dead grapevines, and other weeds. I had gotten to be a big shot, able to inhale corn silk smoke and puff it out "Just like Dad." One day, while showing off in this manner, a kid said, "Here take a puff of this, I have a real one." So I took a big drag and inhaled deeply.

Instant death! I was so instantly nauseous that I almost couldn't sit down without falling. As I sat there gagging, the kid said,

"You've got to do it gradual to get used to it."

"I don't want to get used to it." I whimpered, certain that I was going to die. I sat there for over 45 minutes before I felt able to stand again. It was a valuable lesson, as I never smoked again. I was eight years old at the time.

Macedonia Elementary School only went to seventh grade, and when I finished that, I was assigned to Accommodation School, which was a one-room school of eight grades. It had no plumbing of course, but had two of those three-hole "Necessaries" on opposite sides of the school. We had moved out of Wilford's house and were now in a different school district, but still in Franklin County. The school had a large coal stove in the center of the room. Eighth grade students were assigned to bring in coal, while Mr. Jesse Neal, the only teacher, started the fire, stoked the stove and took out the cinders. Each grade of two to six students came to the front row when their class was to be taught.

Friday afternoon was my favorite time, as Mr. Neal had us play Geography Games, as he called them. On a given map, a student would find an obscure name and write it on the blackboard. The first student to find it on the map was awarded points. I learned a lot of geography that year.

I hated the cold winter weather in that area for good reason. One morning while walking to Accommodation school, which was over two miles from home, a sudden northwest wind came up, blowing twenty or thirty miles per hour. The temperature was near zero, and I had gone out without my earmuffs. By the time I got to school, my right ear was frozen solid, and Mr. Neal said it looked transparent. He wanted to rub snow on it to keep it from thawing out too quickly, but it hurt so badly that I would have none of that. I sat in back of the room, away from the stove until my ear thawed. The next day my ear had swollen to twice its normal size and I was sure that it would drop off, but it didn't. For the next several weeks the kids called me "Elephant ear." All the skin peeled off that ear before it returned to its normal size about two weeks later.

As if that wasn't enough, a few weeks later I froze both feet going to school, and this time Mr. Neal rubbed snow on them for a while until they thawed. Not much teaching got done those couple of days. What some kids will do to get attention and skip class.

There were only twenty-four kids in all eight grades at Accommodation and so I made the basketball team. My cousin, Martha Miller was on the team as well, and she was the star. She could run faster than any of the rest of us, so she became our star forward in our games with other nearby schools. We won most of our games.

But one day during scrimmage we had a small mishap. A kid with the famous name of Charles Boyer had front teeth protruding so badly that he had trouble closing his lips over them. During scrimmage that day the basketball hit the ground and I grabbed it and came up just as Charles was bending down for it. His front teeth struck the left side of my head just above my ear, which wasn't involved. His teeth went through the skin above my ear, cutting to the bone and taking all his upper front teeth out like shelled corn. Mr. Neal ran over to see what could be done and asked Charles if it hurt.

"Not a bit." he said. Mr. Neal then asked me if it hurt, and I said the same thing.

"I can see the mark of his teeth on your skull bone." He told me. He patched us up to prevent bleeding and we both stayed for the rest of the school day.

A week or so later, Charles came to school sporting a new partial plate with four new incisors. He looked like a different person, very good looking.

"You did me the biggest favor of my life He told me, "those teeth had always been a sensitive thing for me."

I suppose that braces could have eventually corrected his malocclusion, but I never saw braces on a person until I met Betty "George" Hogan when I went to McLeansboro High School the next year. Of course the first thing I told her was,

"Try not to smile during a thunderstorm." She hit me.

In those two summers of 1935 and 1936 I spent a lot of time on the Little Muddy River, fishing and exploring. Most of the time I was alone, since such things didn't fascinate my brother. One day I decided to do some Indian style "Hogging" as we called it when we lived in Missouri. Carrying a burlap sack, I went into the murky water of a tributary and felt along the bottom until I touched a fish. It wouldn't flee unless I flinched, as it probably thought I was another fish with amorous intent. At any rate, I would ease my hand along its side and slowly reach my fingers around it until I was at its mid section. With a quick squeeze I would capture it and put it into the burlap bag. One day I had captured about a dozen eating-size Goggle-eye Perch from under a stump that was in the water. Suddenly I felt another, much larger one. I carefully slid my hand along its side until I felt I could capture it. I squeezed down, and immediately realized that this was a very nice, fighting fish. I stood up, and lifted out of the water, a very large Cottonmouth Water Moccasin.

This is one of the most dangerous snakes in North America. It turned its free end, the one with the fangs, and looked me right in the eye. But not for long. I dropped it with a flourish and it took off in one direction and I in the other. It must have thought that I had a culinary intent for its future, and we had eaten a few of its kin in the past. I knew that these pit vipers bit more people than any other snake, both in the water and out. It put a little damper on my hogging for that day, since I knew that it had to have been watching me with its head out of the water in the root tangle of that stump.

In the spring of 1935 after I finished the seventh grade, my Grandfather took me fishing in the river one Saturday. As we were going across a field to the fishing hole, I found a fine Indian ax. I had assumed that all Indian artifacts had long since been found. When I learned how wrong I was, I wanted to forget about fishing, and hunt "arrow heads." Grandpa said that nobody was interested in "Indian rocks," and we came to go fishing, so we went fishing. After we went home from fishing, I ran back to the site where I had found the ax, and in a half-hour I found four fine arrowheads. I already knew that Grandpa was at least one quarter Cherokee, since he had told me that his Grandfather Zopher Johnson Jr. had married a Cherokee woman during the Indian removal in 1838. My non-Indian ancestors were already living in the area before that time. One of the three "Trail of Tears" came through that part of Southern Illinois in 1837. It was the Goshen Trail. This made me at least one sixteenth Cherokee, the same as the great Cherokee Chief, John Ross if grandpa's tale was true. There is some controversy about this Indian connection but I guess a DNA test will clear this up. This "connection" helped spark my interest in collecting artifacts. I had barely turned thirteen at that time.

After every rain, I could be seen at various fields along the river. I obtained the owner's permission when possible, and this often paid off as they sometimes gave some of their own finds to me since they only had a casual interest. I got so that I could recognize Indian sites as we drove past them. The soil color was the clue, and I would soon hitchhike back to the site after a rain. Fishing took a distant second to this new obsession, and my collection built rapidly.

I finished the eighth grade at Accommodation school in the spring of 1936, and that fall I entered the ninth grade at McLeansboro Township High School, or MTHS as we called it. Being a High School student was a great adventure, but I quickly found that the boys were to enter the school in one set of doors, and the girls entered from the opposite end of the building. There was a strong disciplinary penalty for going in the wrong doors. In the assembly or study hall we were also segregated by gender, the boys to the left and the girls to the right as you face the raised stage where the monitor sat. When the bell rang, those with first period classes left for their respective classrooms. The others remained in the study hall preparing for their first class.

In the classrooms the students sat alphabetically, and so for the next four years I sat next to Orland Ray Johnson on one side, and Mary Elizabeth Jones on the other in the classes that we shared. Orland and I enrolled in the agricultural class, and joined the Future Farmers of America, or FFA. This caused my social life to be almost non existent. On our very first field trip, Orland and I captured a large, but harmless Corn Snake, which we instantly named "Snek." We installed Snek in a terrarium in Miss Woodruff's Biology class and offered to dissect him if Mary Elizabeth would agree to do him in, but she declined. On the next field trip, we captured three mice and placed them in Snek's cage.

He seemed quite appreciative as he swallowed two of them the first day, leaving the third to contemplate his fate. The girls thought this was gross, but this was not the fatal blow to my social life. We handled Snek so much that he got fully gentled, and stopped trying to bite us. Often, we would take Snek for a "walk" to let him clean himself by slithering in the dew-covered grass.

My turn came one day, and I picked Snek up and let him go up my sleeve for concealment. As I walked out into the hall, Frances Lasater was coming toward me. She was one of the most popular girls in our class but didn't seem to know that I existed. She picked this time to talk to me, but Snek soon decided to check things out by peeking out my collar. Suddenly, Frances let out a shriek and fled down the hall.

After this incident, when any girl met Orland or me in the hall, they crossed to the other side. For the next four years we were known as "the snake charmers."

Principal, Marvin J Carlton decreed that Snek was to be returned to the wild at the end of the school year, and this we reluctantly did, because we figured that Snek, being so gentle, would have his name changed to "Hawk Bait." We didn't get into trouble over this snake incident and I hope it wasn't because Mr. Carlton was my distant cousin. My freshman year was otherwise uneventful, as was my sophomore year.

We finally moved into McLeansboro, near the fair grounds, in order to be nearer to school and work. During the summers, I found a way to make a little money. A pharmaceutical company in St. Louis was buying various herbs and weeds for drug manufacturing. One of these weeds was the very poisonous Jimpson Weed that was used as a dangerous narcotic in prehistoric Indian times. I walked from farm to farm gathering the leaves of this plant, taking them home to dry in the loft of the barn that was on the premises. After they dried, I bundled them into a burlap bag and sent them to the factory, whereupon they sent me a small check. All this went well until the second summer. One unusually hot day, I was picking Jimpson Weed leaves and sweating quite a bit. I must have rubbed my left eye with a contaminated hand. Soon the pupil of that eye expanded to its limit, and I had to walk home with that eye closed with my hand over it to keep from being blinded by too much light entering my eye. It was several hours before my eye returned to normal. At this point I decided to try to make a little summer money in other manners.

In my junior year I took the villain's part in the junior class play, called "Bolts and Nuts." The Bolts were a sitcom family while I played the part of the Nut. Some said I wasn't acting as it came too naturally for me. Fame is fleeting.

In my senior year, I was appointed Editor in Chief of the newly re-established school paper, "Letmetellya." I also played the villain in the senior class play called "Life begins at sixteen." In this play, I was the suave Crandall Smythe, trying to woo the oldest daughter of a well to do family. Of course I was foiled in my attempt to steal the family business.

The year was 1939 and President Roosevelt decreed that Thanksgiving be moved up a few weeks to separate it farther from Christmas, and therefore many people had two days in which to celebrate Thanksgiving that year. I had dabbled in poetry before, and so I wrote a poem about it, which found its way into the yearbook. It was titled,

DOUBLE HOLIDAYS.

We had Thanksgiving twice this year, It really seemed quite nice. And now that Christmas is coming near, We'd like to have it twice. We'd eat our Christmas dinner twice, And have an extra day of cheer. Go sledding, and skating on the ice, And add to fun and lessen fear. But we must think of Santa Claus, He'd be double dosed. We can't do that to him because, He's the one that suffers most. Maybe we'd better steady things, And have them both but once a year, Enjoy the fun a holiday brings, And thank God we have the holiday here.

Despite the bad poetry, that last line shows that I was already mindful of the war that was beginning to rage in Europe. A war in which I was to become personally embroiled in <u>four short years</u>.

During weekends I went on hitch hiking trips to various Indian village sites with Emmett Mayberry, and later with a sophomore named Charles Mitchell. He had sort of looked up to me and I didn't quite live up to his expectations. One day we were quite a few miles from home and the weather was hot and dry. We got so thirsty that we finally decided to drink from a puddle in an old farm road.

Charles then said that he was so hungry that he "Just had to have something to eat."

 · I told him that I didn't see anything except "Those Indian turnips over there." I was pointing to some jack-in-the-pulpits growing along the edge of the trail.

"Are they good to eat?" he asked.

"Indians ate them all the time." I told him, whereupon I pulled up one of the larger ones and peeled the small bulb on the bottom. Grandpa Johnson had initiated me to their taste a few years earlier.

"Have a small taste to see if you like them," I said, handing him the bulb. Instead, he put the entire bulb in his mouth and started chewing vigorously.

"Spit it out! Spit it out!" I yelled. Too late! There is no fire hotter than the juice of an Indian turnip. It is so bad that the inside of your mouth feels like it is puckering up. I had neglected to tell him that the Indians always cooked them to remove the oxalic acid that they contained in abundance.

Poor Charles was in such pain that he drank nearly all the water out of our puddle, but to no avail. The damage was done and it was a half-hour before he could feel well enough to continue our trip. I never felt so bad about a practical joke as this one, and I will never forget the look on his face. And, oh yes, he wasn't hungry anymore.

We hiked back home that day, pretty much in silence, but he forgave me, and later on a trip he found a mint-condition 1912 Liberty nickel on one of the old wagon roads while we were on one of our artifact hunting trips. Too bad it was not a 1913 one.

Graduating in late May of 1940, I was determined not to try for a job in one of the textile factories in McLeansboro, so Orland and I decided to hitchhike to St. Louis, Missouri, in search of work. We applied for jobs at several factories, including a fire arms factory (Remington) and a major glass factory (PPG, or Pittsburgh Plate Glass), but no one was hiring. My Step-Grandmother Johnson had a brother, George Fahnestock living near St. Louis. He had a floor finishing business there, but he didn't have enough business to hire us. The frenzy of WW2 had not yet reached the Middle West. We flipped a coin to see if we should go to Kansas City, or to Paducah, Kentucky. Paducah won, but we first went north to Hannibal, Missouri. We tried to find work in Hannibal, but the only position available was painting Tom Sawyer's fence, which paid nothing.

Hannibal is a small town on the Mississippi River, famous for being the locale of Mark Twain's novels. It was illegal to walk across the bridges of the Mississippi River, so we gave a man fifty cents to row us across, which took two hours, and we headed south for Paducah.

While on this odyssey, we slept in fields and barns, and after arriving in Paducah, we slept in the large courtyard at the police station. We were down to ten cents, with which we bought a large bag of day-old donuts. That night a rustling in the bag of donuts awakened me. I made a noise and the rustling stopped. I couldn't see what it was since it was pitch dark. I placed the bag on my chest and went back to sleep. A little later I was awakened again by the rustling, plus an animal was sitting on my chest. I lay there for a while, petrified, until I realized that it must be a rat or a squirrel. Not wanting to get bitten, I made a big sweep with my arm, knocking the intruder off my chest, and scattering donuts around the area. This commotion awakened Orland who wanted to know "What in the hell is going on?" It was just starting to get light in the east, so we gathered up the donuts, and ate the un-nibbled ones. We then left Paducah and headed north for McLeansboro. We were convinced by then that no one was hiring two inexperienced kids, just out of high school.

Back in McLeansboro, Orland went to his father's farm in the small village of Dale, while I was offered a job with a man in McLeansboro who made tombstones. He demonstrated how the carving was done, using rubber masks and sandblasting the openings. He offered me forty cents per hour, and I accepted. He said that I could start in two weeks. It was then early October 1940.

Grandma Johnson's brother, George Fahnestock that we had visited in St. Louis had two sons, George Jr. and Vernon, and an older daughter named Esther, who was named after my mother. We always considered them to be cousins, since we were about the same ages. Esther was the oldest of George's children. Although George had a floor finishing business in St. Louis, they lived on a farm outside of town.

Esther was a beautiful girl and at age eighteen won the county beauty pageant in the late 1930s. She had started dating a young man who lived near the farm. But when she found that he was abusive and extremely jealous, she decided to break off their relationship.

Hurt Hardy (his real name) was extremely possessive and would not let her go. One day when Esther went out to the barnyard to milk a cow, Hurt Hardy had hidden in the barn hayloft with a shotgun. As Esther sat milking the cow, Hurt fired the gun into her back. She screamed and jumped up, running toward the house while the wounded cow ran into the field.

As she ran to the house, Hurt ran the full length of the hayloft and swung the shotgun around the end of the barn and fired a second shot, hitting Esther full in the back from just a few yards away. Hearing the shots, George ran out and rushed Esther to the hospital, but after they removed over two hundred pellets from Esther's back, she succumbed to the wounds.

Meanwhile, Hurt Hardy disappeared, and so the sheriff got a posse together to hunt him down. Three days later he was captured in a willow thicket near a creek and some posse members begged him to "reach in your pocket for a handkerchief." He was almost lynched on the spot, but eventually went to trial and was convicted of first-degree murder. He was sentenced to death by hanging, and in less than a year the county staged a public hanging in the town square, thus ending the life of Hurt Hardy. Mom and Dad and all our adult relatives attended the hanging, but they didn't allow Harold or me to go.

Norfolk, Virginia

A day or so after I accepted the job as a tombstone carver's assistant, I got a letter from Orland, and was surprised to find that he had taken a bus to Norfolk, Virginia to work in the Standard Bag Corporation there with his uncle. This factory made paper bags that are the same as those seen today in grocery stores. Orland said that I could get a job in that factory where I could make at least fifteen dollars a week and up doing piecework. I immediately went back to the tombstone manufacturer and turned in my resignation to a job that I never took. He was pleased that I would give him notice, and said that the job would remain open for me if things didn't work out in Norfolk. It was the first week in November before I was ready to hitch hike the eight hundred miles to Norfolk, having no money for a bus ticket. I started out with light clothing, a small bag, and six dollars. Mom and Dad always worried about my hiking around, but never tried to stop me. I was eighteen years old, and they had also left home at about that age.

My first ride was all the way to Paducah, and by nightfall I managed to get to Lexington, Kentucky, where I slept in a bus station. The next morning I got a ride to Charleston, West Virginia, and from there a man in a pick-up truck took me to the middle of the Allegheny Mountains, near Cass, West Virginia. As we arrived at his destination, near the top of the mountain, he took me into a small diner and announced to the owner,

"I'm going to buy this boy a hamburger, are you going to buy him one?" The owner agreed, and fixed two huge hamburgers, and the driver paid him ten cents. I ate both hamburgers, thanked them both, and decided to go on my way since the diner was about to close. It was bitterly cold at the four thousand-foot elevations and the sun was almost down to the horizon. These were secondary roads and the traffic was next to extinct. It was so cold that I decided to walk down the mountain to get to warmer elevations. After walking about two miles, I heard a car coming up behind me, and I turned to stick out my thumb. The car was a coupe with two people so I started to turn away. The car passed me a small distance and stopped and I broke into a run as they started to back up. I was never so grateful for a ride, as the sun was nearly gone and the temperature was plummeting and a light snow was starting to fall.

In this coupe was a schoolteacher and her father who were heading to Richmond, Virginia for her job. They were driving a coupe that had a baggage area behind the seat, but they insisted that I get behind the seat with the baggage and I didn't resist, being nearly frozen by then. I rolled myself into a little ball behind the seat, which was cramped, but warm. I had thought that I would never feel heat again. We talked for awhile about my plans and I soon fell asleep.

An eternity later, that seemed only a few minutes, the teacher awakened me and said that we were in Richmond. I looked out and saw that it was raining lightly. They had gotten to their destination and were to turn off the route to Norfolk. I thanked them profusely for saving my life, and took a position along the road leading to Norfolk. The coupe went across the street and stopped. After a short while it came back and I trotted to the door, thinking I had left something behind. Instead, this young teacher thrust a dollar bill into my hand. I protested that they had already done more than enough for me, but she insisted, so I took it. This increased my bankroll to two dollars. The great kindness of these two strangers has remained in my memory for life. Again, I took a stance along the road to Norfolk while the coupe remained parked across the street. Soon a car stopped to pick me up, and the coupe, with two sainted people, went on its way. This incident will remain in my memory forever.

My new ride was with a salesman who was headed to Norfolk. It was the best of luck, as he took me within a few blocks of my destination, which was 414 Mowbray Arch, located along The Hague, which is a waterway in the residential part of Norfolk. I walked the remainder of my eight hundred-mile trip and arrived just after dawn. I knocked on the door at 414 Mowbray Arch just as the boarders were having breakfast. I soon learned that a room with Orland had an extra bed, and that room and board would cost me seven dollars a week, one dollar per day.

Mrs. Robinson had about a dozen men boarding at the house, and she fixed breakfast, packed them a sandwich, fed them supper, and gave them a bed. All for a dollar a day! She fed me breakfast that first morning and told me that I could pay her when I started work at the bag factory.

Unfortunately the job was not available for two weeks, and when I finally got started, I found that I could only make thirteen to fifteen dollars a week. It took me six weeks to pay the fourteen dollars I owed Mrs. Robinson for past room and board.

And then the bag factory closed down for two weeks over Christmas, so I knew that I would get two weeks behind again. Then Orland and I decided to hitch hike back to Illinois for Christmas. We started out one morning and got rides fairly easy, since people were in the spirit of Christmas. But when we got to Louisville, Kentucky the next afternoon, a fifteen minute snow shower dropped about an inch of snow, and the rides were not forthcoming. We were alongside a freight yard when a train started moving in front of us. We asked a man on the train where it was headed, and he yelled,

"Paducah." Several empty boxcars were going past, so we ran alongside and hopped into one that was lined with brown paper. It was cold, so we closed the door, hoping to keep out some of the cold. That was only partially successful so we stripped all the brown paper off the sides and wrapped ourselves in it. We lay down and tried to sleep, as soon as it was dark, but the vibration made our hips sore. As it turned out the train was a local, stopping at least a dozen times. At daybreak it made another stop, and we slid the door open a bit. As the train started moving we passed a man and I yelled at him,

"Where are we?"

"Paducah," he yelled, "Next stop, Kansas City."

We quickly grabbed our stuff and jumped from the train that was going about ten miles per hour by then. We got back to McLeansboro almost exactly two days after leaving Norfolk. Orland went to his home in Dale, and I walked the two miles to our house near the fairgrounds. Orland and I had agreed to meet in one week for our return to Norfolk. We decided to ride no more freight trains, and it took us three days to get back to Norfolk.

We went back to work at the Standard Bag factory in the first week of January, 1941, and after a few days, the manager approached us and asked if there were any more good workers out there in Illinois, and I replied, "My brother." He said,

"Get him here, and he has a job." So I wrote to Harold, and he took a bus to Norfolk and went to work at the bag factory. Unfortunately, we only worked until January 11, 1941 when we took better paying jobs. The manager of the bag factory was angry, and I felt guilty about it. My first paycheck from Standard Bag Corporation was $4.58, with a nickel withheld for Social Security tax. This was for two days work. My last check there was for $18.57 with 19 cents for Social Security.

We had answered an ad in the paper from the Norfolk Naval Air Station where Virginia Engineering Co. Inc. was building two large hangars and they needed carpenter's helpers. We only worked there three days when two men were killed when they fell from a broken scaffold fifty-five feet high inside the hanger where we were working. At this time we heard from another contractor where we had put in other applications. This was William L. Shepheard & Co.'s Sheet Metal works, which made duct work and iron chimneys. Orland and I went there to work, but Harold took a job driving a truck for Railway Express.

We worked at Shepheard's until spring, 1941, when Orland went by bus back to Illinois, where he soon married Elizabeth Ann Jones, his childhood sweetheart. I didn't see Orland again until after the war. He had also entered the Army Air Force and became a bombardier. I continued to work at the sheet metal job all that summer, and then took a job with the Prest-O-Lite company. This was the acetylene-manufacturing branch of the Linde Air Products Company, part of Union Carbide and Carbon Chemicals Corporation.

In the spring of 1941 I had a habit of sitting on the front porch of 414 Mowbray Arch to read. I noticed one day that a young, pretty girl had a habit of walking her dog near the water there, so I started sitting on the grass where she usually passed by. Soon we were speaking and eventually she would stop for a short conversation. I was about to ask her out one day when her dog hoisted his leg and peed on my ankle. This young lady was so embarrassed that she couldn't talk to me, and nothing ever came of our meetings. After that she walked past me at some distance, barely speaking. Damn dog!

Dad and Mom drove to Norfolk in late summer of 1941 to visit Harold and me, but they never returned to Illinois, except for a later trip that Dad made to gather our few belongings and my Indian artifacts.

I had bought a bicycle while working at the sheet metal job, and this was my only mode of transportation, except for electric streetcars. I was living at 630 Bossevain, by then, which was another rooming house. As a family, we moved to 1514 Granby Street that had a streetcar track at that time. The house was a four-unit apartment that my parents agreed to maintain in order to have free rent in one unit. Dad took a job as maintenance man for the Thomas Nelson Hotel in downtown Norfolk. It is located on Granby Street also, and this made a straight shot for Dad to go to work on the streetcar. I was soon working the night shift at the acetylene plant, because it paid ten cents per hour more than day shift.

On Sunday morning, December 7, 1941, I was just finishing my night shift, when at eight o-clock the other crew came in and told us that Pearl Harbor had been bombed by the Japanese. I didn't quite know where Pearl Harbor was, but I definitely knew that the war had finally reached the U.S.

One of the first things we did at the plant was to paint all the windows black on the inside so that no light could escape. We used a casein-based paint that was water-thinned. This paint was the forerunner of modern latex paints. The city of Norfolk was almost instantly blacked out, so that no enemy plane could see the potential target. There were many violations of the blackout order, and they were hard to police.

Almost immediately after this, there were submarine scares. It was reported that subs may have gone into the Chesapeake Bay, so the Navy had a submarine net installed across the mouth of the bay just out from Willoughby Spit. There was an amusement park there on Willougby Spit at that time, and several marinas. I had often taken the streetcar there on weekends to ride the roller coaster.

Not long after the submarine net was built, Aunt Bernice and uncle "Zip" came from Piqua for a visit, and to go fishing. One weekend they all rented a rowboat from the Willoughby marina and rowed around the Spit to fish in Hampton Roads. They decided to tie up at the sub net to fish, but soon a wind came up from the north and they were unable to row away from the net. The net was of heavy steel cable with twelve-inch spikes that resembled giant barbed wire. Soon the boat started being ground to bits and it was all that the four of them could do to hold the boat off. The owner of the marina finally decided that the wind was too rough and went out in a motor boat and rescued them.

This submarine net, kept at the surface by a string of large steel buoys, was opened when a surface transport needed to get into the harbor, and was then re-closed by a net tender, a large tug boat. I later heard rumors that German subs got into the Chesapeake Bay by tagging along close behind some of these transport vessels and entering the bay before the net could be closed again. There also started to be rumors about dead sailors washing up on coastal beaches, but nothing ever got into the news about it. I later learned about the awful loss of life inflicted on American Merchant Marines by German subs who used the not quite blacked out cities to profile their quarry at night. American civilian aircraft were conscripted at about this time, and the Civil Air Patrol was formed. Later they were credited with sinking a submarine.

My brother Harold was drafted at about this time and went into the Infantry at Fort Eustis, Virginia.

Chapter 5

OFF WE GO - into the wild blue

"From the President of the United States, Franklin D. Roosevelt," the letter read, "Greetings! You are hereby directed to report for induction into the Army of The United States at Fort Eustis, Virginia, on August 21, 1942."

"Good grief," I thought, "that is just next week. I don't want to be a soldier in the infantry. My brother, Harold is already a 'Dog Face' soldier, and he says 'it ain't no picnic.' I had always dreaded the thought of marching through mud and dust, and slithering on my belly under barbed wire, through weeds and over briars. And maybe even get shot for my troubles. I had already thought about joining the U.S. Army Air Force and thought perhaps I could get into aircraft repair and maintenance. Although I had never so much as touched an airplane I was sure that I could learn.

Without further ado, I grabbed the induction notice, hopped on my bicycle and headed for the Army Air Force recruiting station in downtown Norfolk. It was located on Granby Street, about two miles from my home at 1514 Granby St. I went into the recruiting station with the induction notice in my hand and approached the only person there. He was a soldier with a lot of stripes on the sleeve of his shirt. He seemed very congenial when I told him why I was there. He took the induction notice and said,

"I'll take care of this for you. Just sign on the dotted line, then hold up your right hand and repeat after me."

It was over in a moment, and here I was, a twenty-year old kid, a brand new member of the United States Army Air Corps.

"And now," he said, "go back home and wait for us to call you. As soon as we get a slot for you, we'll be in touch."

I was working the grave-yard shift at Prest-O-Lite, and when our plant superintendent, Maurice Van Osselar arrived just before eight o-clock the next morning, I told him I had joined the Air Corps to keep from being drafted. I remember his reaction quite well.

"Why would you do such a thing?" he asked. "I could have gotten you a deferment, and another and another. This welding gas we make here is vital to the war effort, and you are a skilled worker that I will have to replace and train."

"Well," I said, "I'm single and healthy, and they will get me sooner or later. Besides, most of your other workers are family men, so you may take this as my two weeks notice."

"These things take longer than you think," he said. "You had better stick with us until you get your notice. If it takes a couple of months, you will run out of money. Also it will give me more time to find a replacement and get him trained before you have to go."

This made sense, so I came back to work the next day. And the next. It was six months before I got the notice, and I often wondered if Mr. Van Osselar might have been instrumental in the delay. At any rate, I worked through February 27, 1943. My last check was for that day, and I had worked 53 and a half-hours that week. My gross pay was 47 dollars. Out of that came 47 cents for F.O.A.S. tax. That is Federal Old Age Security tax, now called Social Security tax. Victory tax was $1.60 every week, regardless of income. Also withheld was 65 cents for Group Health Insurance!

I was making enough money that, each week, I had them withhold $18.75 for a war bond, and through payroll deduction I had bought an extra $50.00 bond in December 1942, and two others in January 1943. My total income for 1942 was $1767.85. For that, I paid $210.00 income tax, being single with no deductions.

On the bottom of my check stubs from Linde Air Products is the message: "IT IS IMPORTANT THAT EMPLOYEES DETACH AND RETAIN THIS STUB." Naturally I still have them, since there is no date mentioned that I could dispose of them.

My total income for 1941 had been 1112.60, for which I paid only $29.00 income tax. And now my income would drop to $75.00 per month for the next nine months or so. That was the pay for an Aviation Cadet, as opposed to $21.00 per month for infantry privates. They had a song called "Twenty one dollars a day--Once a month."

My notice had finally arrived in the mail on February twenty third, 1943, and I was instructed to go by bus to Richmond, Virginia to the Army Air Force Classification Center.

Once we arrived in Richmond on March first, things got busy. Many different doctors gave us physical exams. We were given dozens of shots, or so it seemed. On my very first physical I was told that I was three pounds too light for my height. I was six feet tall and weighed 137 pounds. The doctor told me that I would be examined again in two days, and that I should eat lots of bananas, and drink all the water I could hold before the next exam.

So I stuffed myself with bananas and drank lots of water before the next exam. The doctor had me get on the scales then told me that I was still two pounds light, and would have to go into the infantry. After seeing my long face he brought the metal rod that is used for height measurement onto the top of my head and started pressing down. Finally it started to hurt, so I scrunched down a bit. Suddenly he said,

"Wait a Minute, I have misread your height. You are not six feet, you are only five feet, eleven inches tall. You qualify for the Aviation Cadet program by one pound." Thus, my records indicate that I was seventy-one inches tall. Those records are finally correct, as I have shrunk that much. However, the record of my weight is now grossly in error, as I now weigh about 175 pounds.

The doctor who examined my eyes put a gadget against my nose and told me to read the writing on it as soon as I could. I told him that I could read it right there. He said,

"Nobody can read it right against their nose." So I started reading it. He said that he had examined thousands of recruits, and that I was the first that he had seen who could do so. This was a focus-convergence test, so he wrote down the first number, which was fourteen millimeters. I had always been blessed with good eyesight, and at my present age, eighty plus, still read without glasses. It is all in ones' genes, I suppose. When my father died at age seventy, of emphysema, he was still reading without glasses.

After a few days in Richmond, we took a train to Nashville, Tennessee to boot camp. The train took us south, and stopped dozens of times. It seemed to be a converted cattle car and was filthy dirty. It took us two days in this circuitous route to get to Nashville. We arrived just after midnight on March sixth, 1943, four days before my 21st birthday. And no one was expecting us! The weather was bitterly cold, so they put us in a barracks that had one small, unlit coal burning stove. We were issued blankets and a sheet with which we shivered the night away on a thin army cot. "A noble start into the Air Force." I thought, sarcastically.

The next morning before daylight, just as the room was nearly warm, they routed us out to start our routine. First they gave us uniforms and told us to send our civilian clothes back home. Then we had to take an Officer Recognition course. About an hour after the first class, we were milling around waiting for the next session, when I spotted a Second Lieutenant. I saluted him smartly, and he returned it, seeming pleased. We were told how important it was to salute officers. "Especially Second Lieutenants."

They showed us films about various things regarding military life. I remember one with the young Glenn Ford doing a bit about venereal diseases. Very graphic! And a medical officer on stage was telling us how to prevent the possibility of catching one of these dreaded scourges.

" The only sure way to keep from getting the Clap or the Syph," he said, "is don't do it. Put it away. Keep it in your pants. Go home early. --And when you finish, be sure you use one of these silver nitrate kits--." He was drowned out by laughter. The film had just showed us how to use one. Ugh!

The latrine was a primitive affair with about ten commodes in a row in the open room, with a single trough-like urinal. Already mindful of toilet paper, and other shortages, the supply officer had placed a sign near the commodes that read,

"Waste and want, we must abolish.

Take two to wipe, and two to polish."

I liked Army food and couldn't understand the griping by some of the new recruits. Military people had already named chipped beef and gravy on toast "SOS" long before I arrived on the scene. It was "Something On a Shingle," if I may be allowed to clean it up a bit. But I liked it, as I knew a bit about food shortages from my childhood, having gone to school in Ozone, Arkansas with a bean sandwich for lunch on numerous occasions. I had learned to treat food as a necessity rather than a luxury.

After four weeks testing and pounding on us, we were sorted out for our various destinations. Many of the recruits had been to college for two or more years and all the tests were based on that assumption. I only had a High School Diploma and had to pass the same tests. Fortunately I had always been an avid reader of anything scientific and thus was able to pass the same tests with comparative ease. I passed all the coordination tests and was deemed fit to try for pilot training. Pilot candidates were to go to Maxwell Air Force Base in Montgomery, Alabama, class of 43 K. If we all passed the various requirements, we would graduate in the December class of 1943.

Aviation Cadet
Richard R. Johnson, 1943

ZOMBIES!

"You guys are, without a doubt, the crummiest bunch of Zombies I have ever seen." These were the first words that greeted us as we stepped off the bus at Maxwell Field. Our leader, an ex-corporal named Cole, had formed us up at the administration building, and after a few minutes a young man with funny looking stripes on his sleeve, that I didn't recognize, came out to check us over. We were standing at attention while he walked up and down in front and behind us before he spoke.

"You Zombies," he finally said, "are going to be sorry you were ever born before you leave this place. Most of you will probably wash out here, and the rest of you may wash out later. If you survive, which I doubt, you will be men when you leave here. For the next five weeks, you will be Under-class men-Zombies-The Walking Dead. As Aviation Cadets, you have no rank, so we will call you 'Mister,' -with tongue in cheek, of course." He emphasized his speech with scornful looks.

As we stood there, taking this all in, he suddenly yelled,

"Mister Cole, front and center." Our ex-corporal took a step forward, did a left face and marched to the center.

"Mister, sound off."

"Sir?"

"Name, rank and serial number."

"Cole, R. B., Corporal, 1305---"

"At ease, Mister Cole, you are not a corporal, you are an Aviation Cadet, and that will be your rank. Zombie, Are you standing at attention?" He yelled.

"Yes sir."

"I can't tell if you are or not, now, hit a brace."

"Sir?--"

"Pull in your gut, stick out your chest, shoulders back. Now screw your chin down and try to touch your chest with it, hat two fingers off your nose."

Our tormentor walked around Mister Cole and approached another "Zombie" standing next to me.

"Mister, are you smiling?"

"No, sir."

"Don't even think about it." he said, and making one side step was directly in front of me, with his eyes about six inches from mine.

"Mister, are you spying, or do you want to buy this place? "Did I see your eyes wandering around?" His voice was deceptively soft for a moment.

"No sir, I was just--"

"When an officer or an upper class man is talking to you," he bellowed," your eyes will be on his, and nowhere else. And when he is talking to someone else, your eyes will be straight ahead. DO YOU UNDERSTAND?"

"Yes sir." I said meekly.

"What?"

"Yes sir." I repeated.

"I CAN'T HEAR YOU." he bellowed.

"YES SIR." I shouted. I wondered if I could possibly be this overbearing in just five weeks. We quickly learned that we were only to speak when spoken to.

We marched to the barracks from this point and were assigned bunks. We also learned that we were to polish our shoes before every formation even if they were ten minutes apart. We each had been issued a blitz cloth at Nashville, and were now told that our brass belt buckle was to be polished before every formation as well. Underclassmen were to be at attention at all times when outside, except at PT, Physical Training. We had to shave every morning whether we had whiskers or not.

It soon came time for lunch, and we were told to "Fall Out" in front of the barracks. It was a short, hundred-foot march to the mess hall, but we had to go in formation. At all times while marching, we were to sing to the cadence, and continue singing until we reached our destination. If the destination was reached before the song ended, we had to march "In Place" until the song was ended. On the short march to the mess hall, the leader chose to sing a parody on "The Stars and Stripes Forever." Instead of singing "Three cheers for the Red White and Blue," we would sing,

"Be kind to your web footed friends,
For a duck may be some body's mother,
Be kind to your friends in the swamp,
Where the weather is cold and damp.
Now you may think that this is the end,
Well, it is---"   And we left it hanging there.

In the mess hall, the upper-classmen occupied every other seat along each side of a long table, with under-classmen on each side. Therefore, each "Zombie" had an upper classman on each side, and one directly across the table. Most of the meal was family style. Upperclassmen sat at ease, while "Zombies" sat at normal attention during meals. Their eyes were only allowed to go up to the upper class man's eyes opposite, and down to the plate that they were eating from. The left hand stayed in the lap, except when cutting meat, and then it was returned there. There was no allowance for left-handed men. The penalty for glancing at another under classman was to count the windows in the mess hall. This meant that most of your meal was forfeited, as you weren't allowed to eat at the same time. The mess hall had a bunch of windows. 238 actually.

The penalty for looking higher than the eyes of your monitor, or below your plate, was to eat a "Square Meal." The same penalty applied if you were "Dive-bombing." Dive-bombing was the act of leaning over your plate when taking a spoon or fork of food to your mouth.

A "Square Meal" required that you sit at stiff attention with your eyes glued to the eyes of the upper classman directly in front of you. Your fork must be placed in your food in the blind, bringing it up to his eye level and then straight to your own mouth. If the fork came up empty, the mission was completed as if it contained food. The empty fork was then moved straight back toward his eyes until over the plate, at which point it made a vertical descent, back to the plate

for another try. If any under classman had to suffer one of these in-
dignities, he was allowed to stay after the others left until he finished
his meal. It got real quiet after a while except for rattling of dishes
of the clean-up crew.

The academics at Maxwell "pre-flight" were nothing short of
high pressure. We had all the theories of flight, mathematics, Federal
air regulations, Army air regulations, engine mechanics, plus we had
to learn to send and receive Morse code. More practice was allotted
to Morse code that any other subject.

Because of the incidents of "Americide" in the past, Maxwell's
Preflight program included an extensive identification course, so
that friendly aircraft and ships would not be mistaken for the enemy.
Using flash cards and a projector, silhouettes of various ships and
aircraft were flashed on a screen for one twenty fifth of a second,
while the aviation cadets wrote down their answers. There were
several dozen ships and hundreds of aircraft to be learned.

Physical training was intensive. Before an Aviation Cadet could
graduate from "Pre-flight" he was required to demonstrate his ability to do a hundred sit-ups, ten pull-ups and twenty-five push-ups.
The cross-country was a one-hour "dog trot" around the perimeter
of Maxwell Field, which was eight miles. This "dog trot," as we
called it, had to be completed non-stop in order to pass the physical
requirements. My habit of riding a bicycle around Norfolk for years
aided me in passing this test on the first try. It was with considerable
pain, however. As we jogged along I was fine for the first three or
four miles until a pain developed in my right side. It got so bad that I
thought that I would drop out and ride the truck back. I looked at the
next ridge and decided that I would at least go that far before dropping out, or dropping dead. Then came another ridge, and I decided
to try for that one. Finally the pain disappeared and I made it all the
way.

Aviation Cadet C. D. Saxon of our previous class wrote a poem
about life as a zombie underclassman:

MARTIN MINCE, ZOMBIE

"Aeroplanes," said Martin Mince, "are certainly my meat."
"I'd rather fly," said Martin Mince, "I'd rather fly than eat."
"It's in my blood," he would declare, but still we might explain
That Martin Mince (The Flying Prince) had never touched a plane.

So Mince decided modestly he'd give the Force a break;
He got a pretty send-off with a party and a cake,
And Martin came to Maxwell Field one evening just at Taps.
"Give me a plane!" cried Martin Mince, "I'll kill a dozen Japs!"

But Martin was a Zombie; he discovered with dismay
That Zombies have no flights to make-a great deal less to say,
And Martin's upper class found out that Martin "wanted wings."
Then Zombie Mince was taught the ropes, and several other things.

"One forty on the rat-line, you; take in that belt line slack!
Screw in your chin, get on the beam, and straighten up that back!"
And Martin Mince (The Flying Prince) got feeling mighty small,
For Zombies' wings won't ever sprout 'til they get on the ball.

Now First Lieutenant Martin Mince is quite a different guy;
He poured some training in his head before he got to fly.
Oh, aeroplanes are Mince's meat, but still we might explain-
He learned a lot at Maxwell Field before he touched a plane.

One irritating aspect of being a Zombie was the restriction to base. Upper-classmen got to go into Montgomery on Saturday evenings, and as a Zombie you could be assured of being rudely awakened in the middle of Saturday night by an upper-classman coming into the barracks and yelling, "Piss call!" Or, "Wake up and piss, the world's on fire!" This was a regular Saturday night feature, repeated several times.

Finally, after thirty-two days, five hours and fifty-five minutes, the command is shouted:

"Upper class dismissed. Lower class, parade rest."

The "Zombie" has graduated. He is upper class now and for the first time he turned his head to see what Maxwell Field looked like without fear of being gigged. There were new "Zombies" at parade rest in the formation. They were the grossest of the gross, and would need plenty of training. Our class was never so gross, and we had the job of whipping them into line in just five weeks. "Look at those turning heads. Misters, are yo-o-o-u spying? Do you want to buy this place?"

All classes looked forward to Mail Call, and just a short time after I became an upper classman I went to check my mail. This was the very day that the new "Zombies" arrived. I got a letter from Mom and I heard the clerk call a Mr. Jones. I knew of no Mr. Jones, so I went back to where the Zombies were standing at parade rest. I called for Mr. Jones to sound off. One Zombie snapped to attention and identified himself as Mr. Jones.

"You have a letter at mail call," I told him, "Go get it."

"Thank you, sir," he said as he started to walk the ratline, making square corners around the perimeter.

"Cut across," I yelled, "and run, it's almost over." He made a mad dash on the diagonal and I soon saw him coming back on the ratline. As he got back into formation, I asked him,

"Did you get there in time?"

"Yes sir," he said, "It's from my wife. Thank you very much, sir."

On my very first day as an upperclassman I was nice to a Zombie. I needed practice at being obnoxious, so I picked a four-man squad of Zombies for a little close order drill. After having them do right and left flank a few times and a "To the rear, March" a couple of times, often from the wrong foot, one of the Zombies said,

"Sir, may I speak?"

"Sound off." I said.

"Sir, I was a drill sergeant before becoming an Aviation Cadet, and this drill needs work."

Boy, I sure knew how to pick them. First I was nice. Bad decision. Now I'm being humiliated by a Zombie for not knowing my left foot from my right. I quickly figured a way to save face.

"Oh, good," I said, why don't you show these guys how it is supposed to be done and I'll march along to check their progress." I soon dismissed the squad and returned to my barracks to do home work which was less stressful.

The academics of the upper class became even tougher. Added to our already tough schedule of Math, maps and charts, aircraft recognition, ground forces, war department publications and signal communications, were physics, air and naval forces, and chemical warfare.

But there was also the thrill of going out on the gun range, or into the altitude chamber. On the gun range was a high tower that fired clay pigeons toward the gunner to simulate a fighter attack. A shotgun was fixed onto a gun mount having a large ring sight such as would be found on a fifty-caliber waist gun of a heavy bomber. We were required to break a certain percentage of those clay pigeons. Then came it my turn, with my buddy, Horace W. Peppard in the tower loading and firing clay pigeons. The tower was three hundred feet from the gunner, and had a large plate glass window to protect us from birdshot which often struck the glass. I passed the gunnery test without too much trouble, having been raised around shotguns. I killed more than half of the clay pigeons during my turns with the mounted gun.

The altitude chamber was large enough to seat six men, plus the instructor. As air was pumped from the chamber to simulate high altitude, oxygen masks were worn from the ten thousand-foot elevation and more air was removed until thirty thousand feet was simulated. At this point the instructor had each cadet in turn remove his oxygen mask and perform small tasks. Mine was to take a yellow lined paper and write my signature on each line. After about five lines were filled, my mask was removed, and I continued signing my name. Presently, I had reached the bottom of the page, but I noticed that my mask was back on, and in the middle of the page, my signatures were unreadable. I could then report, with complete confidence, that anoxia could not be detected by the victim, despite the erroneous depiction in the latest Memphis Belle movie where the gunners were without oxygen for over a minute at high altitude. I suppose that the movie director wanted us to see those handsome young faces. But there are no symptoms of oxygen starvation, and the victim can die without even knowing that there was a problem. This was brought home to us several times over Europe in the next year.

As upper classmen, we could enjoy "Open Post" on some weekends. Away from the post in Montgomery, we usually ate our meals at attention, since the training we received as under classmen would never be forgotten. The Cadet Club in the Jefferson Davis Hotel was the favorite hangout in Montgomery, while the "rec hall" was the favorite on base. It was here that we studied, played pool or Ping-Pong, and made serious plans about how to take the "grossness" out of the Zombies.

Just before graduation day, we each filled out a questionnaire asking if we preferred "Light, Medium or Heavy." I had always thought that the B-17 was the finest of the fine, and I wanted to be associated with it. I was fearful that if I marked "Heavy, I might end up in a B-24, so I wrote the word "B-17" in the place I was supposed to put a check mark. Similar questionnaires came up twice more during later schools, and I always marked them the same way. Evidently they got my message although most of the cadets opted for fighters but some were assigned to bombers anyway.

One of the zombies that we were trying to straighten out was a little difficult, but he made it to upper class. While we were packing to go to flight school, we decided to punish him yet one more time. As a new upper classman, he was out hazing the new Zombies, which gave us time to dismantle his cot. Peppard and I removed all the springs around the edge of the cot and replaced them with a weak twine lacing, so that he would fall through when he lay down, he being quite a sack hound. We remade his cot and short-sheeted it, leaving it looking pristine. We never learned the outcome, but got plenty of mileage from our imaginations.

The big graduation day parade was an impressive event, with a big band, notable speakers and a "Buzz" job by three P-51 Mustangs. These were the early models with Allison engines and three bladed props, before the bubble canopy of the later versions.

As they came roaring down the runway, the low man was a little too low and his propeller struck the runway for several dozen feet. He managed to ease up a little higher, and they went on their way. After the parade, I walked out and looked at the runway and could see the diagonal slashes that the prop had made every twelve feet. He almost gave a very exciting show that day. I often wondered if it was my grammar school friend, Don Gentile that I had known as a child. He always seemed to push the envelope.

There always seemed to be a shady character in any group of men during training. One particular cadet asked to borrow ten dollars from me and said that he would pay me back the following month at primary flight school. So I loaned him the ten dollars against my better judgment.

I later found that he had done the same scam to several other of my classmates. What really took the cake, though, was that he forgot to tell us that he had flunked the pre-flight course and was to be returned to the infantry. Naturally we never saw him or the money again.

We learned that a large portion of our class of 43K was destined to go to Albany, Georgia to fly the PT-17 "Kaydet." This is a tandem seated open cockpit biplane built by Boeing Aircraft Company. It is called a Stearman after its designer, and has conventional landing gear, meaning that it has a tail wheel. The main landing gear is fairly close set, and the planes will groundloop fairly easily if landed poorly. The lower wing is a scant three feet off the ground and when a ground loop is "Accomplished," the aircraft will spin around on one wheel and one wing tip, usually in a large cloud of dust. Usually when this happens, little or no damage is sustained, but it surely gets the attention of the instructor.

It is now the last week in May 1943, and if we stay the course, we will graduate from flight school in December as full-fledged pilots, and maybe even as Second Lieutenants. Some cadets who wash out for physical or scholastic problems will go on to bombardier or navigator schools. The hype at every school was always aimed at staying on course, with a constant threat of washing out.

It didn't seem to occur to any of us that if we washed out from these various schools that we could end up as non-combatants in a cushy job. Perish the thought!

On the day of our graduation from Pre-flight there was a B-17-F parked by operations and after the parade I walked over to examine it. To me it was a thing of beauty with gracefully flowing lines. The dorsal fin started about midway down the fuselage and swept upward in a graceful curve to the top of the vertical stabilizer, nineteen feet above the ground. Could I ever learn to fly one of these huge machines? As it sat there it seemed to beckon me to come aboard, but I never touched it. I was awed by the graceful look of so large a machine, and wanted more than ever to learn to fly one. How could one man fly such a heavy bomber with its complex systems? The famous Memphis Belle was already back in the US on a war bond tour. I had seen it in the Movietone News at the theater in Norfolk.

This complexity was one of the things that critics of the design had brought up early in the development of this aircraft. And yet, here was a twenty-one year old that thought he could pass muster on it. And indeed, as I look back on those days, it was practically all flown by young men barely out of childhood. The zeal of these young men was the deciding factor in the winning of the war over Europe, even with the highest casualty rate of any other military service in WW2.

In retrospect I decided that World War Two was fought mostly by children. I found that I was destined to finish my combat tour of thirty-five missions and become a combat instructor, both in Europe and in America before I was twenty-three years old. Incredible!

But first I must learn to fly! Since I had never so much as touched and airplane, I knew that it wouldn't be easy for me.

My first military ID card taken on my entrance into
flight training - age 21

Chapter 6

Primary flight training

Finally, we were ready to go to primary flight school where I would finally get to touch an airplane. No more upper or lower class hazing. Our group's destination was Albany, Georgia, to the civilian flight school, Darr Aero Tech. Peppard and I were in the same barracks again. There were 160 cadets in our primary class.

Darr Aero Tech was a civilian flight school that leased the facilities from the Army. This was the 52nd AAFFTD; Army Air Force Flight Training Detachment, located four miles southwest of Albany, Georgia, at the new municipal airport on State route 62. It was the oldest Army airdrome in that area, and was one of the largest Army training detachments in the country. Ground was broken for the school in July 1940, it being the third such flight school opened by Harold S. Darr, a pilot with long-time experience in pilot training. He flew in France in 1917 with the U. S. Army, and kept up with aviation technology after the First World War.

On the 14th of September 1940, the first class of 50 Aviation Cadets arrived at Darr to fly their 15 Stearman PT-17s, an open cockpit biplane. At that time, this was their entire inventory of aircraft. Most of the civilian personnel were transferred from Mr. Darr's school in Glenview, Illinois. Within six months of opening, additional personnel were transferred from Mr. Darr's school of aeronautics in Chicago, and additional buildings were built.

From opening, in September 1940 until July 1941, only U.S. Aviation Cadets were trained at Darr, and seven classes completed the course of instruction. From this time until October 10, 1942, United Kingdom cadets were trained, so that they could supplement their comrades in the Battle of Britain. On September 15, 1942, U.S.

Cadets resumed training at the base. My arrival at Darr was in the last week of May 1943, four classes later.

After a bit of schooling, Peppard and I were assigned to the same instructor, Mr. S. D. Davis, an easy-going pilot instructor. He was one of the seventy-nine civilian instructors on duty at the field.

The first time I touched an airplane was when Mr. Davis had a few cadets out to examine a PT-17 trainer. This open cockpit biplane had no electric system, and was started by cranking a handle on the left side of the engine cowl. The crank turned a heavy flywheel which was wound up until it gave off a high pitched whine. At this time, with the engine being primed with a couple of shots of gasoline, the starter was engaged, and after a few cylinders turned through, the magneto switches were turned on. The engine usually started, but if not, the whole procedure had to be repeated.

June first, 1943 was my big day to take an orientation ride with Mr. Davis in ship number 41. It was one of those sunny, warm days with cumulus clouds which we called "summer puffs." This meant that the air would be bumpy.

Within ten minutes after take-off, I started getting queasy, so I told Mr. Davis that I was getting airsick. Before he could get us back to the field, I tossed my cookies over the left side of the cockpit while Mr. Davis tried to stay unimpressed.

Total airtime for my first flight: 28 minutes. Wash airplane time: one hour.

The next day was June 2, 1943, my Mother's forty third birthday. I was to fly again, in ship number 49 this time, and was to handle the controls. I did pretty well for about a half-hour until I started getting airsick again. Mr. Davis quickly returned to the field and landed.

Total airtime for my second flight: 44 minutes. Wash airplane time: one hour. Amazingly, in exactly one year from now I would have eight combat missions under my belt. But today, Mr. Davis sent me to the Medical Officer to see what I should eat before the next flight. He said that if I defaced another airplane, I would probably wash out. So I went to see the Medical Officer, 1st lt. Daniel F. Shea. He gave me a pep talk, and told me to eat a light breakfast the next morning, with nothing greasy.

June third, I was assigned ship number 46 for my third flight. I did a little better this time. Flying and handling the controls helped stave off the airsickness for over a half-hour. All I got was a gut wrenching dry heaves, but at least I didn't "decorate" the airplane. Total flight time was 50 minutes this day. The next day was a repeat of day three, and after that I didn't get sick again.

Most Cadets were able to fly solo in the Stearman in eight to twelve hours. My solo came after ten hours and forty-nine minutes on June 17, 1943, just seventeen days after my first orientation ride. Then after several days of dual and solo flights, it came time for my first check-ride.

This check-ride was to be with one of the few military officers at Darr, and Mr. Davis had warned me that they were looking primarily for safety in their new pilots. Knowing that I wasn't a very good pilot candidate, I was determined to be safe. The air around Darr seemed always to be congested with PT-17s, so after I took off with the check pilot, he told me to make a left turn. I cranked my neck all around to be sure that I wouldn't run into another plane before I turned. I then turned left and repeated this maneuver every time he asked for a turn. Although my air work was a little sloppy, he was duly impressed with my safety and he gave a good report about me to Mr. Davis.

At this point we started doing aerobatics in the Stearman. I was taught loops, slow rolls, snap rolls and spins. The spins were supposed to come out on the same direction after a given number of turns.

One day we went to an auxiliary field to do "Hurdles." Mr. Davis got out of the airplane and gave me over to another civilian instructor, Flight Commander, R. G. Parker. Two other instructors held up two poles that were twenty feet high with a ribbon between them. In order to pass the course, the fledgling pilots had to control airspeed well enough to make a three point landing within 200 feet past this twenty-foot obstacle. I watched as the instructors hastily lowered the poles when some of the cadets came in too low. It was required that we do three of these full stall landings out of five tries. When it came my turn, I was able to do three out of my first four solo tries, and so Mr. Parker got back in the airplane with me and said,

"That was pretty good air speed control and so now we deserve

a little play time. I'm going to show you how do it on one wheel."
So, up we went around the pattern, and on the approach he put the
airplane into a full forward slip. Just as we were about to touch
down he yelled,

"Oh, shit! I'm on the wrong brake!"

With this, the Stearman touched down on the right wheel and
right wing tip and did an impressive ground loop. It did a 720-de-
gree, two complete turns, before it stopped, making beautiful figure
eights with the wing tip. The cloud of dust was impressive. The
other instructors, along with Mr. Davis walked up and gave Mr.
Parker, my unfortunate check pilot, the "Haw haws" and asked him
what he would do for an encore. With that, two instructors took the
right wing tip and yanked the airplane up and down until the wheels
bounced off the ground. The ground loop had only scuffed the fabric
on the bottom of the wing tip.

I was still in the airplane and Mr. Parker got back in and we
took off. We climbed to about two thousand feet and Mr. Parker said
through the Gosport, the speaking tube,

"I'm going to show you a couple of aerobatics that I don't want
you to try." With that, he did an outside snap roll, which felt like it
would fling you into orbit if the seat belt hadn't been fastened. I did
a momentary "red-out" which is opposite the familiar "blackout." A
blackout is caused during a severe pullout, which forces the blood
downward from the brain. Forcing too much blood to the brain and
eyes, causing a momentary red tinge to your vision causes a red-
out.

This was my first, ever, red-out. The second came in short order
when Mr. Parker did an inverted immelman. He pushed the stick
straight-ahead into a dive and held the stick there until the plane
reversed its direction upside down. Of course with gravity feed to
the carburetor, the engine quit until he righted the airplane into normal flight. This red- out was really red, and I realized that the first
one had merely been a "pink-out." I was glad that I was wearing
a parachute, but the airplane never complained. It is truly a tough
airplane.

Some days when we had a bit of free time, someone would say,
Let's go over to the field and watch a few ground loops. We were

seldom disappointed. Ours was a large circular field with a wind
sock in the middle so that we could always land into the wind.

Toward the end of the primary course the operations officer was
reviewing documents and told me that I had a shortage of solo aerobatics. I needed an hour and fifty minutes to complete the course
and graduate to basic. So He told me to get a PT-17 and go do the
aerobatics time that I needed. This was July 20th, 1943, one month
and three days after solo.

Ship number 97 was on line, so I did the required pre-flight,
cranked the starter, primed the engine and pulled the mesh handle,
turned on the ignition, and the engine started. I climbed into the
cockpit, strapped myself in and started to taxi when I advanced the
throttle too quickly and killed the engine. I un-strapped, got out,
cranked the engine again, scrambled back into the cockpit and was
on my way. I flew out to the practice area, climbing to three thousand feet and started doing aerobatics. Three loops in a row, two
slow rolls in a row, a few hammerhead turns, a couple of immel-
mans and a bunch of snap rolls. The PT-17 fed gas to the engine by
gravity, so that any inverted or negative "G" forces would cause the
engine to stop until positive "G" forces were re-established.

After a while this all got a little boring, and I had only done fifty
minutes of my required solo aerobatics, so I decided to improve
on the loops. I knew that what seemed like a loop to the pilot, only
looked like a "flip" to an observer on the ground, so I decided to
make a truly round loop. I went into a dive, adding full power, then
pulling up into a steep climb over the top. As I neared the top of the
loop I slowly added forward pressure on the stick to cause negative
G force. Of course the engine stopped, which I expected. What I
didn't expect was to find myself drifting out of the seat of this upside down airplane, hanging by the stick with my right hand and the
throttle with my left. In my hurry to restart the engine I had forgotten
to re-fasten my seat belt! And now, here I was hanging upside down,
floating six inches out of the rear seat in an open cockpit biplane
with nothing above me except the earth.

This was the perfect scenario for an inverted flat spin, from
which I had not the skill to recover. It was enough to cause an

involuntary colonic spasm, but finally I took my left hand off the throttle and pushed it against the instrument panel, thus giving me enough pressure to push the stick back. After hanging weightless for a few seconds that seemed an eternity, the airplane tucked under the backside of the "loop" and I fell back into the seat. It scared me so bad that I spent the next hour just riding around at five hundred feet, sightseeing. How could I tell them back at base why I had jumped out and left their perfectly good airplane up there? Of course I was wearing a parachute, but with my luck I would have had an experience like that of another cadet.

He was flying solo one evening near dusk when he thought the airplane was on fire, never having seen the exhaust at night. He parachuted out and left the airplane to fend for itself. It flew on for over an hour before running out of fuel, made an acceptable landing in a cornfield nearly a hundred miles away. It ground looped, sustaining only minor damage, and was flown home two days later.

I never told anyone about nearly falling out of an airplane until many years later, and I still owe Darr Aero Tech one hour of solo aerobatics.

I had my sixty-hour check ride on July twenty-second, and on the next day did a fourteen-minute flight from the front seat. This was my final flight in a Stearman, PT-17. I had accumulated sixty-five hours and thirteen minutes in less than two months. During those flights I flew thirty-nine different PT-17s.

Two friends from Darr were later killed in a mishap with an AT-10. Another was killed in a P-40. Two were killed in B-17s before going overseas. My best buddy at the time was Horace W. Peppard of New Jersey. He was killed in Labrador while flying as copilot for another friend while they were ferrying a new B-17 overseas.

There always seemed to be an inordinate number of fatal accidents in training phases, some from landing accidents, and some from foolhardy buzz jobs. One cadet from a previous class thought it would be fun to buzz down a country road while meeting a car or pickup truck, touch the roadway with the wheels, and pull up at the last minute. On one such buzz job he met a pickup truck which slammed on the brakes. Just as a man sitting In the back of the pickup stood up to see what the problem was, the lower wing of the

PT-17 struck him under the chin, killing him instantly. The cadet was given a court-martial and given a life sentence at San Quentin military prison.

Another cadet made an illegal off-airport landing. His family lived not very far from Darr Aero on a large farm, so one day he decided to land in their pasture and take a few family members for a ride. He first took his father for a ride and after landing was getting ready to take his mother on a short flight, when his excited twelve year old sister ran into the turning propeller and was killed.

These tragedies were drilled into us during the early stages of our solo flights, and very few cadets did any unauthorized flights. This is also the reason that few cadets were ever stationed close to their own homes.

Just after solo, June 13, 1944

Chapter 7

Off to Basic

Bainbridge, Georgia was to be my next stop, and one of my worst traumas. We were to fly the BT-13, Vultee Valiant and the similar BT-15, the only difference between the two planes being the engine. The BT 13 has a Pratt and Whitney engine and the BT 15 has a Wright engine, both having 450 horsepower. Of course, they had long since been nicknamed "Vultee Vibrators" which we used only in our own circle, as the officers at Bainbridge AAF frowned on the use of such nomenclature.

My first flight in a BT-13 was on August 2nd, 1943, exactly two months and one day since my first flight in the PT-17. The Vultee is a much more complex and unforgiving airplane than the Stearman and therefore takes more dual instruction to solo. I didn't solo in this plane until August 21 after more than fourteen hours dual. We didn't start practicing landings until we had done eight days of air work and flying other systems in the airplane.

After forty practice landings with an instructor, I did two solo landings on August 21st, 1943. This solo was in a BT-15 after having only flown in BT-13s except on two other occasions. There is no difference in the handling characteristics of the two aircraft, and they look identical except for the difference in engines.

Mostly, the academics were tougher, and the airplane was more complex. Perhaps I had reached the limit of my training ability. Then I found that nearly all the cadets were having equal trouble. We finally figured that the commandant of cadets was harder on us than most. My own grades were average or below average, while no subject was above average. I was able to fly the BT-13 as good as most others, but fell into an easy trap. Before landing the Valiant, the canopy is supposed to be opened on final approach. This is the

final item on the "before landing check list." It is to be open in case
of a mishap so that the rescue people can drag you out easier. I forgot to open the canopy on one landing and got the attention of the
commandant. It was placed on my record and I was reprimanded by
radio at that time. Three days later, I gave a repeat performance. As
I was nearing the flare point, the radio came alive.

"Who is that cadet landing with the canopy closed?" I immediately reached up and unlatched the canopy and slid it back, but was
too busy to answer.

"WHO IS THAT CADET LANDING WITH THE CANOPY
CLOSED?" I was on roll out and could finally answer.

"Richard R. Johnson, sir."

"Report to my office as soon as you park that plane, Mr. Johnson."

"Yes sir." I responded, knowing that I was going to receive the
attention of our feared commandant of cadets.

I walked into the administration building and knocked on the
open door of "Old Iron Pants" 1st. Lt. "Breaker." And now, the
trauma.

"Enter." I marched in through the open door and went straight
ahead until I was directly in front of lieutenant Breaker, at which
point I made a "Left face," and made two steps toward his desk. I hit
a brace, saluted and said,

"Aviation Cadet Johnson, Richard R., 13065783 reporting as
ordered sir." I knew I would be standing in a brace for this lecture,
but I had no idea how long it would last. Lieutenant. Breaker walked
around me several times talking as he went. He called me every kind
of pond scum that ever pervaded the Earth. He asked me where I
was from. When I told him I was from Norfolk, Virginia, he talked
at length about how the Mayor and all the City Council must have
been relieved to get rid of me. Without ever uttering a cuss word he
called me every sort of low life that had no business in an airplane
or on the planet. If I ever flew in combat I might cause great losses
to our own side. This harangue went on for forty minutes without
let up until another cadet walking down the hall glanced through the
open door to see who was getting chewed out.

"MISTER," called lieutenant Breaker, "Step in here." The unfortunate cadet marched in and reported.

"If you are so curious to know what is going on in here, you just stand alongside Mr. Johnson and find out." He then proceeded to rant and rave at this new victim for twenty minutes just for glancing through an open door. Unbelievable, but I was grateful for the interlude in my own torture. Finally, after exactly one hour he ran out of expletives and said,

"I can't stand such gross behavior. Both of you get out of my sight, dismissed." We saluted, did an about face and marched out.

"Wow." was the only comment of the other cadet as he went on his way. As for me, I instantly hated lieutenant Breaker, and could think of all kinds of dire things that should happen to him. His tirade got through to me, however, as I never again came even close to landing with the canopy closed.

I could be a little devious at times if I thought it necessary. I was to fly a dual cross country with the instructor on a dead reckoning flight without the advantage of the four course radio range that I had gotten used to. After I flew for about an hour I noticed that I could see out a small corner of the windscreen and see the ground on the right side. I had to get the time and direction just right in order to find the destination airport. So I flew about a quarter mile to the left of the course at that point and luckily saw the airport in that little corner of the windscreen. At this point I eased the plane a little to the right and then told the instructor that I thought that we should be there, so he said to remove the hood. I did so and looked all around as if looking for the airport.

I must have missed it," I said, knowing that I was directly over it. The instructor banked the airplane steeply.

"Look down," he said, "you hit it dead center." I did get a good one once in awhile.

One day I was scheduled to fly solo aerobatics, and as I taxied to the warm-up area I noticed a P-47 on the ramp. This huge Republic Thunderbolt was taxiing out to take off after a BT-13 had finished landing. The tower was talking to him on another radio frequency while talking to the BT on our regular frequency. As the P-47 started his take off roll the BT was still rolling slowly down the middle of the runway.

"BT, get off the runway." No answer. "BT, GET OFF THE RUNWAY." There was still no answer and the BT stayed on the runway. I suppose the instructor in the BT was talking to the student and wasn't listening to the radio.

As the P-47 gained momentum to about seventy miles per hour, the pilot raised the tail and saw the obstruction for the first time.

He immediately hauled the plane off the runway, and lifted by the screaming, four bladed propeller, it staggered over the BT-13. But he didn't quite make it. His right landing gear caught under the right wing of the BT and tore it off, tossing it at least thirty feet in the air. His left wheel tore the canopy off and sent it sliding and spinning down the runway. Incredibly, the P-47 remained in the air and the pilot flew around the tower a few times, raising and lowering his landing gear. After about four cycles, he went on his way, apparently with no major damage. Tough airplane! I would be glad to see it as one of my escorts when I got into combat.

Meanwhile, the instructor and cadet climbed out of the wounded BT, seemingly uninjured. The plane became a salvage job except I imagine the two pilot seats were not usable after this mishap. I was diverted to another runway and continued my air work. When I returned to base the wreckage had all been cleared, and I never learned what the outcome was. I often wondered how close the giant four-bladed prop came to the two occupants of the BT-13.

On September 1st, 1943 I was to practice dual night flight, so I checked out BT-13 number 156. I had just made two solo flights that morning. One was an hour and the other was an hour and fifteen minutes. Between flights I went to ground school. With the instructor aboard, I was to make my first night flight. In fifty-five minutes we shot three landings and then I did six solo landings in an hour and five minutes. I had already had several instrument flights. On September 5th I did eight night landings in two hours. That same morning I had dual cross-country, practicing navigation by pilotage. After a couple of formation flights I did a solo cross-country in daylight, landing at another air base. This trip took nearly two and a half-hours. On September ninth I shot seven night landings in preparation for the big night cross country that was required of us. On September thirteenth I did a dual cross country of two hours and twenty-minutes. All went well, and I was finally ready for the big event.

September fourteenth was a clear day with a nearly full moon at night. This was it! The big cross-country. It was to take two hours to do a "Round Robin" following light beacons. These beacons flashed a letter in Morse code, and could be seen for thirty miles or more. A piece of cake, I thought. I drew the course on the air chart and was ready to go. In retrospect, I should have made a sequential list of the beacons, since there was six or seven of them. After taking off in BT-13 number 162, I flew directly to the first beacon. I turned to the second beacon, and could see four or five others in all directions.

"Let's see now, what was the third beacon supposed to be flashing? I forget. Let me check the chart. Wow, they call this thing the Vultee Vibrator for good reason. And the cockpit light is not too good. Okay, I see that the next light is supposed to be flashing 'L', dit-dah-dit-dit. That's an easy one. In Morse code they said to think of it as 'to hell with it.' But now the airplane has wandered off course while I was trying to read the chart. Maybe I can skip 'L' and go to 'B.'"

Needless to say, I lost all track of the beacons that I was supposed to be following, so I just flew on and on. I was sure I was over Georgia, or Alabama, or--. Suddenly I saw some blue runway lights off to my right. I didn't know what field it was, but I suddenly saw the reflection of the moon on a body of water. After a minute it disappeared for a few seconds and reappeared almost instantly. Only this time it didn't go away, and there were absolutely no lights or beacons ahead of me. And the blue runway lights were almost out of sight behind me.

Suddenly like a bolt of lightening, it struck me. The Gulf of Mexico! The blue lights were at Tyndall Field, near Panama City in Florida's panhandle. I did a quick one hundred eighty-degree turn to reverse my course, keeping the blue lights of Tyndall Field off my left wing. I decided to run a reverse course for awhile, and if I stayed lost, I would land at Tyndall before running out of gas, although I couldn't imagine the embarrassment that would accrue by landing at a strange base and asking "Where am I, and how do I get home?"

After a little while I saw the moon's reflection on a body of water again, which appeared to be a rather large river. Our base at Bainbridge was on the Apalachicola River so I followed it, using the moon as a guide. After getting almost out of sight of the blue lights, I came to a fork in the river. I knew that the Chattahoochee River came into the Apalachicola from the left, so I followed the right fork. In a little while I saw a lighted area ahead and as I flew closer, I recognized our base. I quickly got into the pattern and landed a half-hour past my estimated time of arrival. I figured I'd have another session with "Old Iron Pants," but nobody said a word, and neither did I.

They all thought that I had done a wonderful cross-country. I knew however, that I had almost ended at the bottom of the Gulf of Mexico, and they would always have wondered what happened to old number 162 and the inept cadet character that was flying it. That was my last night flight at Bainbridge, which is probably a lucky thing for them. And me.

Aerobatics is something the military emphasizes. It is a good thing for training and discipline. And for fighter pilots, it is essential for survival. At this point I had already asked for B-17 assignment a couple of times, but you could never be sure of what you would be put into until the time arrived. My best chance to be a B-17 pilot was based on numbers of cadets requesting fighter school, as most did.

On September 17, I was sent to do solo aerobatics, so I got BT-13 number 175 and headed for the practice area. I had already flown two other planes that morning, doing dual instrument work in one of them. I needed only one more aerobatics flight after this one to complete the course.

After I got to the practice area I did a couple of loops and a series of barrel rolls, and a hammerhead turn or two. About this time, my noon coffee was asking for attention, so I leveled off and unhooked the relief tube that is between the pilot's legs. I was soon feeling much better and decided to do a nice snap roll. I reduced power and pulled the nose up slightly, and just before the plane stalled I reversed the controls. The BT did a vicious snap roll, grinding and vibrating something fierce. Only on this particular snap roll I had the added burden of urine spraying out of the relief tube, covering the entire cockpit, and the pilot in it. Me. It even dripped off the canopy, which I opened right away Some "friend" had plugged the vent that was supposed to empty the relief tube as it is being used. As I flew back to base to shower and change clothes, I was hoping that it was all mine, and not the last two or three cadets who had flown this plane this morning.

These kinds of tricks were not unusual in the life of an aviation cadet even with all the pressure of homework and flying training. There was always time to short sheet a neighbor or play some other kind of trick. I think though, that plugging the outlet of the relief tube was one I never would have thought of. At least until it happened to me. After this incident I always added this one item to the pre-flight inspection.

"Be sure relief tube vent is open."

Whereas civilian instructors did the primary training at a civilian field, with military pilots used only as check pilots, the basic training was done at a military field with military instructors. Most military instructors were second lieutenants with an occasional first lieutenant being employed as check pilots.

Our commandant of cadets (Lt. Breaker) was a first lieutenant who seemed bitter about not being a captain since he had been there for a couple of years without being promoted. We always felt that he picked on us unnecessarily, but probably he was trying to protect us from ourselves. I was always a little putout by my report card saying that I was a below average student. At my primary flight school I had a mix of average and below average grades which came out to a grade of C+. I was beginning to think that my patron saint was Mediocrates.

So how will I make out at our next school? The PT 17 was a fairly simple airplane with no electrical system and the BT 13 was quite complex by comparison. I survived basic training by the skin of my teeth and now I am to be sent to advanced training to fly a twin engine trainer of even more complexity.

Chapter 8

Off to Advanced flight training

Here I am back in Albany, Georgia where I did ten weeks of primary flight training in the Stearman, PT-17 "Kaydet." Only this time, The base is Turner Field. Army Air Force, instead of Darr Aero Tech. And the airplane that I will fly is a Beechcraft AT-10 "Witchita." The AT-10 had already received its derogatory nickname, "Beaverboard Bomber" from previous classes. This aircraft was a twin engine craft, built primarily of plywood and other non-strategic materials. Even the gas tanks were of plywood with neoprene cover. The large radial engines were placed on the wings so that they were nearly even with the nose of the airplane, giving it an odd look.

My instructor was a young second lieutenant who had just the opposite opinion of me than did First Lieutenant "Old Iron Pants" Breaker, who had ranted at me for an hour because I had landed with the canopy closed on the BT-13. With only six hours dual in the AT-10, Lt. Hall told me that I was ready to "solo" the twin engine machine.

Lt. Hall was wrong! My very first solo flight took me to an auxiliary field where we were to practice take off and landing. My co-pilot was a new kid on his second flight in the Beechcraft. The auxiliary field was a wide concrete strip aimed into the prevailing winds, except this day the wind was blowing from about forty five degrees right to left.   The concrete strip was so wide that, as an air-craft landed in the center, another would be taking off on the right edge, and another would be taxiing back on the left edge. On my first approach I crabbed into the wind enough to maintain a straight heading down the runway. At the last moment before touchdown I was to apply left rudder to align the plane with its direction of travel, and thus avoid the possibility of a ground loop, or placing a side

78

load on the landing gear. At this time there was another AT-10 just starting his take off roll on my right as I passed over.

When I pushed the left rudder to align with the runway, nothing happened in time, and my aircraft struck the runway in a forward slip, making a loud "lurch" noise with the tires. It also "lurched" to the right, putting me on a collision course with the aircraft taking off. My aircraft bounced off the runway a bit and staggered in front of the other craft. I immediately jammed both throttles to the firewall and flipped up the landing gear switch in the same operation. The AT-10 engines reacted instantly and the gear came up at once. The aircraft on the take off roll saw the problem and kept his craft on the runway. I cleared his canopy a bare three feet and staggered off at a diagonal and re-entered the pattern.

Just then the radio came alive and instructed me to report to the operations officer's command post and to report to First Lieutenant Jones, who was not only the operations officer, but also the commandant of cadets.

"Well, like in Basic, here comes another hour of ass chewing," I thought. I landed successfully this time, having given the rudder more lead-time and modifying the approach with crossed controls with a little right wing low against the wind. My poor co-pilot had never uttered a word during all of this operation. I figured that he must have been struck dumb, or was thinking about how he was going to clean himself up.

I entered the command post trailer and reported to Lieutenant Jones who was behind the desk.

"Sir," I said, while hitting a brace, "Aviation Cadet Johnson, Richard R., 13065783, reporting as ordered –Sir." I repeated.

"At ease, Mister Johnson, he said in a deceptively soft voice, "What happened out there?"

"No excuse sir." I said in my most military voice.

"Now, now," he said, still softly, "I don't need that kind of response. What really happened?"

I explained to him that I hadn't landed in a crosswind with the AT-10 before, and it being a heavier plane, didn't react as quickly as the BT-13 would have.

"Well," he said, "that was the most remarkable recovery I have

ever seen. I had written off two planes and four pilots until you
saved yourself. We're not going to have any more trouble with you,
are we?"

"No sir." I replied with great relief.

"Okay, Mr. Johnson. You are dismissed."

I couldn't believe my good luck as I quickly saluted and departed. After this incident, my training went smoothly, my instructor, Lt.
Hall having been a witness. My grades and scores were all "above
average, smooth, confident," which is on my grade card. They had
a lot more confidence in me than I did in myself. Lt. Hall even
recommended that I be made an instructor in the AT-10. I quickly
vetoed this idea as I figured that flying combat would be dangerous
enough.

After flying a dozen or so AT-10s for seventy-seven hours and
six minutes, I finished the advanced course. My last flight was on
December third and graduation was to be December fifth. A few
days before graduation we were all given interviews to see who
would become Second Lieutenant, and who would be made Flight
Officer which is equivalent to the Navy Chief Petty Officer, or the
Army Warrant Officer, the top enlisted rank. Since I was young
and had only a high school diploma, I knew that there was a strong
chance that I would make Flight Officer since only a small percentage in my position graduated to officer rank. And I had my grade
card declaring that I was a below average student in basic, which
would offset the scores of "above average in advanced.

When the interviewing officer asked if I would feel bad if I made
Flight Officer instead of Second Lieutenant, I told the interviewer
that, yes, I would feel very bad, since I had worked very hard and
did my very best. I kept emphasizing the adjective, Very. The Officer who interviewed me told me to watch the bulletin board, so in a
few days I went to the bulletin board when I heard that the lists had
been posted. I crowded in with about fifty other cadets and checked
the list.

"Gloriosky," as Little Annie Rooney would say, "I made Second
Lieutenant." I soon found that my candor had worked, as I made
Officer rank. I felt that if I had told the interviewer that I wouldn't

mind being a Flight Officer, he would have known that I was lying, and I would have made that rank. As it was, most of the younger cadets made Flight Officer and I was one of the youngest, still being 21 years old.

Mom and Dad came down to Albany by train to see me graduate, and it was a grand affair with music and noble speeches, and we visited quite a while. As I left the ceremony I had a dollar bill in my left hand to present to the first enlisted man to salute me. It didn't take long, as the tradition was well known, and many enlisted men hung around the graduation ceremony to make a few dollars. I went back to Norfolk with Mom and Dad to spend a couple weeks leave before going to B-17 transition.

Avon Park, Florida

I arrived at the B-17 transition school four days after Christmas, 1943 and had my first B-17 ride on New Year's Day, 1944, just three days after arriving. The complex systems of the B-17 required a great deal of learning before even starting the transition process. In just a few days the pilot was expected to do a blindfold test of the cockpit. This meant that any component or gauge, or switch had to be physically touched by the blindfolded trainee when called off by the instructor. There were thirty nine items on the list, and the score had to be 100 percent correct but it is surprising how quickly most of us were able to accomplish this bit of training, since all we had done for the past nine months was eat, sleep and talk airplanes. Peppard and I had sat in the cockpit for hours testing each other. I had accumulated a little over two hundred seventy hours in the training planes before arriving at Avon Park, which is more than enough time to qualify as a commercial pilot in civilian life.

The B-17 that we used for training was an F model, the major difference being the addition of a chin turret on the later "G" models that we would be flying in combat. It had been determined earlier that my buddy, Horace W. Peppard and I would become co-pilots for some of the older and more experienced pilots. Peppard and I were both among the youngest in the graduating class and both barely made second Lieutenant despite only having a high school education.

I was assigned to fly co-pilot for 2nd lt. Aubrey A. Alexander on crew number 15 and Peppard was assigned to crew 16 which was piloted by Theodore R Beiser. As soon as we saw the listings, Peppard said,

"Hey, I know Alexander. Would you mind switching crews?"

"I don't know either one of them, so it doesn't matter to me." I replied. At this point we went to the operations section and asked the officer in charge how we could exchange crews.

"What crew are you assigned to?" he asked Peppard.

"Sixteen." Peppard replied.

"What crew are you on?" he asked me.

"Fifteen." I replied. With that he merely slid our names out of the crew roster and switched them.

"It's that simple," he said.

This simple action may have saved my life, but cost Peppard his. Such are the whims of fate.

We met our crews later that day to get acquainted. The pilot of crew 16, Theodore R. "Bud" Beiser was an easy going type who soon let the other officers on the crew know that we were to call him "Bud" when we were not around others. In front of others we called him Lieutenant Beiser, as did the enlisted men at all times.

I soon discovered why Beiser's nickname was Bud. I have several pictures of him with a bottle of "Bud" in his hand. He was from Fairhope, Alabama, which is on the lower part of Mobile Bay. He loved fishing and golfing, and still does to this day. He doesn't like to leave the area, saying, "Why should I leave Utopia?"

Our bombardier, Edward G. Cooper, was a second lieutenant from Portland, Oregon. He was a happy-go-lucky type, always quick with a quip or a joke. His ancestors came from Germany, and he said that he was looking forward to "Visiting Uncle Max," although he reasoned that "Uncle Max" wouldn't be too happy about the visit. Later, on some of our bombing missions to his ancestor's area of Germany, he would take a piece of chalk and write "Uncle Max" on one of the bombs, and "Aunt Sophie" on another.

Our navigator was 2nd Lt. Isadore Gepner, from Birmingham, Alabama. He had no middle name or initial. Lt. Gepner was all business when it came to navigating, and was very good at it. When he got excited he often spoke in Yiddish, which none of the rest of us understood. He may have saved us later, on our overseas trip, with some first class navigation.

Our flight engineer, Lenny J. Buchanan was about ten years older than most of the rest of us, so naturally, we called him "Pappy." He was from the Poplar Bluff, Missouri area. "Pappy" was a very good engineer, and worked with the ground crews in all phases of maintenance and repair. In the air, he was the chief repairman. Buchanan's job was in the top turret as long as the airplane didn't need attention.

Benny J. Gorchesky was one of the best radio operators in the business. He also manned one of the waist guns when the need arose. Benny, from Johnstown, Pennsylvania, was also one of the youngest in the crew. He kept the radios in order and made emergency calls if necessary. He also tested our "Gibson Girl" radio before each flight. This was the radio carried in the inflatable life raft. It had an hourglass shape for holding between the knees while cranking its generator. The hour glass shape is what gave it the name, "Gibson Girl."

James W. Haines, from the Dayton, Ohio area was the assistant engineer and was the other waist gunner. He and Buchanan nearly always helped Lt. Cooper and the armament crew with bomb loading. Also he assisted "Pappy" with maintenance on the B-17 during flight and helped with installing fuses in the bombs after take-off.

Charles W. Latta was too big for the ball turret position. Or, so everybody thought. He was young and agile, and proved that he could not only get into the ball turret, he showed that he could fire it quite easily. Charlie was from the Durham, North Carolina area, and was one of the youngest on the crew, next to Gorchesky. I was third youngest on the crew, being 21 years old at the time.

Carroll H. Brackey from Lake Mills, Iowa was one of the older men on the crew, next to "Pappy" Buchanan. His job was to slither back past the ball turret and the tail wheel box, to his position in the tail. He had his own little world back there, with his twin fifty caliber machine guns and his own jettisonable escape hatch. We usually didn't see him, or any of the other gunners for that matter during a flight, but we kept in constant touch with each other on the intercom.

After ten days at Avon Park, eight crews went to MacDill Field, just outside Tampa, Florida where we were to train for combat in the B-17. After flying some fifty hours in ten days at Avon Park, we first flew from MacDill Field on January 11, 1944. During the rest of the month we flew a little over forty-six hours, which included four and a half-hours of pilot in command for me. I did four, day landings and three night landings in that time. On January 11 we did 16 landings in 5 hours. The next day we did 17 landings in five and a quarter hours.

We did a take-off on January 13th and did no landings that day. If this seems strange, it is because we took off at 10:20 PM and landed after midnight. By the end of January, we stopped practicing landings and concentrated on air work.

In February we flew nearly sixty-three hours, twenty-four of which were night flights. We practiced night formation, gunnery, navigation and emergency procedures. Part of the emergency procedures was for feathering a prop, that is, to turn it knife-edge into the wind, thus stopping the engine. On all my later combat flights I never had to use this procedure and was always grateful to the Wright engine designers who made this one of the most dependable engines of Second World War aircraft.

On March 25, 1944, we flew our last training mission from Mac-Dill Field. By this time I had over 153 hours of B-17 flight time. We then boarded a bus to Savannah, Georgia and reported to Hunter Field. On April 5th we flew our first B-17 G. It had a shiny, aluminum finish with its new chin turret. We made a two hour flight that day to check out the newest thing in combat aircraft. Its tail (serial) number, was 42-102392. This was the aircraft that we would ferry to the British Isles.

My good friend, Aubrey Alexander, was assigned B-17 number 42-102414. This was easy for me to remember, since my old address in Norfolk had been 414 Mowbray Arch. His copilot, who was my best buddy at that time, was Horace W. Peppard, we having gone all the way through flight school together. I had been assigned to Alexander's plane and crew, but Peppard asked to switch crews with me since he knew Alexander, and I didn't know either him or Beiser at the time, so we switched.

At this time we received our secret destination orders which we were not to open until we were airborne. We were not supposed to know quite where we were headed or by what route in case a careless remark might find its way to the enemy.

Winter flight gear, December 1943

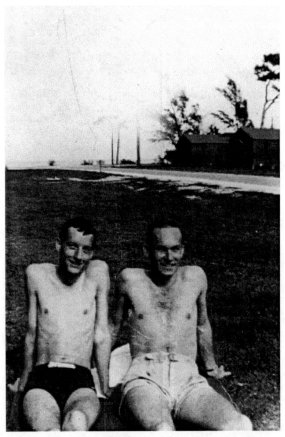

Author (Left) Co-pilot for T.R. Beiser (Right), 1943

Chapter 9

Overseas to Europe

The next day we took this brand new B-17, with the radio call letters, K-TEX Mike, which we immediately corrupted into Kotex Mike, and headed north, behind crews 13, 14 and 15. Alexander's crew # 15 had my best buddy, Horace W. Peppard as its copilot. Taking off every thirty minutes, eight bombers left Hunter Field to take the northern route to Europe.

After heading north from Hunter Field on April 6th, we found that we had a brisk tail wind, so we did a lot of sight seeing on the way up the coast. We flew a circle around Norfolk, Virginia, and I was able to pick out my home there. We then flew to Washington, DC and flew around the Capitol Building and the Washington Monument, staying at about one thousand feet. We soon found ourselves over New York City and decided to fly around the Statue of Liberty. We were still ahead of schedule, so I suggested to Beiser that we fly around the Empire State Building. Staying at a thousand feet, we flew rather close to the tallest building on Earth at that time. Unfortunately, my suggestion got us in a little hot water. Evidently some one with binoculars could look down and read our tail number as we flew below their level, and when we got to England a letter of reprimand was waiting for Beiser. Evidently the authorities in New York were overly sensitive since Yankee Stadium had been recently buzzed by three B-17s during the World Series baseball game. These three B-17s eventually found their way to the Group that we would be assigned to. Beiser never held it against me for getting him into this minor bit of trouble.

After six hours we arrived at our destination of Grenier Field, Manchester, New Hampshire where we spent the night while our plane was refueled and serviced. We spent an extra night and took off on the eighth of April, headed to the town of Happy Valley, Labrador. Our field of departure there was Goose Bay. We arrived at about noon and the ground crews got busy servicing the plane. We were scheduled to take off in the early hours after midnight the next day, April ninth, headed for Keflavijk, near the Capitol City of Reykjavik, Iceland. We went to bed early because of this accelerated schedule. We found that bad weather was expected.

As it turned out, the weather was very bad when we were routed out of bed. It was snowing pretty hard, but the operations people said that the flights were on as scheduled since the runway was cleared and other crews were expected to arrive, the same as we had. We were to take off at thirty-minute intervals, go to eleven thousand feet, and remain at that altitude for the entire trip.

Crew thirteen took off first and disappeared almost at once. Crew fourteen waited thirty minutes and did the same. Crew fifteen, The one that I had been originally assigned to fly with, started engines and taxied into the take off position. After their allotted thirty minutes they took off into the snowstorm and disappeared just as the others had.

We started engines and taxied into position only to be signaled by an Aldis lamp to return to the hard stand. There we found that Crew fifteen carrying my good friend Aubrey Alexander, with my best buddy, Horace W. Peppard had crashed just after take off, killing all on board, including the great grandson of Jim Bowie, inventor of the Bowie knife. Needless to say, we were all pretty shaken up. The inspectors went through our plane with a fine-tooth comb, checking to see if sabotage was maybe the cause.

Nothing was found, and we carefully checked the wheel wells to see if some saboteur might have planted a bomb that would explode when the wheels were retracted. We found no hint of trouble, so we taxied back to the take off end of the runway without topping off our gas tanks. By this time the snow was falling more heavily than ever and we decided to do a three-man take off. Beiser would handle the controls and watch the directional gyro while I watched the rapidly disappearing white stripe down the middle of the runway, with Pappy calling off the air speeds. We made it off after an interminable take off roll, being loaded to the gills with gasoline for our eleven-hour flight.

Immediately after take off the snow was so heavy that we could barely see the wing tips, and looking straight ahead was like looking into the big end of a white funnel. We were never to see any sign of the crash site of crew 15 because of the snow, so we flew on to our assigned altitude of eleven thousand feet and stayed there for the entire trip. We found it comforting that the deicer boots had not been removed from our aircraft, as the snow was just wet enough to form rhyme ice on the wing leading edges. Once in awhile we shined a light to see if the ice was a problem, and when it was, we exercised the deicer boots. These boots consisted of three flat tubes along the entire wing span. When ice formed on the wings, we inflated the center tube and then the two outer tubes, which cracked the ice off and into the slipstream. We also had a bit of trouble with rhyme ice forming on the propellers. We could eliminate this with alcohol deicer fluid, which we could spray from the propeller hub and down each of the three blades. When bits of ice stopped hitting the fuselage we knew the props were clear. These deicer boots were removed in the combat area since they added over 150 pounds to the gross weight.

After about six hours into the flight it started to get daylight, and the snow abated a small bit and we could see the wing tips pretty good. But now we started worrying about our position. We had picked up the leg of the four-course range out of Iceland, but it was a hundred miles wide at this distance. We knew the wind had been from the northeast, but Gepner couldn't give us a precise fix, because he couldn't see the sun. We knew that we couldn't drift a hundred miles off course without the danger of running out of gas. But to climb above the clouds would use even more gas, so we elected to fly the extra hundred miles if necessary rather than risk an almost certain gas depletion in going to a higher altitude. We flew the entire trip on autopilot, since it could maintain altitude and heading, needing only small corrections with a knob to control elevators, and one for aileron and rudder. Letting "George" do it made it a lot easier on the pilot and co-pilot. Lt. Gepner gave us periodic course corrections so that we would fly a Great Circle Route.

While we were discussing the fuel dilemma, the sun suddenly appeared behind a heavy haze of snow. Lt. Gepner immediately grabbed his sextant and stuck his head up in the astrodome in front of the cockpit. Beiser and I could see him clicking away on the tape. The sun went behind the overcast almost instantly, but Lt. Gepner soon reported that he thought that he had gotten some decent fixes and that he thought we were about fifty miles south of course. He gave us a course correction, which we immediately took, knowing that to follow the range leg at that deviation would take us in an immense curve before reaching the narrow part of the radio signal.

After eleven hours and five minutes, we found the "cone of silence" of the radio station that we were following, and thus knew that we had found the field we were looking for. We had not yet started our letdown from the eleven thousand feet, since we had an estimated thirty minutes of fuel left. We were just about ready to go out to sea a few miles to let down, when suddenly we found a hole in the clouds that was about a mile in diameter, and we could see snow on some mountains. We immediately let down through this opening in a tight descending spiral at minimum air speed we being lightly loaded at this point. We shortly found ourselves in the clear under the clouds, which were about four thousand feet above the ground. This is when we started celebrating Easter Sunday, April 9, 1944, which was that day.

Snow was piled twenty feet deep along both sides of the runway and as we approached for landing, we found that we had a fifty-mile per hour head wind. This made our touchdown speed of less than forty miles per hour instead of our usual eighty to eighty-five miles per hour. This was fine until we got to the end of the runway and Beiser instructed me to unlock the tail wheel so he could turn off the runway. As soon as I unlocked the tail wheel, Beiser made a left turn onto the taxi way and had to use a lot of left brake and right engine to keep the nose from turning into the wind which was now fifty miles per hour from the right. We had only gone a few dozen feet when the wind driving against the huge dorsal fin of the B-17 caused the tail wheel pin to shear. This gave us even less control over our desired direction, and almost full left brake and right engine throttle was required to get us to the downwind part of the taxi strip. B-17's always taxied on the two outboard engines. At this point it became fairly easy. Just hold the yoke forward and stand on the brakes to keep from going too fast. We shut down in the hard stand just before noon on Easter Sunday.

The base maintenance officer and our own crew replaced the tail wheel pin that evening after we all went sight-seeing in the Capitol city of Reykjavik.

Iceland didn't have the shortages that one saw in the States. The shop windows had all kind of goods that were being rationed at home. Many sidewalks in the town were lined with fish heads a couple of feet deep with paths cut through at doorways. This was their method of refrigerating these fish heads, which would be removed before they thawed. I think they were processed into fish oil that was used as a vehicle for paint making, as well as fertilizer, cat food and many other uses.

That night was my first experience with the Aurora Borealis. It was so cold that I could only stay outside a few minutes at a time, but it was so fascinating that I made many trips out to look. I got hollered at by the guys playing cards for letting in the cold air. These Northern Lights looked as if you were standing at the base of a stage looking up at the bottom edge of a velvet curtain, which was slowly changing color and moving ever so gracefully as if in a fairy light show. The color at the bottom edge of the "curtain" was very bright with the color slowly diminishing, as one looked higher, until directly overhead it couldn't be seen at all. The colors undulated from red to green and back again, in a slow waltz across the northern sky.

The next morning, our aircraft having been serviced, we took off for Prestwick, Scotland. We had expected more B-17s to go with us, but two others of our group of eight never made it to Iceland. We later learned that one had tried to go above the storm and ran out of fuel as a result. They had come back down and just before running completely out of gas, had ditched alongside a tanker ship. Unfortunately the water was so cold that most were lost to hypothermia before they could be picked up. This was in the same area of the north Atlantic that had claimed the Titanic, right to this very day thirty-two years earlier. It was reported that death came in less than twenty minutes to some of those who went into the water.

The other lost B-17 had decided to go below the weather when it got daylight, expecting to make an emergency landing on Greenland. They never made it, having to ditch when their fuel ran out. All of these men were lost. Their May Day transmission was the only clue to their position. April 9th was not a good date for that area.

Our flight to Prestwick was uneventful, as the weather had gotten a little better. We were so proud of "our" brand new Flying Fortress that we thought would be ours to fly all our combat missions in, just like the Memphis Belle. No such luck. On April 22, 1944, our plane, "Kotex" Mike" with the tail number, 42-102392 built at the Boeing main plant in Seattle was taken away from us and assigned to the 91st Bomb Group. It started flying combat missions right away and was shot down on its 7th mission on May first, two weeks before we even flew our first mission. That plane, which had been re-named Cool Papa received a direct flak burst in the nose and went down in flames with only two survivors. When they took the plane from us we had such short notice that we even left some of our gear on board, including our parachutes, binoculars, and a few personal items, part of which we eventually got back.

For three weeks we dallied at Prestwick, going to school to learn all the latest aircraft recognition. They eagerly showed us pictures of the German Me 262 Jet and the Me 162 Komet, rocket plane. We had seen them all at MacDill Field a couple of months earlier. They schooled us in radar technology, and LORAN, which is an acronym for Long-Range Navigation. PFF or Pathfinder was the British Radar that we often used for bombing through clouds. American airmen called it "Mickey," as in Mouse.

The last week of April found us on a bus headed for the Bomb Group to which we had been assigned. It was the famous, 303rd Bomb Group known as "Hell's Angels." As we drove past the little village of Molesworth and turned onto the base, which was a little over a mile from that village, we were greeted with some strange sights. There were so many B-17s that they couldn't be easily counted. The 427th Squadron to which we had been assigned was on the base near a runway, while the other three squadrons were a little farther away. As we approached the barrack area of the 427th, some wag had hung a neatly done sign on the first billet area. The sign read: "GIRLS WHO VISIT ON A WEEK END MUST BE OFF THE BASE BY TUESDAY." I have tried to find someone who might have a picture of this sign, but to no avail. I don't even know who the artist was.

Along the taxiway near the armament section was row upon row of bombs out in the open. Some of these larger bombs were fitted with wings and a double tail to be used as glide bombs.

After we got settled, and after hearing "You'll be sorry" a few times, we did the latest schooling. We learned that we had a forty percent chance of finishing our tour of duty without being shot down or wounded, and if shot down there was a fifty percent chance of survival from that, giving us an eighty percent chance of surviving the war. We didn't relish the thought of being part of the twenty percent who would be killed. We later learned that this casualty rate was the highest of any military units in WW2.

On May 5th, after the day's mission had left, we did two short flights to familiarize us with the area. The first flight was for thirty minutes and the second was for an hour and forty-five minutes. The next day we did another flight of an hour and a half. We didn't fly on May 7th, and on the 8th we did an hour of Link Trainer. This was about my zillionth hour in that boring black box. Actually it was about my hundredth hour.

On May 9th we flew another hour and a half for area familiarization. On May 10th we did a flight to simulate a mission, getting into formation and flying to The Wash (practice range). Cooper dropped several bombs on separate bomb runs to the satisfaction of the instructor on this flight of four and a half-hours.

We stood down for the next three days, during which on May twelve, the Eighth Air Force made its first raid against German oil production. On the fourteenth of May we flew a practice flight of two hours and twenty-five minutes.

Tomorrow, May 15th, 1944, we were to start earning our keep, and to learn why we had been trained so hard all these months. Tomorrow was to be our first mission, and I was to fly co-pilot for Lt.

Phillip W. O-Hare in A/C number 42-97391. He was almost finished with his tour and was to train me in all aspects of combat flying. My pilot, Lt. Beiser and the rest of our crew was to fly with an experienced pilot, Steven Bastean, who would finish his tour in mid-June. All crews were thus flown on their first mission.

Little did I know at that time, that on my last eight missions I would be flying seven or eight new crews on their first mission, using their pilot as my co-pilot just as Lt. Bastean and Lt. O-Hare were doing today. O-Hare died in 1985, but Bastean is living in Treasure Island, Florida.

Chapter 10

Count down to D-Day.
Combat Mission # 1
May 15, 1944

Most readers of WW2 history are aware of the V-1, "Buzz Bomb" and the V-2, sub-orbital rocket. What most people don't realize is that in 1944 Hitler was busy building a V-3. This was the so-called "London Gun" being installed in Western France, near the coast at Mimoyecques, which is near Calais. It was to consist of two batteries of twenty-five guns each. The barrels of these guns were each, 416 feet long. Installed along a steep incline, they would be capable of firing a 55 pound shell into the city of London. If the Allies had allowed this weapon to be completed, it would have eclipsed the damage done by the upcoming V-1 and V-2. The multistage explosive propellant would have altered the range and direction so that the entire city of London could be targeted.

Unfortunately for the Germans, the earth removal scars caught the attention of Allied reconnaissance planes, and the site was periodically bombed. My first combat mission on May 15, 1944 was to finish off that German project.

I had been assigned to the 303rd. Bomb Group, known as the "Hell's Angels." My job was to fly co-pilot on the crew of 2nd Lt. Theodore R. Beiser. However, an experienced co-pilot-turned instructor takes all new crews on their first mission. As Beiser's co-pilot, I flew with 1st. Lt. Philip O-Hare who was nearly finished with his tour of duty. 1st. Lt. Bastean flew as Beiser's pilot for his first mission. This policy of flying experienced pilots with new crews was necessary in order to teach the "green" crews how to get into formation. After this first mission, the new crew was re-united for subsequent missions.

Our bombardier had the job of arming the six, 1000 pound bombs after we were in the air. Each bomb had an eight-inch vane or propeller on the nose fuse, which was prevented from turning by a cotter pin through a hole. Each cotter pin had a bomb tag with warnings. As the pin was removed, a wire attached to the bomb bay was inserted through the cotter pin hole. When the bombs were dropped, they slid off the arming wire, which allowed the propeller vane to turn in the wind. After falling about five hundred feet, the propeller vane wound itself off the fuse, which was then armed, and this would explode the bomb upon impact.

After he removed the bomb tags from the nose fuse, the bombardier walked to the front of the airplane and gave each officer a tag to keep as a souvenir. Our ball-turret gunner did the same with the tail fuses for the rest of the crew. I kept my mission diary on mine. On this first mission each B-17 carried seventeen hundred gallons of gas, and six, 1000 pound bombs. The bombs were fused at one tenth second at the nose and one fortieth second at the tail. One fortieth second would allow the bomb to penetrate a roof before exploding, and the one-tenth second fuse would assure that the bomb would explode before deep penetration if the first fuse failed.

This day's mission started with a 4:00 A.M. wake-up call. Breakfast and briefing followed quickly, and we were in our plane with the engines running by 6:00 A.M. The lead plane took off at 6:15 and all twenty B-17s were over the field and in formation at twenty thousand feet at 7:40. Our squadron, the 427th, was assigned the high position, behind and to the right of the lead squadron, the 358th. The 359th squadron was low-left. The 360th squadron did not fly in this formation. Each squadron furnished seven B-17s to the group formation, except the lead, which had six. Our squadron also furnished two spares that were to take up any position that might be left empty by an abort. They were to return to base before reaching enemy territory, and if there was an abort later, the other B-17s moved into the empty slots, leaving the tail position empty. On this day, there were no aborts, and the spares returned to base. Lt. O-Hare's position in the squadron was number seven, -"Tail End Charlie."

"Tail End Charlie" is one of the most vulnerable positions in the formation. "Purple Heart Corner" is the next plane on the outside of the formation. There was an undercast at the target so we had to bomb by radar. The lead plane borrowed from the 306th Bomb Group was equipped with this system, and all following planes dropped at first appearance of bombs from that plane.

Just after "Bombs away" from about twenty five thousand feet, we encountered some flak. However, it was light and inaccurate, the nearest burst being at least a quarter mile away. The German gunners may not have had their radar working, and so were shooting at the noise of our engines. None of our aircraft sustained damage and all planes returned to base and landed before 10:30 A.M. Total flight time was just over 4 hours. We were over enemy territory barely seven minutes.

My first combat mission was truly a "Milk Run," so called because it was no more dangerous than delivering milk.

My second mission, on May 19, was not so uneventful as the target was "Big B," - Berlin! American bombers had only bombed this Capital City a few times before.

Of course, Berlin being the capital city of Germany was heavily defended. When the curtain was drawn back to show the target there was a moan from all the aircrews who would fly this mission.

Chapter 11

Mission # 2, Berlin
May 19, 1944

Beiser, our pilot, and I, his copilot was re-united for our second mission. The 427th squadron was assigned lead, and we were to fly in position # 5. Berlin was the primary target, with Kiel as the secondary target in case Berlin was socked in. Each B-17 was loaded with twenty seven hundred gallons of gas, and twelve, five hundred pound bombs. At six pounds per gallon, the weight of fuel for each plane was sixteen thousand, two hundred pounds, and bombs weighed twelve thousand pounds, for a total of over 14 tons. The B-17G carried more than five thousand rounds of ammunition for its 13 machine guns. The weight of these 50 caliber machine guns, plus oil for the engines, and oxygen for the crew, often brought the take-off weight of these aircraft to over sixty five thousand pounds. Empty, they weighed a little over thirty five thousand pounds.

Our route north over the English Channel was hampered by dense and persistent vapor trails of the preceding groups. Our cloud ceiling at departure was two thousand feet, which altered our forming up a bit. However we departed the English coast with eighteen aircraft plus two radar ships from another group. Soon, the lead ship of the low squadron aborted due to a supercharger problem. Our route to Berlin took us up the English Channel past Hamburg, and across the Jutland peninsula to a southeasterly heading. This took us about mid-way between Hamburg and Kiel.

Our escorting fighters were P-38 "Lightenings" and a few of the older P-51 "Mustangs." Their fuel range would not allow them to escort us all the way to Berlin, and they dropped off just past Hamburg. Fortunately, we saw no enemy fighters close enough to identify, and so our main problem was flak.

As we approached the target the flak was unbelievable. It was as if someone had painted a thin black line across the sky at our exact altitude of 26,000 feet. As we approached Berlin, clouds covered over half the earth below us, which made the target difficult to see. Many of our aircraft dropped "Chaff", which is bundles of tin foil cut to the exact length of the German radar signal. This only helped during cloudy weather, as the German anti-aircraft gunners preferred visual aiming. Their "Final Aimer" usually aimed for the left wing-root or number two engine of the lead plane. These 88MM cannon were all on pivots and all the guns turned in unison. The gunners were so good that they could fire a burst every three seconds or so. While the aim was done from a control site, all the guns pointed parallel to each other and did not converge on the target. This allowed a wider pattern of bursts, which could cover an entire group of airplanes.

The big disadvantage for the flak gunners was the necessity to lead the target by two or more kilometers. That was how much they had to allow for the interval of travel by the target until the explosive shell arrived. The gunners had to assume that the target would be at a given point when the explosive shell arrived. A slow turn by the target aircraft was usually enough to cause the flak to miss.

On this day, however, one of our B-17s was hit by a direct burst and went down. This was Lt. E.L. Roth and his crew on aircraft number 42-31386, "Sky Duster," from the number three position of the high squadron. Only five parachutes were seen to emerge from the stricken aircraft. This was shortly after bombs were dropped. As co-pilot, I was able to see this loss for a short while, but our ball-turret gunner, Charles Latta and others got a first hand view.

We had heard rumors that civilians had murdered some of our bailed-out crewmembers and this was confirmed after the war. After leaving the hell in the air, many were faced by an equal hell on the ground.

Berlin had large numbers of 88-millimeter flak guns all around the city. Also, many fixed guns of larger caliber were deployed in the area. Many of these were 105 mm and some were 128 mm. They were not as accurate as the 88s but made a larger explosion. When the target aircraft couldn't be seen, these guns fired a burst that would explode at or above our altitude, thus forcing us to fly through a rain of shell fragments, or "Flak." Many of these guns were mounted on railroad cars for mobility.

Our Group Commander, Col. Stevens was leading this mission against Berlin. He was flying with Lt. Bordelon of our squadron, which led the group that day.

Of the nineteen aircraft from our group who flew this day, one was shot down by flak, three received major damage, Eleven suffered less severe damage and only four B-17s came back unscathed. Our aircraft had several flak holes in the leading edges and a few in the sides, but ours was listed as "major damage." due to the fact that during the bomb drop our B-17 was forced out of position by a neighboring aircraft. This put us directly behind the lead plane so that when he dropped his bombs, his "Sky Marker" bomb enveloped our plane with a white acid fog, which ruined all the Plexiglas in our plane. Flying home was difficult due to the milky looking windshield.

Also, due to six-tenths cloud cover over Berlin that day, our bombing results were not very good. We felt let down that our effort was largely wasted after facing such battle conditions. Total flight time was over eight hours. We were over enemy territory, three hours and a half. We reported "Hot News" of a German naval convoy in the Hamburg Fjord on the way in, but couldn't see it on the way out, because of the ruined Plexiglas. All of our flying efforts were in staying in formation with such limited visibility.

Mission # 3, Blainville France
May 25, 1944

"Target for today is the marshaling yards at Blainville, France."
Since this would be a rather long mission, our take-off time was
a little earlier than usual. The first B-17 took off at 5:47 A.M. and
the last at 5:58. The 303rd Bomb Group was to supply only twelve
aircraft, with two spares, for the 41st Combat Wing, of which we
were a part.

London is sixty miles south of our field at Molesworth, and our
departure course took us straight south, past London. At that point
we turned east and passed over a suburb of London, climbing to
19,000 feet at 7:31 A.M. From here we crossed the English Channel in a climb so that we penetrated the French coast at 23,000 feet.
Our penetration was at a point about half way between Le Havre
and Boulogne as there were no flak guns nearby. Just out of range,
we saw a few bursts of flak as we continued on a course that took us
within sight of Paris, which lay to the south.

At the target we had taken an earlier lead, since the other combat wings had overshot the penetration course, which put us almost
first to the target. We were low group on this mission and since the
lead group overshot the IP (Initial Point) we had a longer than usual
bomb run.

During the bomb run, the formation is most vulnerable to enemy
action, since the bomb-bay doors are open from the IP to the target.
This alerts the German anti-aircraft gunners that we will be flying a
long, straight course to the target. This day, the bomb run was eleven
minutes, and we expected to have a great deal of flak come up.

But nothing happened. Evidently the 88-mm guns that we
thought were there, had been moved elsewhere. The weather was
CAVU (Ceiling and Visibility Unlimited), therefore if there had
been flak guns we would have been "Sitting Ducks."

This was my third mission, and was the first that I saw bombs exploding on the target. The extended bomb run allowed the lead bombardier to kill his drift to perfection, and the Norden Bomb Sight did its job flawlessly.

There were no damaged aircraft and no aborts on this mission, and all twelve of us returned to base just after noon. All the aircrews were hoping for a bunch of these "Milk Runs."

Total flight time, five and one half-hours. Over enemy territory, almost exactly three hours. We did our part to damage the German war machine for the upcoming invasion.

Next: Another "Flak City"

Chapter 12

Mannheim, Germany, Mission # 4
May 27, 1944

On this mission, our fourth, we were assigned to position number 6 in the low squadron, known as "Purple Heart Corner," because it is lowest in the squadron, and farthest out.

Mannheim, Germany was a heavily defended city on the Rhine River near Ludwigshafen, just a few miles northwest of Heidelberg. Mannheim was a bottle neck for transportation in that area, and our mission was to destroy the marshaling yards that would feed supplies that were to defend the coast during the upcoming D-Day invasion. We did not yet know when that invasion would be, but knew it would be soon. Our assigned secondary target was the nearby city of Ludwigshafen.

"If overcast, PFF (Pathfinder, or Radar) on Ludwigshafen. Target of opportunity-Florennes-Juzaine Airfield. Last resort, any military installation in Germany not adjacent to built up area." (!) We were trying to spare German civilians! This phrase was usually reserved for use in occupied countries only.

Thirty-seven of our B-17s were loaded with ten each, five hundred pound bombs. Engines were started at 08:15 and take-off started at 08:45. We assembled the group over Molesworth at six thousand feet, and departed base at 09:45. We were two minutes late, due to keeping Division battle order. The logistics of forming up, joining your Wing and staying on course is almost mind boggling. The Eighth Air Force put up almost a thousand bombers this day, using about two million gallons of gasoline.

We departed the English coast at Beachy Head at 10:39 and 16,000 ft. We climbed as we crossed the English Channel and crossed the enemy coast in France at 11:00 AM at 20,000 ft. At the

Initial Point or IP we made a 30-degree turn to the target and opened bomb bay doors. Ten minutes before the target, the code word for visual bombing, "Stud Horse" was given by radio. This meant that the Wing formation would be broken into the three groups who would bomb individually. A six-minute bomb run was made on a straight line to the target, and the flak started coming up. As we approached the city of Mannheim, the flak became intense, and shell fragments struck many of our B-17s. The ceiling and visibility was unlimited, so the German flak gunners were aiming visually. As a result, the radar jamming "Chaff" that we dropped did little good. The air sparkled as far as the eye could see because of the sun glinting on this falling Chaff. Only a few German fighter aircraft were seen in the distance, but didn't attack, as our escort kept them at bay.

Our thirty-five B-17s dropped a total of 350 bombs on the target with good results. One B-17 jettisoned his bombs over Germany after they failed to release over the target.

One B-17 received major damage and seven had minor damage. None were shot down. In my diary I had underlined the words, Very Lucky, as our plane escaped damage. A Milk Run to a Flak City!

Total flight time, seven hours. Time over enemy territory, Three hours and Thirty-five minutes.

And no damage!

Dropping 6, 1000 LB bombs

Chapter 13

Mission 5. Glide Bomb mission to Cologne.

Today, May 28, 1944, the Eighth Air Force would lose 32 Bombers and 14 fighters to the German defenders, including one from our group. The weather over Europe was predicted to be mostly clear, and targets would include fuel and transportation systems. Our crew was assigned a special mission this day, and would not participate in the regular effort to destroy Nazi war materials.

When our crew arrived at the 303rd Bomb Group in early May, a strange sight greeted us. The barracks for the 427th squadron to which we were assigned, were on the airdrome, and all along the armament roads, were stacked row upon row of some strange flying machines. They consisted of wings and a double-boom tail mounted on a two thousand-pound bomb. This strange device was supposed to be mounted in pairs under the belly of a B-17, and dropped on the enemy from a distance, thus sparing the air crews from the intense flak that was encountered over many targets. The idea had merit, but there were many problems.

The visibility at the target had to be fifty miles, which is rare in Europe, and this caused a couple of other attempts to be scrubbed in the past. The bombs depended on inertial guidance for directional control after release. This consisted of a series of gyroscopes driven by a battery.

This was a special project that Eighth Air Force commanding general, Hap Arnold, had adopted, so it had to be tried. One couldn't guess how many millions of dollars this project cost. This day the predicted fifty-mile visibility arrived over Europe, and the mission was on. We were part of the 41st Combat Wing, along with two other groups. In the night, the armorers attached two of these bombs to the belly of each bomber, using special bomb shackles. The bombs were side by side, with their wing tips only four inches apart. They had a twelve-foot wing span and were almost twelve feet long.

Our group, as well as the other two groups in the 41st Combat Wing was expected to put two battle formations in the air that day. The 303rd put 19 planes in the glide bomb formation, which left the base an hour earlier than the second element going to oil targets. Our takeoff time was about 09:30, so that we could be out of the way of the next element.

We crossed the French coast two miles south of Nieuport at 19,500 feet and proceeded to Cologne. We were to bomb by groups and our squadron, the 427th went in first. Starting at 140 miles per hour, indicated air speed, we started a shallow dive until we reached 208 mph. At this point, we leveled off for a few seconds and released the bombs nearly 18 miles from the target while flying at 195 MPH. Unfortunately, our bombs, as well as those of the other two groups following, mostly spun in and exploded in fields 15 miles from the target.

Of the 59 B-17s of the 41st Combat wing, 113 glide bombs were released at the target, the Eifeltor Marshaling yard in Cologne. Not one bomb came within a mile of that target, however 42 hits were scattered throughout Cologne, killing 82 people, and injuring over 1500 others. Many of the bombs fell into sections of the city already bombed out by night missions of the RAF. I saw one bomb explode near a bridge on the Rhine, but not close enough to damage it.

Unfortunately for the Germans, the bombs arrived before their air raid sirens had sounded.

Upon our return to base, one engine on our "Betty Jane" had to be replaced due to flak damage on the way to the target.

Later that evening on German radio, which we always listened to, William Joyce, or "Lord Haw-Haw," as we called him, reported that Cologne had been bombed by allied bombers from an altitude of 40,000 feet. We had quite a laugh about that, since the B-17 wasn't designed to fly quite that high. Three nights later they had figured what really happened, and Lord Haw-Haw said that any airman shot down during such a mission, would be executed the same day. He said that it was a terrorist raid, which, indeed it turned out to be, but this was not our intent. This was not the reason that the attempt was never repeated, however. The failure of the system was evident from the results.

The eleven-second delay in the fuse meant that this two thousand-pound bomb would possibly skip through town for eleven seconds before exploding. The glide ratio of these bombs was an amazing five to one, which meant that if we dropped them from four miles high, they would travel twenty miles before striking the ground.

An interesting aside on this mission concerns the batteries that ran the gyroscopes in the guidance system of these "Grapefruit" bombs. The stacks of bombs sat on the ground for so long that many of the batteries failed to hold charge, and so the Wing ordered a hundred new ones from the States. The Exide Battery Company said that they no longer made this type of battery, and that they would have to set up a complete assembly line, and therefore could produce no less than several thousand batteries. After the entire hassle back and forth, the batteries arrived at Molesworth after the mission was over. When it was decided to not fly any more glide bomb missions, the mechanics of the 427th Squadron used these batteries in an innovative lighting system for the barracks. Also, the wooden crates that the bombs were shipped in were of gunstock grade black walnut lumber. The ground personnel, led by Sgt. Nathan Smith of our intelligence section, made a magnificent bar at the site 5 joint Enlisted/ Officers recreation room from this lumber. The bar was over 2 feet wide and 24 feet long.

Several references to this glide bomb mission have placed it on the wrong day. The date was May 28, 1944, not the 25th as Martin Caidin reports in his book, "The Forts." This same mistake appears in Polmer and Allen's encyclopedia, "World War ll. America at War, 1941-1945. Despite this small error, both of these books are a must for World War Two buffs.

The other mission of May 28th, to oil and transportation targets throughout Germany, was met by fierce resistance. Upward of 300 German fighters flew up to intercept the bombers, and in many cases our own fighters were out of range. The results of those raids were generally excellent, but in the course of the day, 32 of our bombers and 14 fighters were lost. From our group, Lt. Determan and his crew was shot down. This day's operation is detailed in an upcoming book by Dutch author Ivo M. DeJong. The title of this book is "May 28, 1944: A day to be remembered."

Chapter 14

Mission number 6
Posen, Poland. Slugging it out for ten hours.
May 29, 1944

Part of our mission to prepare for D-Day was to intercept and destroy the German fighter force. Had this been accomplished earlier, the invasion would have been in early May, but in order for the invasion to succeed, the Allies had to have mastery of the air, and this had not yet been accomplished.

Today, we were to bomb a Focke Wulf assembly plant and airfield in Posen, Poland, where the dreaded FW190 was being built. We were assigned a position behind and to the left of the high squadron leader. Our group furnished 18 planes for the wing formation for today's flight, which would take over ten hours. We were in our aircraft at 07:10 and started engines at 08:00. We started taxi at 08:10 and took off at 08:25. It took one hour for all planes to get into formation at 8,000 feet over Molesworth, where our 303rd Bomb Group was located. Climbing to 13,500 feet, we crossed the English coast at Cremer. Over the channel we climbed to 21,000 feet, picking up friendly fighters: P-51s and P-47s. We crossed the enemy coast near the Dutch town of Ijmuiden, not far from Egmond, at 10:44.

Our course was due east, aimed directly at Berlin, but while still out of range of their flak guns, we made a dog-leg to the south. We then took a direct flight to Posen (Poznan) Poland, and drew a bead on the FW factory in the Posen suburb of Erzesinki. The sky was cloudless and our bomb run of 38 miles gave the lead bombardier plenty of time to kill the drift, which was 5 degrees to the right of our track. This caused our true heading to be at a compass heading of 64 degrees, while our track over the ground was at 68 degrees, magnetic. The intervalometer was set at the Salvo position, and when bombs first appeared from the lead plane, all the other planes dropped in unison. Despite considerable flak, the Norden bombsight did its job well on this mission. Much of the plant was destroyed, as were several other buildings nearby. We were surprised that we encountered no enemy planes, since our escorting fighters had long since returned to base, the target being far out of their range. Perhaps the Germans didn't expect us to bomb such a distant target. This was the only Poland mission flown during the entire war by the 303rd Bomb Group.

What we didn't know at the time was that the Germans were taking some of their flak guns from aircraft plants and taking them to defend their oil refineries. Despite our constant harassment, the Germans were increasing their aircraft production throughout the war, but they couldn't be flown without fuel. And they couldn't be flown well by inexperienced pilots.

Coming off the target, we headed due north for 25 minutes, while letting down to 14,000 feet from our bombing altitude of 22,000 feet. This was done to conserve fuel, as this was a critical problem on such a long mission. At the lower altitude, the turbo superchargers could be turned off, and the engines leaned out for better fuel efficiency.

After letting down to 14,000 feet, we turned to the northwest, and crossed into the Baltic Sea. At this point we crossed over an island that we thought was undefended. We were wrong! Our gunners reported flashes from the ground from four different areas of the same field. The island contained a four-gun battery of 88MM flak guns, and we flew directly over them. Four bursts at a time were coming up every three or four seconds and the only thing that saved us was a quick turn to throw off their aiming lead. The second burst destroyed an engine on one of our planes and he started dropping back.

We no sooner got over the open Baltic again than we noticed a small formation of planes off to our right, going in the same direction. They were German fighters trying to simulate our own P-51s. After they passed a couple of miles ahead of us, they made a turn to the left, and their profiles gave them away as Me109s and FW 190s. There was three of each, and they made a diving left turn to attack us from the one o-clock high position.

I thought that I was on intercom and said, 'Enemy fighters, one o'clock high.' A voice came back at me, 'Get off the air.' I looked down at the radio and realized my error. I had broadcast my information all over Europe when the rule was to maintain radio silence. I switched to intercom and the crew was already aware of our impending confrontation and talking excitedly.

One Me109 chose our plane as his target and came in firing his thirty caliber machine guns and his 20mm cannon. The bullets from a 20MM cannon will explode on impact, but none hit our plane. From all the smoke pouring out of his wings, I thought that our top turret gunner, Sgt. Lennie Buchanan, had set him on fire. It only took an instant for me to realize what was really happening, Our pilot, T.R. Beiser grabbed the yoke and pulled up a bit. I was convinced that the German pilot had drawn a mental bull's eye on the co-pilot's windshield, so I grabbed the yoke to assist Beiser. All our forward guns were firing at this point, but our gyrations prevented any serious damage to the Me109. More importantly, it also prevented the German pilot from inflicting any damage on us. Our B-17 was very light at this time, having dropped our ten, five hundred pound bombs and having burned most of our eight tons of gas. I always thought that the B-17 was the noisiest thing possible until I heard "Pappy" Buchanan's fifty caliber machine guns blazing away, just six inches over my head.

This Me109 duplicated our every move, but was behind the curve, as he could not anticipate what we were going to do. At the last moment I was certain that he was going to ram us, but he veered off our right wing tip so close that I could see his face, and was startled to see that he was not wearing an oxygen mask. It was our rule to use oxygen above 10,000 feet in daylight, and from the ground up at night. He probably removed his mask at the start of his attack. Whether it affected his aim, I'll never know. A few years ago I saw his gun camera film, and the gyrations that we were doing was remarkable! At any rate we didn't hurt each other.

We expected the fighters to come back, but they spotted our

straggler, and decided to finish him off. It didn't work, as two of the enemy planes were shot down, and a third was damaged by our wounded B-17. The German pilots may have been inexperienced. Many years after the war, while I was a member of the Maryland Wing of the Civil Air Patrol, I met a member who had been a German pilot that had survived the war. He told me that only a fool would fly against a B-17 unless he was forced to do so. Having a gun camera made it mandatory, I guess. He never told me his score, if any.

On the way back to base we saw a B-17 go out of control and explode, and eight parachutes were counted. In the North Sea we saw another B-17 ditch, having run out of fuel. We saw one of the inflatable life rafts that had several men in it. Air sea rescue came and picked them up a couple of hours later.

None of these downed bombers were from our base, and we all got back safely, including our straggler who made it on three engines. Nine B-17s of our group sustained minor damage, while our straggler was listed as major. One aircraft was listed as damaged by friendly fire. This was our aircraft, as another B-17 firing at "our" Me109 fired a 50 caliber, armor piercing, incendiary bullet through our left aileron. Fortunately for us, it missed our gas tanks, which would likely have made us into a fireball. Guns on the B-17 cannot shoot parts off their own plane because of stops built into the mechanism, but it cannot prevent "OOPS" from their neighbors.

On our return trip to Molesworth we were joined by a twin engine P-38 that had an engine feathered to conserve fuel. He indicated that he was out of ammunition and wanted to fly with us so that we could protect him in case we were attacked again. However there was no other excitement and we led him to England where he waggled his wings and flew to his own base. It was pretty neat: a fighter having a bomber for an escort.

Total flight time for this mission was just over ten hours, with 4 hours and 40 minutes over enemy territory.

On this mission, the return flight took us very near neutral Sweden, and from other groups, eight bombers (!) sought refuge from the war by landing at two fields there. One of the damaged B-17s was the now famous "Shoo Shoo Shoo Baby" of the 91st Bomb

Group that was restored at Dover Air Force base in Delaware and now has permanent residence at Wright Field in Dayton, Ohio.

It had been rumored that the Eighth Air Force command was thinking about having our own P-51s shoot down bombers that headed toward Sweden if they appeared to be undamaged. This was confirmed after the war, but the reason no action was ever taken was that it would have put a strain on bomber-fighter relations. As it was, Sweden accumulated several dozen bombers and quite a few fighters. Of course the crews were interred for the duration of the war and the planes were impounded. The History Channel produced a documentary called "Whispers in The Air" that deals with this problem. After the war, the US sold these aircraft to Sweden for a dollar each. During the entire war, over thirty seven thousand cases of desertion were prosecuted, but only one death sentence was ever meted out.

Beiser and I had agreed earlier that if either of us tried to take our undamaged plane to Sweden or Switzerland, The other would pull out his 45 pistol and take over the airplane and return it to Molesworth. Of course, faking an engine failure would be easy as far as the others on the plane were concerned, but such fakery would not work on a cockpit officer. And it probably wouldn't work on the flight engineer. As it turned out, such a discussion on our crew was unnecessary, as none of our crew ever voiced a desire to visit Sweden.

This mission to Poland was the only one that the 303rd ever flew to a target in that part of their country.

Chapter 15

Mission number 7
May 31, 1944, Target, Holland.

The weather briefing for today's mission indicated good weather over the target, but we soon found that towering cumulus clouds had built up while we were en-route. Some topped out at 28,000 feet, well above our planned altitude.

The 303rd Bomb Group was to supply 14 aircraft for the wing formation, and we were on our way by 08:00. As we approached the enemy coast, Clouds appeared on our route, and we had to deviate from the planned course. This took us almost over Brussels, Belgium, which was well defended with 88MM flak guns. Almost immediately, the B-17 flown by Lt. Flick, who was flying off our right wing received a direct hit. One man in his crew was seriously wounded, and they turned back to England, landing at an emergency strip at Chipping-On-Gar.

Due to the clouds, we had to abandon our primary target at Colmar, France, and the secondary, St. Dizier airdrome in France. Our target of opportunity became the airport at Gilze-Rijen in southern Holland because we could see it somewhat.

Unfortunately, the clouds caused us to only do a one-minute bomb run, and our bombs fell between the runways into a wooded area. For some reason, two planes did not drop their bombs, and returned them to base. We saw six enemy fighters but they did not attack since they were being harassed by our P-51s.

Two B-17s of our group sustained major damage and six had minor damage including our "Betty Jane" who suffered a fist sized hole in her tail. Vertical stabilizer, that is. We were over enemy territory for an hour and twenty minutes on this mission.

As an interesting sidelight to this mission, my wife, Marjorie and

I, visited this airfield in 1992, thanks to the legwork by Dutch author, Ivo M. De Jong. He took us there in mid May, almost 48 years after this mission. I was surprised to find that I was the first person to ever officially visit the airport site that had bombed it. Also the historian who met us, said that our bombs that fell into the wooded area, destroyed a large store of fuel that the Germans had hidden there. Our bombs nearly struck the fire station, and one fell into the hundred foot wide pond that supplied water to the fire fighting equipment. This 500-pound bomb struck the pond so centered that it blew all the water out of the pond without changing its contour. This left very little water for the fire fighters to put out the gasoline fire that our bombs caused. And, talk about flying fish!

There is now an American F-16 squadron based there, and very little of the German presence can be seen. One item of interest was a small section of the old German taxiway, which had a two-inch wide florescent stripe in the middle, so that their fighters could taxi in the dark without exposing their lights to the Allies.

The main avenue on the air base is called Piper Cub Wey (Way) which led to the F-16 maintenance hangar that we were privileged to visit. German headquarters at the field in 1944 were built next to a Dutch school just off the base, so that the Allies would not bomb it. It worked, as their headquarters building never was hit in the half dozen times that the field was bombed. I'm not sure if the Allies knew of this headquarters, and I think that they might at least have been strafed by one of our fighters if they knew of it. As members of a combat crew we had very little information about targets other than the ones we were assigned to attack.

On a mission to this field on August 19, 1943 the bombs from another group in our wing fell short, and landed in the Dutch hamlet of Hulten, killing twenty-one civilians. This Hamlet is almost at the outer gate to the field. The 303rd group also missed the target and lost two bombers to German fighters. Nine men were killed and twelve were made prisoner. Bombs of the 303rd fell outside the perimeter of the field, but injured no one. This was one of the unfortunate aspects of high altitude bombardment. Every group missed on that day due to poor visibility.

These are escape photos to use for IDs after a bail-out. All crew
members carried 6 or more on each mission.

The Germans knew the clothes well enought to identify our bomb
group as all crews wore the same shirt, tie and jacket
during the take.

Mission # 8: Paris!
Prelude to invasion.

June 2nd, 1944, my Mother's 44th birthday, and the first anniversary of my first airplane ride at Darr Aero Tech in which I decorated the side of the primary trainer. It seems unbelievable that I could be co-pilot of so large an airplane and be on my 8th mission in just one year after touching an airplane for the first time in my life.

Today we are to bomb a large marshaling yard in the outskirts of Paris, our aim being to delay German movement to the front lines during the up-coming invasion. My diary for that day reads,

"Paris, France (Marshaling yards) five tenths cloud cover. Moderate flak-no damage. Saw hundreds of landing craft on English coast. Invasion soon maybe."

Fourteen B-17s from our 303rd Bomb Group were furnished for the 41st Combat Wing. The 427th Squadron, to which I was a part, was to lead our group. Each of our B-17s had been loaded with six 1000-pound bombs and 1700 gallons of gas. Our target was the Juvissy Marshaling Yards eleven miles to the southwest of downtown Paris.

Our time schedule for this mission was pretty tight, as we were to take off at around 5:30 PM, double wartime, and arrive at the target before dark. The days were long at this time of year, so we were confident that we could make this schedule. We departed the English coast over Selsey Bill, at an altitude of 18,500 feet. Selsey Bill is a point of land just east of Portsmouth. We crossed the English Channel, climbing to 22,000 feet, and crossed the enemy coast just across the harbor from Le Havre, France. We encountered a layer of clouds at our altitude, and decided to drop down to 18,000 feet. We made a feint toward Chartres, and just before reaching their outer defenses, made a dogleg to the left, and made a direct flight to our target. We bombed at 8:32 PM well before the sun went down. England was on double war savings time, which made our bomb drop at the real time of 6:32 PM. We flew a circle around Paris at 21,000 ft and headed toward Le Havre, where we departed the enemy coast a few miles north of that town. It was starting to get pretty dark on the ground by then, and no lights could be seen anywhere. There was still plenty of daylight at our altitude and just before dark we saw a large group of British Lancasters below us, heading out to do their nightly bombing.

This had been the first day of "Operation Cover" during which we were trying to convince the Germans that the invasion would be at Calais. The morning mission had been a tactical one for the first time for the 303rd Bomb Group.

Our track back to Molesworth took us a mile west of London, which was so totally blacked out that it could barely be seen, even though there was still a glimmer of daylight. We landed at nearly 11:00pm, double war time, and headed to the debriefing room and later, to the mess hall for a late snack, having eaten our box lunches on the way to the target. I was somewhat miffed to find that the mess hall personnel had gone to bed, leaving a large pot of coffee into which they had put too much cream, and too much sugar. I was unable to drink it, since I always drank mine without sugar. This was my only gripe about food, since the Mess Sergeant had always done a great job.

Recon photos the next day showed that we had done a good job on the railroad marshaling yards. Our total flight time was five and a half-hours, with one hour and forty minutes over enemy territory. In the next few days, the weather turned really bad, but the 303rd flew missions on June 3rd and 4th but our crew got a reprieve until June 5th.

We learned later that the invasion of France was scheduled for June 5 after having been canceled from its original schedule of early May. Of course we didn't know the exact day until being briefed for the actual D-Day invasion. In retrospect, it might have been better in May except for logistic problems in getting poised along the English coast. Also, it was not considered prudent for May since we had not yet achieved mastery of the air. It is incredible that the Germans were not expected to know the exact place of the invasion, since the thousands of ships were easily seen from the air and from the sea on the south coast of England.

We also suspected that there might be a spy on our field since some of our plans seemed to be compromised. In the mess hall was a worker who came and went with the rest of the civilian workers. We called him "The Limey" because of the way he acted. If we did indeed have a spy, he was never found out as far as I know.

I don't know that a spy could have gotten much information since the aircrews seldom had any hints of tomorrow's destination. And we never discussed plans outside our own crew.

Chapter 16

Mission # 9, June 5th, 1944
To the invasion coast.

"Cherbourg Peninsula, France," my diary read, "Heavy gun batteries on invasion coast. Made 3 bomb runs. Meager flak, no damage. Four tenths cloud cover on target. Saw hundreds of ships on English coast. Things may pop open very soon now."

This was to be a short mission, so we traded fuel for bombs. Each B-17 was loaded with sixteen, 500 pound, semi-armor-piercing bombs. We took off at 6:15 AM with 12 scheduled B-17s and one spare, which would fill in if there were an abort from our group. Since there were no aborts, the spare returned before reaching enemy territory. We departed England at Selsey Bill at 24,500 feet, and headed to our Initial Point in the English Channel, which was determined by LORAN. This was a less sophisticated version of modern LORAN (Long-Range Navigation) using only two radio stations. This could take us within a quarter mile or so, of our destination. Modern LORAN uses three stations and can get you within a few feet of your destination.

Due to clouds, we tried three times to hit the primary target, each time returning to our IP in the channel, to no avail. Just ahead of our last attempt, was a heavy gun emplacement, next to a landing strip. They received the attention of the nine aircraft in our part of the group. They received 144 semi-armor piercing, 500-pound bombs, just because the weather was bad elsewhere.

After bombing, we let down over the channel, through clouds, and crossed the English coast at Portland Bill at 2,700 feet. We flew a direct course to our base at Molesworth, arriving just before noon.

Over the target area, there was moderate flak in several places, but none close enough to damage any of the B-17s of our group. Only two fighter planes were seen, and they both were ours. We were in the air four and a half-hours, with thirty five minutes over enemy territory.

Tomorrow, D-DAY! June 6, 1944

D-DAY Missions number 10 and 11

"Today is D-Day," the briefing officer announced. "The invasion has already started, and we are going to try to prevent the Germans from bringing up their reinforcements. The weather is very bad, and we may bomb by radar." he said.

Each B-17 was loaded with twelve, 500-pound, and two 1,000-pound bombs, and we were off at 06:00 with 34 aircraft from the 303rd Bomb Group. Two aircraft aborted due to mechanical problems. This was Lt. Bailie of the 358th squadron, and Lt. Fackler of the 359th squadron. This was my tenth mission with the 427th squadron and Col. Snyder, our commander, led the low flight. Newsman Walter Cronkite flew with Bob Sheets (Illegally no doubt) in "Shoo Shoo Baby" of our squadron on this mission.

We were to bomb a bridge near the invasion coast, but the cloud cover at the target was total, so we were to bomb by PFF (radar). Sixteen aircraft of the lead group dropped 192 X 500 GP, (general purpose) bombs and 30 X 1,000 GP bombs on the target, with unobserved results. Our flight had a radar failure, and dropped no bombs. We flew our bombs back to base and made ready for our second mission of the day.

Since we tried to bomb, and went over enemy territory for 30 minutes, we got credit for a mission, which was number ten for me.

By bringing our bombs back, we avoided "Americide" which is the accidental killing of our own troops, such as the one during the invasion of Sicily, on July 11, 1943. On that night, the paratroops and infantrymen of the 504th regiment, boarded C-47s and headed for Gela. Even though warned in advance, American anti aircraft gunners on ships and ashore, shot down 23 of the 144 troop transports, killing 93 paratroopers and wounding over 400.

After today's invasion, -on July 24th, 1944-, bombs from another group fell short and killed 16 American soldiers and wounded nearly a hundred others. Worse yet, the next day, Lt. Gen. Leslie J. McNair was killed along with 101 other infantrymen when bombs fell short. Three hundred and eight others were wounded in that mishap. General McNair received a direct hit, and his only identifiable remains were a portion of a finger with his West Point ring attached.

Norman Polmar and Thomas B. Allen have compiled a complete record in their book by Random House. It is called "World War II, America at War, 1941-1945.

Afternoon, June 6, 1944. Mission number 11.
Same target as this morning.

Our target near the invasion coast this afternoon was a bridge near Caen, France that we were unable to bomb because of an equipment failure on the lead aircraft. We saw flak again, at a distance, but were not affected. The weather over the French coast was bad with five-tenths cloud cover, but we could see bits of the invasion activity. The number of wakes from ships and landing craft covered the entire English Channel for miles. We could see smoke on the French coast from all the artillery. To prevent being fired upon by our own gunners, the fighters and medium bombers had wide, white stripes painted across one wing and around the fuselage. The heavies didn't bother with this, as we were too high to be seen easily, and the Germans had no bombers of this size, and all our gunners knew this. (We hoped.)

We had achieved the desired mastery of the air by this time, and the Germans had a bitter joke amongst themselves.

"If you see a camouflaged airplane, it's British. If you see a shiny, unpainted airplane, it's American. If you don't see any airplane at all, it's German."

Much of our mission at this stage of the war was the attrition of experienced German fighter pilots. As they rose up to defend their country, our fighters shot them down. With their shortage of fuel and experienced pilots, they had large numbers of new airplanes that couldn't be flown. I saw several of their jet propelled, Me262s in unarmed training flights, but it was too little, too late.

The rocket propelled Me163 Komet which was developed by the Germans in the late 1930s did not see service against our bombers until July 28, 1944. I was still flying missions and I saw two, but never encountered one close-up. I heard that they killed more German pilots, than American, since they often blew up at launch.

On the first day of the invasion, one hundred fifty thousand Allied troops landed on the beaches. A week later the total was a half million men. Six weeks later the total had reached two million men and a quarter million vehicles. (See "The longest day", by Cornelius Ryan).

And so, on this day, the destruction of Hitler's Third Reich began in earnest, and the outcome is in the history of Earth's greatest war.

In the years since D-Day, much has been said about this historic event. It was the greatest invasion in the history of man. It ultimately established the United States as the premier super power that it has remained.

I feel that my own participation in D-Day was important, but both of my missions on that day were milk runs, as it was for most of the heavy bomber crews who flew that day. Penetrating the thick overcast over England and the Continent was a much greater danger than the Germans had to offer that day.

The ground troops who did the fighting on that day deserve the bulk of the credit. Our mission to neutralize the German Air Force had worked very well, but there would be resurgences in future missions.

Chapter 17

Mission number 12, June 7, 1944

My diary for this day reads: "Cherbourg again. Invasion coast. Bombed German escape route. Target seven tenths covered. Used PFF method of bombing. No opposition from Nazis. Big operations. We are wholly supporting ground troops."

Beiser and I were assigned to the B-17 with the tail number 42-39875 named "Buzz Blonde." I would ultimately fly twelve missions in this plane. Each of the eighteen B-17s of our group was loaded with six, 1000-pound bombs to be delivered to a road junction near the invasion coast close to Conde Sur Neireau in western France. Eighteen other B-17s from our field were loaded with 500-pound bombs that they dropped on a road and railroad junction near Flers, France. Two of our aircraft failed to bomb because of malfunctions. Due to overcast at the target, we bombed by radar from an average altitude of 21,000 ft. Our "Buzz Blonde" was assigned position number three in the 427th squadron. This is just behind the lead plane of our squadron.

Although the target area was totally clouded over except for very small holes, one crew reported bombs exploding in the target area, which could be seen during one of the brief openings.

We were over enemy territory for forty minutes, but saw no flak or German fighters. We saw a few friendly fighters above the clouds that were our escorts. We could only get occasional glimpses of the invasion activity.

I might explain to the reader that our group was capable of putting forty B-17s in the air at any given mission, and on one mission actually put up sixty. However since a group of that size would be cumbersome, we always made two groups, which we called the 41st combat wing "A" group, and 41st combat wing "B" group.

On this particular day, the "B" planes bound for Flers, took off starting at 0931 and ending ten minutes later with nineteen aircraft in the air at 0941. Without a break, our "A" group took off between 0941 and 0954. Each group had a spare, but since there were no aborts on this mission, they both returned before reaching enemy territory, and thus got no credit for a mission. Our route to the target took us due south, although we did a slight dogleg to the west of London and headed to France and arrived just out of flak range of Le Havre. As we approached the target at 21,300 ft. indicated, (21,000 actual) the wind was 63 miles per hour from 340 degrees, giving us a left drift of 18 degrees. Our indicated air speed of 150 MPH gave us a true airspeed of 208 MPH and a ground speed of 207 MPH at the target according to readings from the Norden bombsight.

The outside air temperature was a relatively mild, minus 7 degrees Fahrenheit. Bombs were away at 1208 PM and we returned to base, arriving at 1432 with all planes on the ground by 1503. Each aircraft had carried 1,700 gallons of gasoline for this five hour and twenty minute mission.

Mission 13, June 8, 1944
Orleans, France

Diary: "Orleans, France (South of Paris). Marshaling yards supplying Germans for anti-invasion. Weather over continent is still pretty bad, but seems to be improving. Encountered no opposition. Six, one thousand pound bombs."

This day we were to try to blow up the train tracks and the rolling stock carrying war goods to the front lines. We also hoped to drop a railroad bridge into the rubble. Beiser and I were again assigned to the "Buzz Blonde" and our crew was complete. Sgt. Gorchesky, our radioman missed yesterday's mission with us because his radio expertise was needed in our squadron's lead plane. But he was back with us today.

Our assembly was modified from plan because of two cloud layers. We finally assembled the group between these two layers. We flew thirty six aircraft in three groups on this mission, taking off from 0431 to 0522 and were all back on the ground before noon, having largely wasted the mission because of a problem with the Norden Bomb Sight in the lead plane. We did visual bombing with an eleven-minute bomb run, but in the last minute and a half the bombardier discovered that he needed two more degrees of drift correction. As he tried to crank in the correction nothing happened, so he tried to crank in more turns with no results. He then decided to turn the mission over to the deputy lead to do another bomb run. His decision was too late however, as the Norden sight released the bombs and all the other eleven planes dropped in unison. Our bombs struck even with the target, but too far to the left by at least five hundred feet, destroying some large unknown buildings. We later learned that something was against the drift knob with enough pressure to prevent the corrections from being made. It was probably the bombardier's parachute harness that caused the malfunction, since the sight checked out fine at the repair shop.

Hogan was the hero of the day. The 359th squadron that held the high group position rescued the mission when the eleven planes of that group laid a perfect pattern on the Railroad Bridge. Lt. Hogan was the bombardier of the day for that feat.

The low group did just as badly as our group's effort. They had to make a second pass at the target and had a short bomb run. Some aircraft were still jockeying into their positions when bombs were away. Some of the planes were in slight banking positions, which tossed their bombs to one side, making a poor pattern. Some days it just doesn't pay to get up.

The lead plane in our squadron, the 427th, was called "Shoo Shoo Baby" after the song by the Andrews Sisters. Nearly every group had an aircraft with that name. The 360th squadron's lead plane was named "Sack Time" after our favorite indoor sport in those days. The lead plane of the 358th squadron was "Princess Pat," with the usual seductive nose art. Hogan's hero was "Heller's Angels," flying lead in the other 360th formation.

Mission number 14, June 13, 1944.
Target, Evreux, France A/D

The weather was finally clear over the target for today's mission, and opposition could nearly always be expected on clear days. We were to bomb the airdrome at Evreux (pronounced Ev-row) in order to harass the German fighter planes stationed there. We had missed a mission on June 12 because of maintenance problems with our "Buzz Blonde." A B-17 with no name was shot down on the 12th when it was hit by a direct flak burst at the left wing root, and another directly in the bomb-bay, while the bomb-bay doors were open for a drop one minute later. The aircraft burst into flame and disintegrated. Only the tail gunner survived.

Today, we were assigned the number two position next to the lead plane flown by 1st Lt. P.E. Mitchell. Off our right wing, the deputy lead was flown by 2nd. Lt. W. T. Means. Before we reached the French coast, the plane flown by the leader, Lt. Mitchell, had to abort due to a failure in his number two engine. Lt. Means moved up to the number one position, and our spare flown by Lt. Lehman moved into the formation to complete the mission. Of the forty planes we put up that day, only three aborted; Our 427th squadron's "Miss Lace" in which I would fly my last mission, flown by Lt. Mitchell; "Old Glory" from the 360th Squadron; and "Helen Heaven" from the 358th Squadron.

We flew to France after climbing through a solid overcast and hit the coast headed toward the French town of Amiens, but turned south in a feint to Paris, and finally to the target which was a few miles southwest of Paris. We each carried 18, 250 pound, general-purpose bombs, and 1700 gallons of gasoline to hit the airfield.

Just before we got to the target, the skies cleared, and the visibility became unlimited. We could see the target from the initial point and the bombardier did a superb job, putting the pattern of bombs across the airfield, ruining both runways. The lead bombardier said that we bombed the target through the only hole in the clouds over Europe. We saw flak in the distance, but had no direct opposition. It was a real milk run. We were over enemy territory for an hour and ten minutes, on a four hour and forty minute flight.

Our bombardier, Lt. Ed. Cooper was training a new toggalier on this mission, Staff Sgt. J.W. Donnelly. Also, our radio operator-waist gunner, Gorchesky was training a new man, Sgt. M.A. Sutton, so we had two new men for the day. Our navigator, Lt. Isadore Gepner, was flying with another crew on this mission, so we flew without a navigator. We stayed close to the formation through the overcast and didn't get lost, but two planes from other squadrons landed at another field.

I "flew" the Link Trainer after my mission of June 8th and was scheduled for the same thing tomorrow, June 14.

Today, June 13, 1944, the first "Buzz Bombs" started arriving in the London area. Of four missiles on that day, only one inflicted any damage, killing six civilians and injuring nine others.

Mission 15. June 15, 1944

On this date we were assigned a railroad bridge in Tours, France, carrying two, two thousand-pound bombs on the belly of the planes, since a two thousand-pound bomb wouldn't easily fit into the bomb-bay.

My diary for the day reads: Tours, France, Massive railroad Bridge across Loire River. C.A.V.U. (Ceiling and Visibility Unlimited). Destroyed it completely. Stopped a train from crossing it. Meager but accurate flak. No damage to us.

We flew over a single flak battery at St. Martin and the flak gunners aimed visually. Our evasive turns were sufficient to ruin their aim and they only did minor damage to a few of the 12 planes in our squadron.

Our bombs were fused at one tenth second at the nose and one hundredth at the tail. We did a twenty mile bomb run and all three squadrons hit the bridge with a good pattern. This was one of the longest bomb runs that I remember, being 14 minutes in a straight line. Lucky for us there was very little defense at the target, as we would have been sitting ducks on such a clear day flying at fifteen thousand, five hundred feet. Usually, when the bomb-bay doors opened on a clear day, the flak would come up in bunches, because the German gunners knew that we would not make any evasive turns. They could lead us by about one and a half kilometers so that the bursts would be right in our formation.

As we approached the bridge with our bomb doors open, a train that was headed in that direction suddenly stopped and started backing up. We were amazed that they were so desperate as to venture out in broad daylight. We worried that they might be carrying prisoners but since there were no enemy fighters to harass us, some of our escort planes went down to see what they could break. We were so busy getting into wing formation for our return home that we couldn't watch much of the ground activity. I sort of envied Charlie Latta, our ball turret gunner, as he had a ringside seat, as did some of the other gunners.

Ed Cooper, our bombardier, was flying with the crew of 1st Lt. C. T. Savage on this mission, for what reason I don't remember, however we had another bombardier that day. His name was J. B. Parker. Crews were often mixed for training purposes.

At any rate, we had no failures that day, except that the aircraft flown by Lt. C. E. Johnson aborted for mechanical reasons and our spare took his position in the formation. All 36 aircraft returned to Molesworth and were on the ground before noon.

When we arrived back at base after a mission, the field was always lined with personnel who were "Sweating us out." This also put the onus on the pilots to make decent landings since all spare personnel on the base would be there to count planes and check the damage. Planes with wounded aboard landed first. When wounded were aboard, radio silence was maintained, but the plane involved would fire a red flare to denote wounded aboard. They would be met with ambulance and doctors to tend to them. This became a common sight as we taxied past after landing.

Total flight time was six hours and fifteen minutes with two and a half-hours over enemy territory.

Mission 16 (Abort) June 16, 1944

This was the first and only time that we had to abort a mission for mechanical or any other reason. Our target was to be an airdrome at Juvincourt France. It should have been a near milk run with us scheduled to bomb from 25,000 ft. Our assembly was to be at that bombing altitude in order to clear other groups going to other targets. Beiser and I were assigned to the tail end Charlie position in the aircraft named "Buzz Blonde." As we neared the 23,000-ft. altitude, the number three engine started losing power. When we found that we could climb no higher, we turned back to Molesworth and landed. When an aircraft aborts or gets lost there is always an inquiry in the operations section.

Following is Beiser's report: To: Commanding Officer, 427th Bombardment Squadron (H) AAF.

1. The abortion of A/C 42-39875, piloted by 2nd Lieut. Theodore R. Beiser, was due to the loss of No. 3 Turbo. We could only get about 20" manifold pressure at 23,000'. I could not continue to climb. (29 inches of Manifold pressure was the norm.)
2. The first indications of trouble started at take off when No. 3 turbo ran away but then seemed to settle down OK. At about 10,000', No. 3 began to lag.
3. The Engineer (Buchanan) went back and changed the amplifier but this did no good. I then took my knife and turned the No. 3 turbo screw full on without any results. I then turned the turbo to 10, and increased the R.P.M. to 2500, but could not get any more boost on No. 3 engine.
4. I finally decided at 23,000' that I could not get to assembly altitude, which was 25,000'. I turned back over Molesworth at 23,000'.

5. No spare aircraft filled this position. I was flying No. 7, in the low squadron, lead group.

Signed, TR Beiser
1st endorsement.

1. The Engineering Section of this squadron makes the following report: Upon checking No. 3 engine a supercharger failure was discovered due to No. 3 Waist Gate Motor burned out and a bolt sheared in No. 4 mixture control.

2. In the opinion of this squadron, Lieut. Beiser was justified to abort.

For the Squadron Commander:
Robert W. Sheets
Captain, Air Corps
Asst. Operations Officer.

I rather imagine that the ground crew for "Buzz Blonde" had an extra session. Had we not aborted, the sheared bolt in the no. 4 mixture control could have been a critical item. If the mixture could not have been leaned out, the engine would have been too rich at altitude, and use extra gas. Also the plugs would foul and cause the engine to run too cold.

This supposed "Milk Run" resulted in damage to fourteen planes from this group, causing one plane to land at Nuthampstead with a wounded crewman.

Mission number 16, June 19, 1944, Monday morning.

My diary entry for this day reads: "Pas De Calais, France Robot plane installations. Target overcast. No opposition, no damage. Observed flak. Altitude 25,000 ft."

Just yesterday, on Sunday June 18, a Buzz Bomb killed and wounded nearly 200 Wellington guardsmen when it struck their barracks. The V-1 missiles were now arriving in London at about 100 per day.

Our previous mission was supposed to be number 16, but since we aborted over friendly territory, we didn't get credit for a mission. We only flew two hours and thirty-five minutes that day.

Today we were loaded with thirty-eight, 100 pound, general-purpose bombs. These bombs were to be dropped through the clouds to try to destroy a V-1 (Buzz Bomb) site, using special navigation and identification equipment called "Gee-H." This type of mission was called a "No Ball Target" which is tactical rather than the usual strategic missions that we were trained to do. We were still trying to support the invasion forces and stop the V-1 assault at the same time. I suspect that this mission scared a lot of people but did little damage. The forty aircraft of our group dropped 1513 bombs and were over enemy territory thirty minutes with a total flight time of four hours and forty five minutes.

Mission number 17, June 19, 1944
Monday afternoon.

Although this afternoon's mission was considered a milk run, it was anything but that, as far as I was concerned. The lead plane in our group, and others, always carried a co-pilot in the tail gun position to check on formation. This was because a cockpit officer could name any ship by position to tell the lead pilot who might be out of formation.

Today was my turn in the barrel. I was assigned to fly with Captain R. S. Harrison and Captain R. P. Dubell in the 359th squadron's lead aircraft number 42-97291. They were leading the group in this afternoon's mission. The target was the same as this morning's mission, a Buzz bomb station near Fiefs and Predefin, which are in the Pas De Calais area.

My diary reads: "Pas De Calais, France. GH Robot Plane installations. Target five tenths covered. Same as this AM's mission. Flew as tail gunner on lead ship to check formation. Temperature -26 degrees centigrade. Saw flak again, but no damage."

This brief description shows a milk run all right, but when I got into the tail gun position with electrically heated suit and gloves, I was out of my element. I made out OK during formation and departure. But when I was about settled down, after advising the pilot that everything seemed good about the formation, I noticed that the AFCE (Automatic Flight Control Equipment) or Autopilot that we called "George" was causing a good bit of movement at my new position. The swaying and yawing soon made me airsick. Not only that, I couldn't figure out how to fire the tail guns. I tried several times, finally giving up, as I figured that no enemy plane would attack from the rear, since all I could see behind me was hundreds of B-17s filling the sky for as far as I could see.

I soon developed the dry heaves, and it got so bad that I thought that I would barf my cookies with nothing to barf in. At that point I took off my flak helmet to use for that purpose, but managed to contain myself. It got to the point that I wouldn't have cared if I were shot down. I even contemplated taking off my oxygen mask for a while to see if that would ease the airsickness, but decided against it, since I knew that oxygen starvation was insidious, with no warning of any sort. We had periodic oxygen checks during all altitude flights, and when some one didn't answer, the nearest crewmember took a walk-around oxygen bottle to check him out.

Beiser and most of our crew didn't fly this mission, and for a brief moment I was resentful for having been assigned this position. It gave me new respect for our tail gunner, Carroll H. Brackey. Ed Cooper was flying with 2nd Lt. D. D. Sayers on this mission, and David Glass, our assistant radio operator, right waist gunner was flying with 1st Lt. A. G. Raistrick.

I guess it didn't help matters that gale force winds had arrived over the channel, making flying even bumpier than usual. The winds were so strong the next few days that the "Mulberry Harbor" at Omaha Beach was destroyed, and the British one was severely damaged. Parts of the American harbor were used to repair the one for the British at Arromanches. A large number of landing craft was also sunk during this stormy period.

A few missions later I had gone to the Key Club near the town of Molesworth for a little relaxation, knowing that I would not fly a mission the next day since our plane was down for repairs. I didn't get back to the barracks until about three AM and discovered with panic that the place was deserted. I quickly checked the manifest and saw that I was again assigned to fly tail gun position in the lead plane for an unexpected mission that morning.

I ran down to the briefing room, since breakfast was already over. I expected to be court martialled for missing a mission, so I ran to the operation's officer for the 303rd Bomb group, Major Schulstad, and told him I was ready to go. He said,

"Oh, that's OK, we found somebody to take your place." I couldn't believe that anyone could be so casual about a crewmember being AWOL, as it were. But it paid off for me since I never had to fly tail gun but the one time. I hadn't told them about my near fatal airsickness and I can imagine what would have happened to me if I had taken this flight today. After having a "few" drinks and no breakfast, I would have been in prime shape for a major barf.

Our attempts to destroy the launching sites were largely failures, since the sites were small and easily hidden. Nearly two thousand allied airmen died in the eighty days of these interdiction assaults. Also, these bombs killed more than six thousand civilians, and nearly eighteen thousand were injured. These flying bombs traveled at four hundred miles per hour, and only the British Meteor, a jet-propelled fighter could catch one. Yet, with over two thousand anti-aircraft guns, some with proximity fuses, nearly twenty five hundred of these weapons fell on London and the same amount on Antwerp, Belgium after its capture by allied ground troops.

Chapter 18

Mission number 18. June 20, 1944. Target: Hamburg

My diary for today reads: "Hamburg, (Yipe!) Germany.

Bombed oil refinery and storage. Made good use of CAVU weather.

Sure went up in flames. Flak so thick you couldn't see through it, but we flew through it. Got plenty of holes. (Over 260). Put our ship out for a few days. Sure earned that cluster." (To Air Medal)

The 303rd Bomb Group put up thirty-nine B-17s for this mission to bomb the Rhenania-Ossag Mineralolwerkes A.G. at Harburg, a suburb of Hamburg. We were to bomb from 25,000 ft. The Eighth Air Force put up eight hundred fifty three B-17s and six hundred ninety five B-24s on this day, for a total of one thousand, five hundred forty eight heavy bombers.

Each of our aircraft was loaded with twelve, 500 pound, general-purpose bombs, fused at one tenth second at the nose and one fortieth second at the tail. Each B-17 was loaded with 2100 gallons of gasoline for the seven hour and two minute flight.

Beiser and I were assigned to position number 4 in a composite squadron. The first three aircraft of the squadron were from the 360th squadron, with us leading our element of four aircraft of the 427th squadron to which we belonged. The 41st wing "A", high group that we were part of consisted of nine aircraft of the 360th and eleven of our 427th. This put us in position number 10 in the group. The lead aircraft carried a K-17 camera and two of our planes carried K-21 cameras. After the mission, these two aircraft left the formation after reaching friendly territory and landed first for photo work. The other group consisting of the 358th and 359th squadrons carried out the same system. In all, planes of the 303rd bomb group carried twelve cameras that day, which was the usual number. One plane, (Named

Banshee), from the 360th squadron carrying a camera had to abort when he suffered an engine failure.

Another of our aircraft from the 360th squadron had a delayed take-off and was not able to find the formation, and so returned to base. One of our aircraft was lost to enemy anti-aircraft fire just after bombs away.

As we approached the city of Hamburg, the flak was unbelievable. The Germans were determined to protect their oil supplies at any cost. The flak explosions were constant and unrelenting, being so close that many could be heard to explode and throw fragments against the sides of the airplane. To see the angry, red center of some of the explosions meant that they were very close. To hear flak explode, it had to be within fifty feet of our plane, otherwise the very loud engine noise would drown out the noise of an explosion farther away. Likewise, to feel a jolt from a flak explosion, it would have to explode twenty-five feet or less from the plane.

I saw plenty of red centers and heard several of them during our 41 mile (!) bomb run. Our ground speed against the wind was barely over two miles per minute, allowing the German defenders over fifteen minutes to track us in the straight and level flight from the Initial Point to the target. This meant that each flak gun could fire up to 300 rounds at us if they didn't burn out the barrel.

Just before the IP, the B-17 flown by 1st Lt. J.T. Parker, nearly dead ahead of us, suffered a double engine failure due to flak damage. He was able to keep up for a short while and dropped his bombs with the formation. He could not keep up with the homeward formation however, and lost altitude while still under control. When we last saw him, he was down near the ground still under control, but he never made it back to base and all nine crew members became prisoners of the German Government for the rest of the war.

We busted the target wide open. One group ahead of us had also hit the target and smoke was visible during the entire bomb run. There were many great explosions among the oil storage tanks and on the cracking plant itself. From our vantage at 26,500 feet, we could see clearly that the target was completely covered by bomb bursts. We hadn't bothered to carry any incendiary bombs on this trip, and it seems that they would have been redundant in any case.

It was surprising that there would be a target of this importance still in existence in the city and suburbs of Hamburg, since it had already been razed by British night bombing, causing a fire storm of tornado intensity that covered most of the city.

Of our 39 B-17s only two (!) escaped damage on this mission. Eleven suffered major damage, three crewmen were wounded by flak and one plane was lost. It is remarkable that only one plane was shot down. The Buzz Blonde that Beiser and I were flying suffered over 263 flak holes of various sizes and yet not a crewmember was hit. And the airplane flew as if nothing had happened to it, even with several cables broken.

Our bombardier, Ed Cooper was again flying with another crew and we had a new man to replace him for the day. Ed was flying with 1st Lt. G.T. Savage Jr. in A/C # 42-107099, "Old ninety-nine" from the tail number. Lt. C. F. Eisel was our temporary bombardier.

Ed Cooper almost lost it all on this mission. Flak was so thick that it fell like rain at times from explosions above the formation. One piece of shrapnel, the size of a thumb, broke through the nose window and struck Ed on the breastbone and drove him six feet back into the navigator's compartment. There is no doubt that the flak suit saved his life, because when we returned to base we helped him cut the piece of flak from the suit. The flak suit is composed of small plates of tantalum or molybdenum steel that overlap each other like scales on a fish. There are always three thicknesses of these plates. The first layer had clasped the flak fragment so that it could not be removed. The second layer was bent sharply around the first, and the third layer was only slightly bent. Ed sported a large bruise on his chest for several days, but was not injured enough to take him off flying status. He didn't even get a Purple Heart for his troubles.

Several crewmembers each received an extra Distinguished Flying Cross for this mission. Beiser and I were also recommended because some of our control cables were cut by flak, but the plane did not react to this damage, and so the idea was dropped. For my part, I lived through the mission and received an Oak Leaf Cluster to my previously awarded Air Medal. The Air Medal was given to each airman upon completion of six missions, and an oak leaf cluster is given to signify another six of the same. This was my third

Air Medal. If you fail to bring the airplane home, even through no fault of your own, you will not get the medal. Our seven hour and two minute flight had us over enemy territory for one hour and fifty minutes of almost continuance combat.

This kind of combat was usually the most scary since there was nothing we could do about it. Flak seldom arrives unannounced as the visibility shows the previous bursts for several minutes. The black line over the target is always exactly at your altitude and you know that you have to fly through it. On the other hand, fighter attacks are usually so sudden that you have little time to get the adrenaline rush until they are past. And if you are not on the bomb run you might be able to avoid the worst of his gunfire by some innovative maneuvering as Beiser and I did when attacked by an Me 109 on another mission.

Chapter 19

Mission number 19, June 21, 1944 "Big B", Berlin, Germany

My diary for the day reads: "Big B" Berlin Germany. -It's biggest raid of war---so far. Flak intense and accurate. Several planes from this field did not return. (Lt. Allen). Passed by Hamburg. It is still burning big and black from our yesterday's raid. We were lucky today. Only a few holes. 26,500 ft. Over enemy territory two hours and thirty minutes. Carried eight, five hundred pound GP and two, five hundred pound incendiaries."

When going to Berlin, each B-17 carried 2700 gallons of gasoline and five tons of bombs. Gasoline weighs six pounds per gallon, giving us a take off weight of sixty five thousand pounds. The empty B-17G weighs about 36,000 pounds.

Beiser and I were assigned to Wing, "B" group, which was in the low position. We were assigned the number four position in the high squadron of six aircraft. There were 18 planes in our group. We had our original crew together for this sortie, which would take eight hours and eighteen minutes from take off to landing.

This was to be my second mission to Berlin where it is never considered to be a milk run, but just after briefing a rumor indicated that the British were going on this daylight trip to Berlin at fourteen thousand feet. We were all elated, knowing that the Germans would be after them instead of us. We figured that our part of the mission would surely be a milk run. We heard all kinds of rumors about this raid. That it would be to retaliate for the buzz bombs that were hitting London at about a hundred a day. We were to drop our bombs "in train" at one every three seconds to spread the damage.

These rumors didn't last very long and the mission went along just like any other large mission, without the British, although we did drop our bombs "in train." This was the only mission that I flew where we did this. They were usually salvoed.

The 303rd Bomb Group sent up 42 airplanes for this mission, eighteen being in our low group.

We assembled in position on the lead group over our base at Molesworth, and departed in combat wing formation. The weather over the target was fairly open, and the city could be seen from some distance. We assumed that visual bombing would be the order, so our group began to take interval. Soon after the IP and opening bomb-bay doors, the order came for PFF bombing, so our group pulled back into wing formation and bombs were away at 10:16 from 25,900 ft.

In the target area the flak appeared to be from at least two flak batteries. It was moderate, but very accurate, being continuously pointed. One three-gun battery was firing directly at our squadron. About a quarter mile to our left I noticed a triple burst, and every three seconds there was another, only closer. Beiser was flying the plane during this bomb run, and I could see burst after burst getting closer and closer, tracking our speed and altitude to perfection. Finally, a burst of three came just off the left wing tip, and I could hear bits of metal strike our plane. I gritted my teeth, knowing that the next burst would be dead center on our aircraft. However I had noticed that the bursts were showing elongated patterns, meaning that we were almost beyond their range. And the final burst never came, as the German gunners moved their sights to another group following us. This was the most fear that I had encountered in combat, because I had too much time to think about it.

Most of the time I was so busy that I didn't have time for much fear. Usually, after we got into formation and headed for the enemy coast, the apprehension would build until the first burst of flak was seen. I then settled down into a grim attention to duty, and thought very little of it unless it got really close. I had to accept whatever happened because I knew that I could not do anything about it.

Three of our eighteen planes were shot down over this target today. One was the leader of our 427th squadron and his number 4 and 5 planes. Beiser and I were often assigned to the number 4 position, but today we were in that position in the high squadron of six planes.

It was ironic that no plane was in the "Purple Heart Corner" of that unfortunate squadron of five planes, and still three of the five were shot down. Lt. Vermeer was scheduled to fly in that slot, but was unable to catch up with us, so he latched onto the 379th Group from Kimbolton, and bombed with them. The 379th was part of our wing. Had he been able to reach his scheduled position, he might have been shot down with the other three. Lt. Allen's plane went down just after bombs away with the ball turret gunner still inside and he was killed. All the others were made prisoners of war.

Lt. Allen's left wing man, Lt. Oranges, was carrying bombs with long delay fuses. He survived the mission, returning home with the rest of us. The long delay fuses were designed to harass the clean up crews and these bombs were only used in the German homeland. The bombs exploded from three hours to three days after being dropped.

The plane flown by Lt. H.G. Way went down about the same time. Both he and his copilot were killed, perhaps by civilians, as were two others of his crew. His navigator, radio operator, ball turret gunner, and tail gunner were all made prisoners.

"Mairzy Doats" flown by Lt. Morningstar disappeared before the bomb run and was not seen to leave since he was the lowest and farthest to the rear. The entire crew survived, being listed as prisoners of war. Morningstar's plane was equipped with a K-21 camera and was scheduled to return early for photo processing.

Strike photos from other B-17s showed a startling scene. Directly below us in the path of our falling bombs was a B-17 out of position. Later pictures show a B-17 having his left stabilizer shorn off by a five hundred-pound bomb dropped from above. That plane went into a steep dive, out of control, and was lost. As mentioned before, the bombs had to fall about five hundred feet or more before the protective vane spun off to leave the bomb armed. If this vane did not spin off in the air stream, the bomb could fall on solid concrete without exploding. If the bomb that struck the tail of that airplane had been armed, the plane would have disappeared in a cloud of fire and debris, perhaps destroying other B-17s as well.

We had observed flak at five other places before Berlin, which was all black in color. Over Berlin, the flak was mostly black from their regular 88MM flak guns, but we also encountered white bursts from larger guns. Some fixed guns, or railroad car guns of larger caliber defended most large cities in Germany. Some were 105MM and some were 128MM, which we sometimes referred to as 155MM for some unknown reason. The German gunners sometimes signaled their fighter planes by using different colored bursts, but occasionally the German fighters would fly into their own flak bursts in the frenzy of battle, trying to press home an attack on a bomber.

We had thrown out a lot of "chaff" to disrupt the German radar, which they used when firing through clouds. Today the chaff seemed to do a little good, as most bursts of flak were low, as evidenced by the loss of most of our low squadron.

In our 41st Wing formation of two groups and one high squadron, our high squadron had only three planes with minor damage and none with major damage. Our lead group, which is at the middle altitude, had nine aircraft with major damage and eight with minor damage.

The low group, in which Beiser and I were flying number 4 of the high squadron, three B-17s was shot down, two had major damage and eleven had minor damage. As the B-17s were shot down, Beiser and I would move ahead into the empty slots, We did this four times until we were in the lead position of this squadron. Our plane was listed as "Minor damage", since we only had a few holes to be repaired. Remarkable!

At de-briefing there is always a gripe sheet that is later printed and given to headquarters. On this mission to Berlin, the sheet was a little longer than usual. Out of nineteen complaints, one was for placement of camera switch. One was for radio buncher, and two were for equipment placement. One gripe was about our crossing over Kimbolton's traffic pattern as we arrived at our base. Three gripes were about need for more passes or space between missions. ("I haven't had a pass for eleven missions in three months.") One gripe was for short supply of ammunition, and six gripes for not enough sleep. (Why do we have such early missions? Why couldn't we have them a little later so we can get more sleep?") (In answer to this last question: The target should be encountered as early in the day as possible before afternoon summer cumulus clouds obscure too much of the area).

There were two complaints about the sandwiches that we carried on a mission. ("More meat or peanut butter instead of jelly.")

Today our liquor allowance after missions was absent and there were three complaints about that. ("Need whiskey, especially after Berlin raid.") ("What happened to the whiskey today?") ("How about liquor?")

Our crew flew this mission with a plane whose guns hadn't been cleaned and Beiser complained about that. ("Crews should have clean guns for next mission. Guns on this A/C were not cleaned today.") I suspect that the harried ground crews were very busy repairing airplanes from our mission to Hamburg yesterday. The plane that we flew to Hamburg yesterday was not on this Berlin mission due to extensive damage that had not been repaired as yet. That was A/C # 42-39875, Buzz Blonde with its 260-odd flak holes. Today's plane that we flew was # 42-102411.

If some of the crews complained about the missions being too close together, just wait. Tomorrow we would fly two missions, losing two B-17s in the morning and three in the afternoon.

Chapter 20

Mission number 20. June 22, 1944--morning

Again we are doing tactical work to No Ball targets trying to slow the rate of Buzz Bomb launches. My diary for the day reads: "St. Omar, France, (Calais area) robot plane installations. Flew low squadron lead. Flak meager, but VERY accurate. Lost two ships, one was leader. Three-tenths CAVU. Only 14 went out...Rough!"

I have no idea why we were carrying two, two thousand-pound bombs on each airplane to bomb a small target, such as a launching site for buzz bombs. Perhaps it was a mission changed from a bridge to a buzz bomb site. My own idea would have been to carry a bunch of smaller bombs inside the bombbay. Of course I had no authority in the matter. And it didn't matter anyhow, since all we did was dig ponds for some farmer.

My diary was wrong about the loss of two B-17s that morning, as only one didn't return. That was our leader, 1st Lt. R. W. Erickson who had Capt. R.J. Lynch flying as mission commander in his aircraft named "Mary Cary." They received a direct hit before bombs were away. Engines number one and two on the left wing were badly damaged, and number two had a runaway prop that couldn't be feathered.

The mission deputy, 1st Lt. J.T. Williams took over the lead and completed the bomb run, but was also hit by flak. He managed to get to the field of one of our other groups, (Grafton Underwood), which caused me to think that he had been shot down. We carried 1700 gallons of gas for this four and a half-hour flight, being over enemy territory for thirty minutes.

The original lead plane was last seen headed for the English coast at Beachy Head. They never made it, as the airplane was vibrating very badly, and finally the runaway number two engine exploded.

The crew was ordered to bail out over the Channel, but before they could all get out, the airplane exploded and half the crewmen were killed. Five men, including the mission commander, Capt. Lynch, were rescued by naval vessels, but the Pilot, Roger W. Erickson was killed, as were the other officers in the front of the plane. There were two navigators on the lead plane for this mission, 1st Lt. Emilio M. Sbrolla and 1st Lt. Lawrence D. Ross, both killed. Bombardier 1st Lt. Dick W. Merz was also killed, as was the right waist gunner, Staff Sergeant Elwood Schoonmaker.

Our 427th squadron had supplied the weather plane for this mission. This was our old "F" Model that had been stripped and sealed. The ground crews had installed 21 high intensity lights on the airplane, which flashed the letter "C" in Morse code while it was acting as formation ship. It was painted with red and white stripes that were ten feet wide in a diagonal pattern. As a combat bomber it had been named "Vicious Virgin." This was changed to "Scarlet Harlot" after the paint job, and I sometimes referred to her as "The Virgin Harlot." Mostly though, we referred to the plane as "The Barber Pole," which we dearly loved to fly. It was so fast that I had said at the time, that if you gave me a five-minute head start, a P-51 couldn't catch me before he ran out of gas. A slight exaggeration perhaps, but not by much.

Mission Number 21, afternoon, June 22, 1944

Having dropped our two, one ton bombs this morning in a feeble attempt to hit a Buzz Bomb site, our planes were loaded with twelve, 500-pound bombs for an attempt to bust a railroad marshaling yard at Lille, France. My diary reads: "Lille, France, Marshaling yards. We flew at 26,500 ft. and got only meager flak. Low group lost 3 planes. My 6th raid in 4 days. That French flak is meager but plenty hot."

Beiser and I were to fly Aircraft number 42-102432, "Tiny Angel," since our usual plane, Buzz Blonde was being flown by Lt. Savage. Tiny Angel would be shot down on the tragic raid of August 15th, with the loss of the pilot, 1st Lt. H.S. Cook, his engineer, Sgt. Slight, and a waist gunner, Sgt. Joyce.

We had a different bombardier again. He was 2nd Lt. G.A. Wellen, Jr. Our regular bombardier, Ed Cooper, was to fly with Lt. Savage in our old, "Buzz Blonde," as was David Glass, our erstwhile waist gunner. Evidently the repairs after the Hamburg mission were not sufficient, as the poor old "Buzz Blonde" couldn't get enough air speed to keep up, and had to abort. Lt. Langford was flying as a spare, and filled Lt. Savage's empty slot.

Beiser and I were assigned to position number 8 for this mission, which made us leader of a three-plane element in the low squadron of the high group. Our 427th commanding officer, Col. Snyder was leading this group, with our two newest crews flying positions number two and three. Lt. Wardowski was to the right of the leader and Lt. Roy to the left. Both of these crews had flown only four or five missions. It is ironic that they were listed alone on the same page of the manifest, and flew side by side on several missions. Yet they were to be lost on separate raids a few days from now.

Just after bombs away, the airplane in the eleventh position of the 360th squadron, flying in the high group, was hit by flak in the right wing behind the number three engine causing a gasoline explosion. Only one parachute was seen to come from the stricken plane. This was the radio operator, Tech Sgt. R. H. Johnson, who was able to evade capture and was returned to American control. All the rest of the crew was killed.

My diary was wrong about the loss of three planes, as the other two were later returned. One that I thought had been shot down was actually hit by flak before the target. He jettisoned his bombs and returned to England, making an emergency landing at High Halden.

The other aircraft that I saw go down was from another wing in our First Bombardment Division.

Beiser and I had taken off at four minutes before four in the afternoon, and landed at eight thirty nine, for a flight of four hours and forty-four minutes. We were over enemy territory exactly one hour.

With double war savings time the sun was still shining when we landed.

Chapter 21

Mission number 22. June 24, 1944

Diary: "Bremen, Germany. Oil refinery. PFF (Radar) Target nine tenths cloudy. Flak moderate to intense. Few flak holes. Hate to go there on a clear day. Another 'Flak City'."

We carried 18 bombs per plane. They were 250-pound general-purpose types. Our target was Oslebshausen, a suburb of Bremen if radar was the required method of aiming. This was all in the industrial part of Bremen. We carried 2100 gallons of gas for this trip.

Beiser and I had the newly repaired "Buzz Blonde" again for this mission, and were assigned the number four position in the high squadron of the low group. On this raid, Capt. Bob Sheets, our operations officer was flying the lead, and again, Wardowski and Roy were flying side by side, behind him in positions number 2 and 3. Bob Sheets took off in a PFF plane and led 17 aircraft to fly low group of the 41st "A" Combat Wing.

We assembled over base at 4000 ft and got into position with the lead group. We flew in Wing formation until the IP was reached. We overran the IP a small amount in order to take interval for bombing by groups. We came to the target behind the lead group and made a straight and level bomb run of seven minutes. Bombs were away at 1:00 PM from twenty four thousand feet on a magnetic heading of 211 degrees. During the bomb run we encountered intense flak that didn't seem to be aimed at anyone in particular. After bombs away we immediately made a turn to avoid flak, at which time we rejoined the Wing until reaching the North Sea, where we fell into trail for the descent. After reaching friendly territory, the lead plane peeled off and returned to Chelveston where it was based.

It was almost solid overcast at the target. We lost one B-17 from our group on this mission. Lt. Harold C. Farthing flying A/C number 42-37654 (No name) was straggling for quite a while, and just before reaching the IP he had to leave the Number 2 position of the low squadron. He was almost directly to our left in the formation, about a hundred feet lower and he gradually fell back, losing altitude until Charlie Latta, our ball turret operator, said that he had gone into the clouds. He never returned to base and we later learned that they all had to bail out. They all landed safely, but the Bombardier, Flight Officer John D. Carson was reported to have been shot by the Germans when they learned that he was a Jew.

On this six and a half-hour mission, we were over enemy territory for an hour and five minutes.

Chapter 22

Mission 23, June 28, 1944. Reims, France airdrome.

This was my first mission in four whole days, as we finally got a pass to get away for a couple of days. We had missed only one day of missions in our absence. On June 25 our group flew two missions, both of which were fairly long. On the morning mission to an airdrome at Toulouse/Francazal, one of our B-17s ran out of gas over England on the way home. The crew bailed out after the pilot headed the big glider, B-17 toward the ocean. All the crew landed safely to become new members of the Caterpillar club.

In the afternoon the group did bridge busting with mixed results. One group dropped 23, two thousand pound bombs with only one hitting the bridge which remained standing. The other group had formation problems as well as personnel problems. The lead bombardier forgot to turn off the salvo switch, and when he turned on the internal bomb rack switches, the bombs on his plane automatically dropped at the IP. One other plane immediately dropped his bombs with the leader, but four other planes held on to their bombs, knowing that there was a malfunction. They dropped their eight bombs on a bridge at Sens, France with excellent results.

The next day, June 26, a mission to the Munich area was scrubbed because of weather information.

Today's mission was destined to be very rough on me. Our target was the Juvincourt airfield near Reims, France. My diary for that day tells it all on one little bomb tag: "Reims, France-airfield south (Juvincourt) CAVU. Caught every flak gun in France. Led high squadron. Lost our left wing man who went down in flames (Lt. Wardowski) Lost one other also. Weather so bad on return we had

155

to land at coast at B-24 base. 5 hrs. Over enemy territory, two hours. Carried 38 X 100 pound general purpose bombs."

Beiser had just been promoted to First Lieutenant and we were in the "Buzz Blonde" again. We led the high squadron of the low, 41st "B" group of thirteen planes in the formation. Captain Packard of the 358th squadron was our leader for this mission. There were no aborts from either group on this raid. We assembled over base at four thousand feet and joined the other group after climbing to 17,000 feet while circling the base. We departed base at 6:23 AM in combat wing formation until just before the Initial Point where we started taking interval for group bombing since the weather was clear at the time. We followed the lead group as it cut slightly short of the IP, but we took aim at a dummy airdrome. When we discovered our error we made a 360-degree turn to the left and picked up the IP again and headed for the real airdrome. On our six minute bomb run the lead plane in our group experienced difficulties with the autopilot and flew an erratic course. The bombardier was able to correct the problem and our bombs were away at 8:32 from 24,400 feet, right on target.

Four minutes later, a flak battery at Laon, France scored a direct hit near the right wing root of "Old Crow" flown by Lt. Wardowski. The Plane immediately became a ball of fire and rolled over in a 180-degree turn to the left. I soon lost sight of it, but Charlie Latta in the ball and Benny Gorchesky in the left waist counted six parachutes. After diving three or four thousand feet, the airplane exceeded its limit and disintegrated into thousands of pieces. My recent friend, P. S. Wardowski was not able to get out. Neither was the Navigator, W.C. Birnbaum or the tail gunner, D.G. Wagner. This was their fifth or sixth mission. Remarkably, the Co-pilot, N. E. Hainlin was able to team up with the two waist gunners, Sgt. A. Willard and Sgt. J. I. Snede and they all evaded capture with the help of the French underground. The Bombardier, 2nd. Lt. C.F. Eisel became a prisoner of war, as did the engineer, Sgt. R.J. Kowatch and the ball turret gunner, Sgt. B.L. Hope. Of course, at that time I didn't know who died and who survived.

Of our twenty-six B-17s, only six escaped damage. Six had major damage and fourteen had minor damage, one being lost. Since the German gunners were aiming visually, the chaff that we dropped to jam their radar did little good.

After all this action, the mission was still not over. The weather had turned sour over England while we were away, and as we started across the English Channel we received word that we should land at alternate bases. Our group got under the clouds and headed for the nearest base, being driven below three hundred feet at times by the overcast. At times we flew over a rise in the ground losing sight of our wing man for a few moments in the cloud, but still able to see the ground. This happened three or four times until one time as we descended into the clear we met another B-17 going in the opposite direction at our altitude and only about three hundred feet to our left. A very close call.

When we found our destination of Debach, a B-24 base, we were flying so low to avoid clouds that we had to make shallow turns to avoid hitting trees with our left wing tip. Amazingly, all of our group landed safely and after a little red tape for landing away from base, the weather improved and we all returned to Molesworth before dark. Nine of us landed at Debach, ten at Hardwick, two at Seething, one at Levenham one at Downham Market and one made it to Bradwell Bay on three engines, -Literally. This B-17 flown by Lt. Mac Connell had been hit by flak, which destroyed an engine and it fell from the plane. It is to his credit that he didn't bail his crew out over enemy territory.

When Lt. E. C. "Al" Lehmann landed at Downham Market in A/C number 42-107099 named "Old 99" (after the tail number), he had two wounded crewmen aboard. He had been flying below and behind Lt. Wardowski.

Our old friend "Betty Jane" flown by Lt. Gallagher was the only one who managed to land at Molesworth this morning.

It was a bad day for me, having lost several new friends who had slept near my bunk in the 427th Officer's barracks. Those empty bunks brought the reality of war home to us more than any other thing. But the bunks didn't stay empty very long since replacement crews were coming in every few days

Chapter 23

FLAK! (Fliegerabwehrkanonen)

During this stage of the war, Germany had deployed nearly twenty thousand anti-aircraft guns throughout Germany and occupied countries. The deployment of these guns for anti-aircraft use instead of against tanks and other ground forces made a great hardship on the German army. Older men manned many flak guns and young boys and even women and volunteers so that able bodied men could be trained for other needs.

Defending the Juvincourt airfield near Reims at this time was a six gun battery of 88MM flak guns. These guns had a range of about ten miles and threw a three and a half-inch diameter grenade with a muzzle velocity of about 720 meters per second. This translates to about 2400 feet per second, almost two and a half times the speed of sound. This velocity bled off quickly as it fought gravity and air friction, so that if fired straight up it would run out of steam at about forty thousand feet and fall back to earth. The German personnel operating these guns could fire each gun every three or four seconds. The wooden boxes for shipping these shells each held three rounds, each of which was over eighteen inches long.

It required six to ten buildings and over 120 soldiers to operate a six gun flak battery. The aiming crew had various duties, including deflection, declination, azimuth and range which showed as a triangle, rhombus, square, trapezoid and a circle on the rangefinder, or Entfernungsnesser, which was a four meter (thirteen feet) wide optical device. When these symbols all came together on the viewfinder, which when focused on the invading bombers gave the final aim, the command to start firing was given by radio. The normal magnification of this rangefinder was 12 power, but it could be raised to 24 power and 36 power to fill the viewfinder with the image of a single plane. The Entfernungsnesser, or E-1, rangefinder operator was the only man in the cannon crew that had to go to school for his trade, all the others being trained on site.

Eighteen year-old Helmut Schade was a member of this Battery on several of our trips across that region of France. He tells of the deep trenches that ran from the barracks to the guns and to a bunker nearby, at Soissons, France earlier in the war. All of their trips were through these trenches in order to avoid American fighter strafing. At the first telephone notice of approaching aircraft, usually seventy five or more miles away, the men dropped everything and raced through the trenches to man their guns. Each of the six guns was on four legs with necessary pivots to turn them in any direction by hand cranks.

The guns could be deflected from the vertical for use against aircraft, to horizontal ground level for use against tanks. All the ammunition was stored in racks alongside each gun. During an attack, the "Farm boys" as Helmut called them, because of their strength, pulled the large casings from the rack and handed them to the second man who plunged the grenade end into a box which set the distance that the grenade would travel before exploding.

The pointed end of the grenade had two small flat spots opposite each other which served as a grasp for the range box to turn the fuse to set the distance the grenade would travel before exploding. This man then handed the shell to the last man who slammed the shell into the breech of the gun and yanked the lanyard at command from the final aimer. All six guns fired in unison. If the grenade hit a plane, it would not explode on impact, but would explode only after traveling the distance set into the fuse. If it missed, it usually exploded at almost the exact altitude of the target.

The final aimer with the rangefinder kept the sights pointed at the left wing root, or the number two engine of the lead plane. The nearly two mile lead was automatically calculated so that the grenade would arrive at a spot in the sky that the target should occupy when it arrived. All the guns operated in unison as the information was fed to each gun through a large umbilical from the rangefinder's position. The guns were aimed in parallel to spread the pattern a little, the guns being fifty feet or so apart. Of course the B-17 was over a hundred three feet wide so that in theory, two hits could be made. A slow turn in either direction by the target aircraft was usually enough to throw off the aim of the flak gunners. This is why it was particularly bad during the bomb run. The German gunners would be tracking a straight line, and if the target aircraft disappeared behind a cloud, the line of aiming was continued as if the target could be seen. If the target aircraft re-appeared, adjustments would be made at that time. Even under the most ideal conditions, the target would only be in range for three minutes. When the bomb bay doors were opened on a clear day, the gunners at the flak battery easily saw them.

These same flak guns were also used against tanks, but Helmut said that the shells used against aircraft were practically useless against a Sherman tank since they had no penetrating power against thick steel. The anti-tank ammunition had an armor piercing core surrounded by a lead case so that if the hit was at an angle, the lead, being soft, would bunch up on impact and hold the core from glancing off.

Early in the war when the German gunners saw the bombs drop from approaching planes, they made a mad dash from the gun and hopped over a low wall into the bunker. They soon realized that the bombs took up to 45 seconds to reach the ground, and so they extended the firing time after bombs away until eventually they didn't go to the bunkers at all, but kept on firing until the target planes were out of range. Helmut mentions that the falling bombs didn't sound like the whistling they make in the movies. Rather they sounded like a surreal strumming, or warbling, like a large swarm of humming birds approaching.

On this particular day, our bombs missed part of the airfield at Juvincourt and almost hit the flak battery, which would have been a lucky accident for us, but not so lucky for Helmut and the others. The last bombs in our pattern hit the ground a bare three hundred feet short of the guns. Helmut said the roar of the explosion was a mighty thud, which felt like a minor earthquake. He said he was surprised that the noise was not nearly as loud as the 88MM cannon would make. And no one wore ear protection!

Helmut says that radar was practically useless as far as hitting a plane was concerned. On overcast days, the Americans dropped "Chaff" which was strips of tin foil cut to the exact length of the German radar signal. He said that one had to have a vivid imagination to make out the pattern of a plane with all the "snow" on the radar screen. On overcast days they relied more on barrage flak, which filled the sky with bursts of shrapnel at or above our altitude. They also used sound detection devices very early in the war, but soon abandoned them, as they did not give them the advantage that visual sighting provided.

The same was true of the American precision bombing which was done best in clear weather. Many of our missions used radar and loran for bombing through clouds, but mostly large targets were the only things hit during these missions. It did serve to notify the Germans that we were willing to waste a lot of bombs and gasoline if we could get a good hit once in a while, which we often did.

The flak battery was protected from strafing American planes by several units of 20MM cannon, each having multiple barrels. I asked Helmut if they were ever strafed, and he said "Many times." I said that I bet the flak boys hunkered down behind their armored shields during a strafing pass.

"What shield?" he said. "There was no shield in front of these guns to protect the gunners. They were expected to keep firing as the fighter plane approached. If they hunkered down during the approach of a fighter, they were giving away their best shot to get the fighter."

"Did you lose any of those gunners?" I asked.

"Yes," he said, " we lost a number of men, but they shot down several fighters in the course of the war."

"Now for the big question." I said. "Did your battery ever shoot down a B-17?"

"Well, we damaged several." He said rather evasively. "One time we hit a B-17 and set his number two engine ablaze and the fire reached back past the end of the tail. We all started jumping up and down, celebrating our good marksmanship. We were certain that we had shot him down. However, in a little while the fire went out and then the smoke stopped and the B-17 never left the formation. As they disappeared into the distance, our celebration turned into glum disappointment. I couldn't believe it! The guy never even got out of formation."

"But," I insisted, "did you guys ever shoot down a B-17?"

"We did manage to shoot down a couple of B-24s during the course of the war." He said, still being evasive. "They were much easier to shoot down than a B-17. Once we were firing at a B-24 group when suddenly a bunch of parachutes started coming out of one of them. The airplane seemed to be intact and on autopilot and it flew on for more than fifty kilometers before it finally crashed. We never did know why they left it."

Helmut had been conscripted into the German Army when he was seventeen years old. He was in the army by the time he was eighteen years old. He was born on May 18, 1926. One night in 1943 a British Blockbuster bomb fell across the street from his home in Dusseldorf, destroying ten houses and filling the street with at least ten feet of debris. The mother of one of his friends was killed when she had refused to go to the bomb shelter. Others were killed, but Helmut doesn't know how many. In the winter of 1943 and spring of 1944 when Helmut went into the German army, they sent him into the Taunas Mountains to train as a cannoneer. They were so short of supplies that they didn't even have coats to protect them from the brutal cold.

Helmut's mother died when he was a young child, and his father was killed in a Dusseldorf night attack by British bombers in 1944. His father was a paramedic at the time, having been refused for army duty because of a non-healing sore on his heel caused by poison gas in the First World War.

When the war ended Helmut came to America to see his future wife whom he had met earlier in Germany. Virginia came to the United States in 1949 as a refugee from Estonia where she was classified as a political refugee, or "Displaced Person." Being a German citizen, Helmut didn't qualify as a DP, but had to go through the regular channels to become a U.S. citizen. There was a five year waiting period before one could take a citizenship test, part of which was demonstrating an ability to speak, read and write the English language. Virginia made her citizenship exactly five years after coming to America.

Helmut came to America in 1952 and had a tougher time, taking over five years. He said that the lady at the Immigration and Naturalization Service was very nice and that he might have had a much tougher time if not for her kindness and understanding. Helmut opened a furniture finishing business in Georgetown in the District of Columbia, until he retired to a waterfront home near Solomons, Maryland. This is how I got to know Helmut and Virginia, since my wife, Marjorie and I also have a place nearby.

After I got to know Helmut better, I again asked him the same question.

"Helmut, did your crew ever shoot down a B-17?"

"Well, yes," he replied, "they were hard to shoot down but we did manage to shoot down a couple of them. One that we shot down came all to pieces with engines still turning, making the eeriest noises, and several parachutes came out. I'm glad that it wasn't the one you were flying."

"Not nearly as glad as I am," I replied, "But I think it must have been your battery that shot down a friend of mine, Lt. Wardowski on June 28, 1944. He and his navigator, Lt. Birnbaum from my barracks were killed along with their tail gunner, Sgt. Wagner. It's strange how we could be sworn enemies at one time and then develop a friendship at another time."

"It's a different time and place." He said. "We were both doing our job, and your job was to break things, while mine was to try to stop you from breaking things in my territory."

Bombers that were shot down often fell into areas that caused more damage than the actual bombing. There was always a great deal of fire during a crash.

On October 14th, 1943 a B-17 was set ablaze near the small German village of Adendorf and most of the crew bailed out. The plane continued to fly on until it crashed into the enclosure of a large castle called Burg Adendorf. The castle built in a square was undamaged by the bomber, but two crewmembers died in the crash. The B-17 wreckage filled the entire enclosure and burned for some time, exploding 50 caliber bullets, but not the six, 1000-pound bombs that it carried. No one of the ground was injured.

The small Principality of Liechtenstein was not so lucky. A bomber was shot down over Austria, and during its death dive drifted into the neutral Liechtenstein, landing squarely on the Royal Palace, completely destroying this architectural prize. Liechtenstein, about the size of Washington, DC, was under the control of Switzerland.

This plane returned to base with rudder and tail gunner gone.

Mission number 24, June 29, 1944

My diary for this day reads: Leipzig, Germany (Hot place) Aircraft plant for Me109s. Flak was intense, accurate. Lost another wingman (Lt. Roy). Direct burst broke him in two at waist. No one was seen to get out. Saw other planes go down, some in flames. No more like this for me--thanks."

Our 303rd Bomb Group furnished thirty-six planes for this mission, including a spare and one PFF plane from the 305th Bomb Group. Incredibly, there were seven aborts, including two from our 427th squadron. "Buzz Blonde" had a fuel pump failure on No. 4 engine, and "Pogue Ma Hone" (Gaelic for Kiss My Ass) had high oil pressure and high oil temperature in one engine. "Duchess Daughter" of the 359th squadron had a supercharger go out. Lt. Carpenter in "Bad Penny" from the 359th squadron had a bad ear problem at altitude, and had to return. "Lonesome Polecat" of the 359th had a fuel shortage. "Fearless Fosdick" of the 358th squadron didn't hear the change in assembly altitude and couldn't form up. "Clover Leaf" couldn't find our group and so latched onto the 379th Group out of Kimbolton, which is part of our 41st Combat Wing.

During our crossing of the North Sea we received a recall order and the 379th returned to base along with our "Clover Leaf." Our 303rd leader was not able to identify the sender of the recall order, even though it was given in authentic language, so we continued on the mission. It was a favorite trick of the Germans to send phony radio messages to try to disrupt our missions. It seldom worked, but today it was partially successful if that is what really happened.

Our group started with nineteen planes but was down to fifteen before we even got into enemy territory. As we approached the IP, the message for visual bombing was received, and we started taking interval for group bombing. It was about this time that a direct burst of flak tore Lt. Roy's "My Yorkshire Dream" in half at the waist. We saw no parachutes, but found out later that the Ball turret gunner, Sgt. L.K. Black, had managed to get out of his turret and snap on his chute while the plane was in its death dive. He later said that the bombardier managed to get out also, but his chute didn't open properly. Sgt. Black said that 1st Lt. L. E. Weiss went past him with a "streamer, and was never able to open the chute properly. Sgt. Black was the only survivor of this ill-fated B-17.

Lt. Roy's co-pilot, R.E. Quint, had told me that he was going to be a father in just a few months. This baby girl was born on January 4th, 1945 and was named Tawny. She was Tawny Quint Young, living in Nevada City, California until her untimely death in 1998.

The crew of Lt. Roy was on about their sixth mission.

In two days, there were eight empty bunks in our barracks. This is what really brings it home to you. In the combat area when a plane went down, my reaction was,

"Thank God I wasn't over there." It was later that it hit me that they were truly gone.

After this disastrous mission I finally got a three-day pass before going for check out in the left seat. A couple of us went to London to see the sights and took a bus to Trafalgar Square and then off to Piccadilly Circus. We went to a stage show just off the main square and afterward went into a small pub. There I met a nice looking young lady and struck up a conversation. Soon we were sitting at a table together and getting even friendlier. Suddenly she said,

"After talking to you for a while I would guess that you are still a virgin." I was startled, but managed to stammer,

"What makes you say that?"

"Well, at least half you yanks are still inexperienced."

"No, I wouldn't say that," I said.

"Look, Yank, you keep flying missions and you may get shot down without ever experiencing the finer things in life. I can relieve you of this burden."

"Really?" I asked.

"Yes, and it will only cost you three pounds." (About fifteen dollars).

After being hit by a two by four, it finally dawned on me that this gal was a mercenary, a Piccadilly Commando. I wouldn't have believed it when we first started talking. She was fairly cute and I was tempted, but there flashed through my mind the movie I had seen in Nashville with the young actor, Glenn Ford. So I lied that I had to catch the next bus back to base. She seemed miffed that I had wasted her time.

Chapter 24

Left seat check out.

My 24th mission had been my last as Beiser's co-pilot and it had been a bad one. Now, I would take two and a half weeks break from combat, take a few days leave, and then start additional training to become a combat instructor.

During my first 24 missions, I had been to London twice for overnight passes, but I preferred going to Bedford, where I had met an English family named Lowe. I don't remember the first names of the adults, but their two daughters were named Beryl and Marjorie. Funny I should remember that.

Beryl was in the Royal Air Force as a WAF, while Marjorie was still in High School. Beryl had a steady boy friend while Marjorie was pretty well protected. A good thing, since she was a very pretty girl. I was attracted to her, but didn't have a chance to get to know her very well.

Mr. Lowe sometimes took me fishing on the River Ouse, the beautiful little river that ran through the heart of Bedford. I caught a three inch fish one day and was about to throw it back when Mr. Lowe reminded me that they never threw back a fish that size. I found it difficult to imagine the rationing and hardships that the British had to endure for so many years. We had rationing in the United States at that time, but nothing approaching that of the British.

Mr. Lowe was the plant superintendent at a local Spitfire Assembly plant, and one Sunday he said that he had to go to the plant and I could ride along. Since Marjorie wasn't home that day, I said that, sure, I would ride along.

The assembly plant was in a converted auto garage. It was a very large building, and inside was about ten Spitfires in various stages of assembly. There were only three or four people in the entire building, and I asked Mr. Lowe where all the workers were.

"Oh, we don't work on Sundays. He said, "They will all be here tomorrow." I was dumbfounded, since I knew that in the United States, defense plants were working 21 shifts per week, every week with no holidays. I didn't comment about this since they had been through so much. Besides, I reasoned that they may have been short on parts, and so decided to take Sundays off.

In my High School at McLeansboro, Illinois, the book, Pilgrim's Progress was required reading. It was here in Bedford, England that the author, John Bunyon wrote this Christian allegory while he was in prison there. I was impressed by this fact, and was dismayed in 1992 to find that this small prison had been torn down. John Bunyon was the rector of a large Church in Bedford.

While visiting the Lowe family in Bedford, I stayed overnight in the Red Cross billet there. One night as I was getting ready to go to bed, Glenn Miller and David Niven walked in to spend the night also. They both spoke to me briefly, and Glenn Miller asked me if I had caught his show. When I told him that I didn't know about it, he said that he had just completed his first band concert in England. And I missed it. Damn!

The couple of times I was in London, I didn't care for the attitude of some of the street people. While walking with a girl on Piccadilly Circus one evening, a newsboy hawking the London Times would yell,

"Hey, get your paper here." Then in a sotto voice he would say to me,

"Rubbers, I got 'em for sale." If I didn't pay any attention to him he would yell,

"Give 'er a go, Yank, she's fourteen." It was very embarrassing to me. And nearly every newsboy or street urchin would yell the same thing. I think that they meant that the age of consent in England was fourteen at that time. I really didn't know. Another thing that an American soldier would hear from the younger children was:

"Got 'ny gum, chum?"

The thing that really caught my eye in London was the incredible number of bicycles. The streets would be full of them as far as the eye could see in the late afternoon. At times it was difficult to find a place to cross the street. It was necessary to go to an intersection and wait for a Bobby to halt traffic before one could cross. It was equally as congested in Bedford and Cambridge. Gasoline was strictly rationed and cost the equivalent of about four dollars per gallon. I found it incredible that we were burning about two million gallons of gas per mission, and I suppose the British were doing the same thing on their night raids.

Back at the 303rd, early on June 30, I started my left seat training. After the daily mission departed, various officers of the 427th squadron instructed me over the next two and a half weeks. It was fairly easy to fly from either seat, once you learned from the other. Captain Robert Sheets, our operations officer had me do two hours and twenty-five minutes of air work, and only one landing on the first day. On another day I did twelve touch and go landings without the use of a trim tab. Rolling the trim tab back would make the landing easier since the elevator on the plane would assist. However, during the transition to take off mode the pilot would not have strength enough to hold the nose down when all four throttles were advanced. Some fast work on the trim tab would, of course, help with these landings and take-offs, but Capt. Sheets wanted us to see how the aircraft reacted. At the end of this day my abdominal muscles were quite sore from heaving back on the yoke to land and pushing it forward to take off.

On July 2nd he had me do two landings in an hour and forty minutes. Then I got to ride in the top turret while another co-pilot was being checked out in the left seat. After about fourteen hours of flight over the next two weeks, I was rated as a B-17 pilot with unlimited ratings. This meant that I could instruct in any phase of the B-17. Being able to fly the plane equally well from either seat was a big advantage.

After a final check ride with Col. Ed Snyder, our squadron commander who gave us our instrument check flight, I, and another first pilot candidate was standing in front of operations discussing details of our check ride when two enlisted men passed without saluting. Col. Snyder stopped them and reminded them that military courtesy was expected at all times. They apologized, saluted and went on their way. Then Col. Snyder turned to us and said that, as junior officers, it was our job to stop them and dress them down. This mild rebuke bothered me, because I knew that I should have stopped them, but this would also mean that I would have had to interrupt Col. Snyder who was just getting ready to have us promoted to First Lieutenant. It was just a momentary thing and nothing more was said about it.

So, I became a combat instructor. I think that they must have been trying to get rid of me, because it became my duty to fly new crews on their first mission, using their pilot as my co-pilot. This is how Beiser and I started our first mission. This duty was a real pain, as I had to brief the new crew at the airplane after the regular briefing.

"When you see white streaks in the sky over the target, those are not German rockets coming up at us, they are our sky markers going down from the lead ship."

Almost invariably, at bombs away, a crewmember would yell on the intercom:

"They're shooting rockets at us!"

"No, I told you at briefing that they were sky markers from our lead ship." I eventually had eight of these dubious honors.

During this early July period, the King and Queen of England came to visit our base, among others. They had Princess (later Queen) Elizabeth with them and all the airmen who had cameras took her picture. She was 16 years old at the time, and rather pretty. I had a large format camera that took the now obsolete 116-size roll film. I took several pictures of the Royal Family, which turned out very good. I still have the camera and copies of the photos are now in our 303rd Bomb Group picture album.

Also in this time period, our operations officer accidentally wrecked our weather ship. This was the "F" model that the 427th had resurrected, and stripped of all the armaments and sealed up the windows and other gun ports. It made this the finest flying airplane of this size in the European Theater of Operations as far as I was concerned. With its red and white, ten-foot wide diagonal stripes it was quite a sight.

On the Fourth of July a group of P-38 pilots came to a party at our base and celebrated a bit too much and couldn't be trusted to fly back to their base, whereupon Our Ops officer offered them a ride home. Taking the weather man along as co-pilot, they delivered the P-38 pilots to their base, but upon returning to Molesworth, he neglected to lower the landing gear during landing at our base late at night. The airplane might have been saved if it hadn't slid off the runway. After sliding down the runway for about a thousand feet it slid off to the right side of the runway into the dirt where it continued on for about six hundred feet. It plowed a great set of furrows in the dirt, rupturing the belly and filling the inside of the airplane with over a foot of dirt. The engine cowlings also dug in, destroying everything of value on the airplane. It didn't take a doctor to pronounce my favorite airplane Dead on Arrival. I grieved a bit and even contemplated getting a lynching party together. Just kidding, Mel! The ground crews eventually took the hulk to a scrap yard in Cambridge after salvaging what they could.

It was also about this time that a Co-pilot from the 359th squadron accidentally flipped up the landing gear switch during rollout after a landing of "Duchess Daughter." Instead of raising the flaps, he raised the landing gear and did considerable damage to the airplane. And his chances of becoming a first pilot or a First Lieutenant.

Also, one day in this period some one came into the barracks and said that a B-17 had nosed up right in front of the control tower. I had never heard of a B-17 nosing up and so I decided to go take a look. I had been told in training that a B-17 would not nose up even if the brakes were locked up on landing because the center of gravity was too far aft. I borrowed the same bicycle that I had ridden out to see the "Barber Pole" that had bellied in, and went to the control tower. Sure enough, there was a B-17 with its tail about sixty feet in the air. It had wandered off the taxiway with the left landing gear and got stuck in the mud. The pilot attempted to move the airplane back onto the taxiway using full power, only to find that the engines forced the nose down, since they couldn't move it forward. Number one and two propellers were bent and the wing tip was damaged, as was the chin turret and nose of the airplane. Those Wright Cyclone engines with their 1200 horsepower were able to lift the thirty six thousand pounds of weight off the ground and destroy themselves. I was impressed.

Finally, I was told that I would have additional duties while I was waiting for the time for my first mission as pilot in command. That duty turned out to be mail censor.

The enlisted men had their mail censored by officers, who looked for information that the enemy might use in case the letters were intercepted, or went to a talkative friend or relative in the States. The letters had to be written on one side of the paper so that offending or obscene words or confidential matters discussed in the letter might be cut out with a razor blade. There were a few high spots in this duty, as some of the letters were very entertaining. Mostly the enlisted men were very careful about what they wrote.

In one letter, the writer was complaining about everything that he could think of, including all the saluting that was required. He said, "This place is just a bunch of bull shit." So, I took my razor blade and carefully cut out the word "shit," leaving the rest of the letter untouched.

Another enlisted man wrote that he was in a foreign combat area that was top-secret and he couldn't reveal his location. I knew that this wasn't the case, so I took my censor's pencil and wrote the word "England" across the top of his first page.

The best was from a Lothario who wrote a very passionate love letter to a girl in the States. I had nothing to censor, so I picked up his next letter, which was almost identical to the first, but addressed, to another girl. And then a third, which was identical to the other two, but addressed to a third girl.

An evil thought passed through my mind.

"Suppose I accidentally put the letters in the wrong envelopes, and sent them on to the States? --Nah."

One day I went over to the maintenance hangar to look around and the Sergeant in charge had some fifty-caliber bullets on the workbench. I watched as he worked the bullet out of the casing and poured the powder out. He then took a dull punch and set the casing on an anvil, placing the punch on the firing pin in the center of the base. With a light tap of a hammer on the punch, he fired the primer, which made a subdued "Pop." He then proceeded to make a base for a model airplane.

I thought this was neat, so I duplicated his endeavor, thus making a base and stand for a Hawker Hurricane that I still have. Also, I made a cigarette lighter by cutting a 50-caliber casing in half and adding the works to the inside. Since I never smoked, I gave one to a crewmember and made another for my father.

These fifty caliber bullets are quite a piece of work with their armor-piercing incendiary projectile. The inner part of the bullet is of hardened steel that has a needle-like point that is so hard that a file cannot cut it. The outer jacket of copper is fairly soft, and as the bullet is assembled, a small amount of incendiary thermite is dropped into the end of the jacket and the steel center is pressed into the jacket and sealed. When the bullet is fired into an object, the copper jacket is slowed down or stopped and the steel center presses through, igniting the thermite. This little spurt of flame then follows the steel jacket through the target, igniting anything that will burn easily. Like gasoline. This was the basic ammunition of most U.S. fighters and bombers in World War Two and later. Tracers were not generally used, especially on bombers, because gunners tried to aim with them and it just wouldn't work because of movement of the target.

Another problem was that when fighters were firing their guns the last few bullets were tracers, thus alerting the American pilot that he was out of ammunition. The enemy also knew that he was out of ammunition. It was not a good scenario.

This is also where I got my only "battle scars" in the war. I had worked the projectile out of a casing and poured the powder out. The sergeant was not around and I couldn't find a dull punch to explode the primer, so I picked up a prick punch for that purpose. A prick punch has a very sharp point for making starter holes when drilling in metal. Bad decision. When I tapped the punch with a hammer the primer exploded, but the sharp point of the punch caused the brass surface of the primer to split and shoot back upward, thus imbedding all the brass fragments in my left thumb and middle finger. Bleeding profusely, I walked over to the dispensary to get a stitch or two, asking the 427th flight surgeon, Capt. Ralph T. Anderson if this would qualify me for a Purple Heart. He asked me if the enemy had done this to me, and I said,

"No, I did it to myself." He told me that one couldn't get a Purple Heart for self-inflicted wounds.

I knew that.

Chapter 25

Mission 25. July 17, 1944

Diary: "St. Quentin, France, RR Bridge. My first mission as first pilot. Saw meager flak. No damage. Target C.A.V.U. Did O.K. but had to bring back one bomb. Rack switch SNAFUED."

I was flying my first new crew on their first mission on this day, with my left thumb and middle finger bandaged from yesterday's self-inflicted wound. Of course my flight glove hid the evidence. 1st Lt. H. C. Clark was the first new combat pilot to benefit from my status as a veteran combat pilot. His co-pilot, 2nd Lt. G.P. Vesy was left behind while I trained Clark in the fine art of forming up into a combat group and wing. The rest of Lt. Clark's crew was with me in a new B-17 with the tail number 43-37666, named "Full House." Three sixes and two threes.

In less than four months this airplane would be involved in a mid-air collision with another, un-named 427th Squadron B-17 on November 9th, 1944, killing seventeen men in the two airplanes with only one survivor. The tail gunner in the other plane escaped when the tail was severed from the fuselage.

But for today's mission, this plane was carrying two, one ton bombs under the belly, as were all the others in our group.

Our group was supposed to drop 72 of these big bombs aimed at a bridge near Peronne, France. One bomb from the plane I was flying refused to release at the target, and so we brought it back to base. It was just as well, since the other 71 bombs missed the bridge despite clear weather and my diary notation to the contrary.

Lt. Clark asked if it would be noticeable to land with two thousand pounds off to one side and I told him that they were so close to the center that we would never notice if one were missing. (I hoped, since I had never had such an experience).

176

"You might notice something if it decided to release at touch down." I said. However nothing happened and I made a normal landing.

Just after I finished my "New Crew" duty in less than a month from today, Lt. Clark was shot down along with eight other B-17's when our group was attacked by 20 or 30 enemy fighters. Clark was killed, as was his co-pilot, 2nd Lt. G.P. Vesy. Also killed were the other two officers on the crew, 2nd Lt. R.J. Davies, Navigator, and Flight Officer E.E. Brosius, Bombardier. They probably got a 30MM cannon shell directly in the nose.

Two of the five enlisted crew were also killed on this August 15 mission. They were the Engineer, top turret gunner, Staff Sergeant H.P. Scott, and Radio Operator, waist gunner, Staff Sergeant F. Roswall.

Three Sergeants, C.A. Sikora, Jr., C.S. Cruttenden, and E.W. Bjorn from the rear of the plane were able to bail out and became prisoners of war for the duration.

On the mission in which Clark and his crew were lost, there were a total of nine B-17s lost to enemy fire, mostly by fighters. The 303rd Bomb Group lost almost a fourth of its B-17s on that raid to an airfield in Wiesbaden, Germany. Thirty-nine were sent out, and thirty returned. Twenty-three men were killed, twenty-two in crashed bombers and one in our squadron's "Flying Bison," which made it back to base.

I was there when it returned to Molesworth on this, its last flight, being so badly shot up that no attempt was ever made to repair it. Some of the newer German FW 190s were equipped with a 30MM cannon on this day. This was the latest modification to that plane. The thirty-millimeter cannon could bring down a bomber with a single hit, unlike the 20MM that could do severe damage, but seldom destroyed a plane with a single hit. This big ammunition is almost identical to that used in our A-10 Wart Hogs today.

I was saddened that my new friends were killed for such a small return on their bombing investment. The airfield was damaged, and a number of enemy planes were burned, but not to the extent that the Germans couldn't repair it quickly. And they had a surplus of airplanes without enough pilots or fuel to fly them.

We usually lived in a day to day existence, knowing that the next mission could be our last. Many men reacted differently to the stress of almost daily combat.

During an earlier mission to Berlin when our 427th Squadron's, Lt. Allen was shot down by flak, my thoughts were not about "Poor Lieutenant Allen," but, "My God, I'm glad I wasn't over there."

When I returned from that particular mission I went into the barracks before I went to de-briefing where I met another pilot who wasn't on this mission.

"Hey Al," I said, "Lieutenant Allen got shot down today."

"No shit? I wonder if his pants will fit me." This was his only comment and I was shocked, but said nothing more. I couldn't imagine anybody being so callous about a friend or acquaintance being shot down and possibly killed. I figured that his attitude might have just been his defense strategy. On this occasion, some of the personal effects of the shot down crew were stolen before the Provost Marshall secured the barracks. They recovered most, but not all of the stuff that was stolen from them. I was considerably distressed by this situation. Lt. Allen and his crew became prisoners of war.

After morning briefing, about half of the combat crews would go to the chapel for prayers or last rites. Some of our crew did this, but I never did, as I always relied on my own silent prayer:

"Thank You, God, for taking such good care of me."

This was a silent prayer I had made as a thirteen year old while living in Southern Illinois, never asking for anything in the future, but always thanking Him for keeping me alive and in good health. I had vowed to repeat this silent prayer every time I thought of it and I still do to this day. I was aware of Christ's admonition about long-winded prayers, in Matthew 6 verse 5.

In today's world the goodbye greeting is apt to be, "Try to stay on the green side of the grass."

Mission 26, July 28, 1944. Merseburg, Germany

Today's mission would take us deep into Germany to the Luena Oil Works at Merseburg, the most heavily defended city in Germany, where strong enemy resistance is always encountered. My second new crew was going with me in the B-17 named "Betty Jane" that I had flown several times before, including the glide bomb attack on Cologne.

This morning the 303rd Bomb Group put up 37 aircraft, taking off between the hours of 0550 and 0619 to make assembly over the Harrington buncher at 9,000 feet. Each B-17 was carrying ten, five hundred pound bombs.

During assembly my aircraft was approached by another B-17 which caused me to fly a 360-degree turn to stay out of his way. By the time I returned to the assembly area, the 303rd Group was too far ahead for me to catch up, so I latched onto the 379th out of Kimbolton, which I knew was going to the same target. Many pilots aborted when they couldn't find their group and I didn't want this stigma attached to me. Had I not known the destination of the 379th, I would have had no choice but to abort. I could have climbed steeply, or dived to get away from the intruding B-17, but being heavily loaded, this would put undue stress on the wings and tail, so I chose to circle. Also, an abort from this mission would have sparked a thorough investigation since it was a prime target. The powers that be looked closely at the reasons given in order to be sure that crews were not avoiding certain targets. Amazingly, very few crews ever aborted a mission. I think that most had the same attitude that I had. What happens, happens, and will only happen to others.

My new co-pilot for the day was J.A. Drewry with all his crew, except his co-pilot who was flying with yet another experienced pilot.

During this mission the 303rd saw no enemy fighters, but the

379th that I was with encountered a few. Our top turret gunner, Sgt. E.H. Koch fired at an FW 190 that seemed to be trying to drag a bomb on a long wire through our formation. That bomb didn't explode and Koch didn't seem to hit the FW190 who was about three thousand feet above us flying in the same direction. The fighters were not attacking for some reason not clear to me unless they were waiting to see the big explosion that never came. There were no P-51s in the immediate area, so we should have been attacked. We encountered flak at seven different locations on this mission, but the "Betty Jane" only suffered two minor flak wounds on this trip.

We had been discharging chaff to foil the German radar and it seemed to do some good. The target was overcast, so the German gunners could not sight visually, nor could we bomb visually. Most of the heavy concentration of flak seemed to always be behind us. Evidently we didn't do such a good job on the synthetic oil plant, as we later learned that we would go back to the same target tomorrow.

Our flight time was eight hours and ten minutes, with four hours and twenty minutes over enemy territory.

Just a few days ago, on July 20th an attempt was made on the life of Hitler. It was a failure, but had it succeeded the war might have ended several months earlier, thus saving thousands of lives.

Mission 27. July 29, 1944. Merseburg, again

My diary reads: "Merseburg, (Gr.) Near Leipzig. Same target as yesterday. (Leuna Oil works). Saw terrific dogfights over target, between our P-51s and the enemy fighters. Target CAVU. And flak was terrific. Got several holes this time. Had third new crew. Carried 20 X 250-pound general-purpose bombs. Flight time, 8 hours and thirty-five minutes. Over enemy territory 4 hours and twenty minutes."

I was flying the "Betty Jane" again today for an assault on Germany's most heavily defended city. My new crew for today was that of Lt. P.F. Curetan, Jr. Ironically and tragically, he was to be killed in action on November 21st at this very same target. The only survivor of his nine-man crew would be Radio Operator, Tech. Sgt. J.A. Ellis.

German farmers would murder most of the others. The navigator was hanged on the spot and Curetan and his co-pilot were stabbed to death with pitchforks. This kind of treatment was not unusual when one bailed out over Germany itself, but it was rare in the occupied countries.

On today's mission the 303rd Bomb Group supplied 13 aircraft for the 41st "C" Wing, High Group. We did a plan "D" Group assembly over Harrington Buncher at 17,000 ft and flew in Combat Wing formation while slowly climbing to 26,000 feet. At the IP (Initial Point) we took Group interval for visual bombing and dropped our bombs from a magnetic heading of 95 degrees.

At the target we saw about fifteen ME 109s trying to attack the lead group, but they were being harassed by our P-51s. Just after bombs away, four of the fighters managed to elude the P-51s and made a single pass, from 12 o'clock high, through the lead group without shooting any down. We were probably lucky that these were Me-109s and not FW190s with their new 30mm cannon.

After we dropped our bombs we made a sharp right turn to avoid flak, and at this time rejoined the wing formation for our return to Molesworth. Over England we dropped down to one thousand feet and eventually had to fly at three hundred feet because of low clouds. We probably scared a lot of live stock and not a few people, including us.

At the target there were no photographs of the actual bomb bursts as they were concealed in smoke and shadows in the target area. The Germans always tried to conceal their important targets with smoke screens, but with limited success. The lead Group's bombs fell a little short of the MPI (Main Point of Impact). They had approached the target at 103 degrees magnetic. The Low Group's bombs appeared to fall right on target. They flew to the target at 102 degrees Magnetic.

Our heading of 95 degrees gave us a good separation from the prop wash of the other groups and our bombs were right on target. The lead group of the "D" Wing following us headed to the target at 98 degrees. Their lead bombardier didn't quite kill the drift and their bombs fell a couple hundred yards to the left of the MPI.

Of the 51 (!) B-17 aircraft furnished by our group for this mission, thirty-two sustained battle damage, but none were shot down thanks largely to the efforts of our P-51s over the target. Several of our B-17s had major damage from flak, and many had flak holes, including my poor old "Betty Jane."

Many times the ground crews repaired the holes so well that I could not find them. I even made mental notes on some occasions and still could not find them. These guys were good! Of course this was much more difficult on unpainted airplanes.

Most of the B-17s built after 1943 were left unpainted except for identifying markings. It was impossible to hide from German Radar or their optical devices. Being new crews, we generally were assigned whatever plane was ready to go. This meant that we flew twelve different B-17s in combat and they all flew about the same. Of course most of the Brass flew in their favorite planes most of the time. I will note here that the Brass never shirked the tough missions, going on some of the most dangerous missions of the war.

When we flew to Berlin or Hamburg there was always a Squadron Commander or equal rank in the front plane. And the front plane was always a prime target for Flak gunners as well as fighter aircraft.

Mission 28, July 31, 1944. Munich!

My diary for this day reads: "Munich, Germany (Rough). Carried incendiaries this trip. It looked like we made big fires too. The flak was really intense. Saw several B-17s go down, I carried quite a bit of flak back with me. I saw a few F Ws, but none attacked. Carried ten M-17 Incendiaries of 500 lb. each. Over enemy territory four hours and thirty five minutes."

The 303rd Bomb Group scheduled 38 planes to bomb the Aero Engine Works by radar. Two aircraft aborted and the mission was flown by thirty-six B-17s for an eight hour and ten minute flight.

We had a late breakfast for this mission, and finished briefing and were at the airplane at five minutes past eight. We started engines at 0855 and started taxi at 0905 with takeoff at 0915 behind the 358th Squadron, which was first and the 360th, which was just ahead of our 427th Squadron.

My former pilot, Theodore R. "Bud" Beiser was the lead pilot for our squadron, with J.E. Fletcher as his co-pilot and J.B. Coffey as navigator and C.M. Webster as bombardier. All four men were 1st. Lieutenants, Tech. Sgt. Lennie J Buchanan was top turret, Staff Sgt. Charles W. Latta was ball turret, Tech. Sgt. Benny J. Gorchesky was radio man-waist gunner, while the other waist gunner was Staff Sgt. James W. Haines. Staff Sgt. Carroll H. Brackey was the tail gunner. All these sergeants were from our original crew and had all been promoted since arriving at Molseworth.

I was flying another new crew for this mission in A/C No. 42-102569, which had no name. This was the first mission for 2nd Lt. T.A. Duncan and his crew, minus co-pilot, 2nd Lt. D.A. Singleton. We were loaded with 2700 gallons of gas and 10 M-17 incendiaries of 500 pounds each.

Beiser was leading us in the 41st "B" Combat Wing, Low Group of 13 airplanes. We assembled over the Harrington Buncher at 7000 feet and departed in Combat Wing formation. Since we were bombing by radar, we remained in Wing formation for the bomb run and dropped our bombs in the target area with the leader. We could see fires through an occasional hole in the clouds.

The flak was always bad at Munich, and fragments hit many B-17s. Of the thirty-eight planes of our group, twenty were damaged by flak, of which eleven were major. I was flying from the left seat on this mission and learned a little lesson on this date.

Part of our protective gear was a "skull cap" of flak resistant plates that we wore under our "fifty mission" caps. It was a heavy and uncomfortable thing, and since I had never seen a hole in the top of a B-17, there were times that I would take it off and place it under the pilot seat with my parachute. Over Munich the flak was very bad, but I still didn't get out my "flak beanie" as I called it. Suddenly an 88MM flak shell passed just about ten feet in front of No. 2 engine, about five feet from my left elbow. The shell exploded about thirty or forty feet above our airplane and the base of the shell came back down on top of the number two engine. It went through the cowling and hit the collector ring hard enough to cut a half moon shaped hole. This caused a small air leak in the exhaust manifold and the pressure dropped back a bit on that engine.

Before I adjusted the manifold pressure, I reached under my seat and got my "beanie." I removed my hat, put the "beanie" on my head and replaced my hat. Then I found time to adjust the manifold pressure. I looked at that hole atop the engine quite a few times on the rest of the mission. The damage to the engine and other small holes in the top of the left wing was negligible, but my ego suffered a bit in front of the new crew. I wore the beanie on all my remaining missions.

My airplane was listed as having major damage, although it was nothing compared to what would happen to it later. On Jan 8th, 1945, after I was back in the US, this aircraft would be involved in a bad landing after a mission to Koblenz. The pilot would land long on the short runway and go off the end, across a road and into a farmer's field, doing major structural damage to the right wing and engines.

All systems on the B-17 are run by electricity with the exception of cowl flaps and brakes, which require hydraulic pressure supplied by an electric motor. On this date the engineer had to drain fluid from the system when he found a limit switch missing on the electric motor that supplied pressure for the brakes. Upon return to base the engineer refilled the reservoir, but air got into the brake line, thus negating the hydraulic pressure needed to operate the synthetic rubber expander-tube which forces the brake pucks to push against the brake drum. Thus, no brakes. Many modern airplanes still use this system today, as do the original Piper Cubs and my Cub-Super Cruiser, PA-12 which was built in 1946.

A few days later our planes were loaded with two, two thousand-pound bombs, which we carried on the belly of the plane, but less than an hour after takeoff, the mission was aborted due to bad weather at the target. Upon returning to base we found that the wind had changed and the landing was to be done on the short runway 32, to the northwest. Due to other air bases in the area our pattern system was to allow each plane to be in the traffic pattern alone while the others orbited the field. If a B-17 had a missed approach, it would remain until it got safely down. On this day I was about fifth to land, but had to orbit for nearly forty-five minutes while several B-17s made missed approaches. One even did three attempts before getting down. I became angry at the delay, which was a bad sign, and could have caused me to make a bad arrival. I decided, however that I would get down on the first try, regardless of the fact that I was carrying most of my fuel, and two big bombs on the belly. A collapsed landing gear would have made quite a sight.

When landing the B-17, the pilot concentrates on the throttles and the runway while the flight engineer leans over his right shoulder, yelling the airspeed into his ear. This is the way I was trained, and was my only thought at that time. Normal approach speed for a B-17 is 100 MPH, basically without power.

I made a long, low approach with partial power and the engineer started yelling,

"Ninety five---Ninety five---Ninety--Ninety----Eighty five----Eighty five!"

I increased power a bit as we were down to about a hundred feet.

"EIGHTY! EIGHTY!" I added more power as I flared for landing, being at about half power by then. This time the tail wheel hit the pavement about three feet inside the turnaround on the end of the runway, and a split second later the main gear hit down solidly and I started touching the brakes. I turned off onto the main runway where they intersected about two thirds of the way down the runway from my landing point.

The Bible in Proverbs 16:18 says - "Pride goeth before destruction, and a haughty spirit before a fall,"- but I got away with it this time.

Chapter 26

Mission number 29. August 4th, 1944
Peenemunde, V-2

My diary reads: "Peenemunde, Germany. Experimental station for Jet Propelled aircraft (V-2). Lots of flak due to CAVU weather. Got only a few holes. Shot down an Me 110 on way back. Ball turret gunner got credit. Long, hard trip. Blasted it wide open. Won't have to go back!"

At least I didn't have to go back. This was one of the most successful missions that I participated in. I was flying another new crew, that of 2nd Lt. L.M. Johnston in A/C number 42-31432, "Jigger Rouche, Kraut Killer." We each carried five 1000-pound bombs and 2700 gallons of gasoline for this nine-hour trip.

The 303rd furnished thirty-seven aircraft for this mission, and we had two radar ships from the 305th Bomb Group, which was a PFF Group that supplied these aircraft to many different groups. It later developed that we would not need to bomb by radar, as the weather had cleared at the target. We had made a plan "D" assembly at 6000 feet over Molesworth and took our thirteen B-17s into the high group of the 41st Combat Wing formation to which we were assigned. We departed the English coast at Louth at about eleven o'clock, intending to fly at low altitude for a while to save gas. However, over the North Sea there was a cloud layer that caused us to start our climb to altitude a little early.

We crossed the enemy coast at 22,000 ft and maintained this altitude to the target, which was on the Baltic coast north of Berlin. Just before the IP we got a radio message that visual bombing would be done, so we took proper interval so those groups could bomb individually. Bombing by Wing formation was an all-or-nothing situation, while bombing by groups gave us three chances to hit the target.

We made a seven and a half-minute bomb run from the IP to the target and bombs were away a few seconds after 1442 from 23,000 feet, we being the high squadron for today's mission.

The bombs from my airplane had delayed action, or "Long Delay" fuses. This is how we added insult to injury. Some fuses of this type had a device built in, so that when the bomb struck the ground without exploding, a plunger in the special fuse broke a vial of acetone. The acetone slowly dissolved a celluloid diaphragm that was spring loaded. When the diaphragm was dissolved, it released a striker that exploded the bomb. The celluloid discs were of different thickness so that the thicker they were, the longer it took for them to dissolve. Thus there were no moving parts to the fuse, and sound detectors could not hear anything except the final movement of the firing pin. By then, everybody within two miles could hear it.

My bombs didn't explode with the others, but one was designed to explode three hours after impact. Each bomb had a different delay, so that my last bomb didn't explode until three days after the initial drop. My aircraft was in position 9, which is near the center of the formation. This same position in the other groups had the same fuses, so that there was a total of fifteen delayed action bombs dropped onto the target. These were intended to harass the clean up crews, and I have no doubt that they were quite un-nerving. We had at least one aircraft carrying these bombs on most big industrial targets in Germany. We did not carry them to targets in occupied countries, as this would put our friends at risk. Much of the clean up work was done by forced labor in the occupied countries.

We had taken off and climbed through a solid overcast in England, but over the target area the clouds were almost absent and visibility was forty miles. The bombardiers flew the lead planes with the Norden bombsight that was hooked to the autopilot and the bombs dropped automatically at the proper instant and position. The seven and a half-minute bomb run gave the bombardiers plenty of time to kill the drift. Of the three groups doing individual bombing on this mission, our high group, in which I was flying, had the best score, having 100 percent of our bombs fall within two thousand feet of the main point of impact, or MPI. Ninety five percent fell within one thousand feet and sixty percent fell within five hundred feet. The low group did nearly as well with ninety five percent of their bombs falling within one thousand feet of the MPI and thirty percent within five hundred feet. The lead didn't do quite as well, with ninety three percent within two thousand feet and twenty five percent within one thousand feet. They only got five percent within the five hundred-foot circle.

As the bombs started falling, a speedboat on the canal turned and sped away in the opposite direction. It was just as well for him, because several of these one thousand-pound bombs hit the canal, damming it up at three places, one nearly striking the speedboat. This was from the Lead Group, which we could see ahead of us.

The Low Group had five near misses on the MPI building, a direct hit on a conveyor system and one on a coal pile. They had two hits on the canal bank, damming it up at these points.

Our group, the high group, had the only direct hit on the MPI building, and three near misses. Four other buildings were severely damaged and there was a near miss on the conveyer system. A thousand-pound bomb is quite potent.

We even thought that we might kill some of the big rocket scientists at the facility. We later learned that Werner Von Braun was at the facility that day. One non-operational Junker 52 was seen near the west end of the east-west runway, but other executive Transports were nowhere to be seen. They were most likely in hangars.

Our group also had the most concentrated bomb pattern, it being 1230 feet by 900 feet, which indicated that we were flying a tight formation at bombs away. The Lead group's pattern was 1800 feet by 1150 feet. The low group's pattern was 1700 feet by 1350 feet. Bomb patterns were always oval due to the different altitudes of the bombers during bomb release.

As we headed home, going over the Baltic Sea, we flew over the Danish Island of Falster and immediately over the island of Lolland Maribo. At this point, the tail gunner of this new crew, Staff Sgt. E. S. Brown reported on the intercom:

"Tail to Pilot, there's an Me 410 coming up behind us. No, I believe it's a 110."

"Are you sure it's not a B-25?" I asked, knowing of the twin rudder configuration.

"No, it's definitely a 110 and he's closing." The Ball turret gunner, Staff Sgt. J.A. Czerwonka, confirmed that it was indeed an Me 110.

"How far back?" I asked.

"About two miles and closing." the tail gunner answered.

"Well," I said, "we are on our way home and haven't fired a shot, so let him have it. With this, the tail gunner and ball turret gunner started firing. After thirty or forty seconds of almost continuous firing, the ball turret gunner yelled on the intercom,

"He's diving away! He's going straight down. He's picking up speed and still going straight down! "He's crashed! He's crashed! I didn't see any parachute!"

It seems evident that some one in our group hit the pilot from nearly one mile away, and after we landed I put in a claim for the Ball Turret Gunner, Sgt. Czerwonka, only to find that several claims were made for this same airplane. I thought Sgt. Czerwonka should have gotten credit, since we started firing first, and the plane was hit while still a mile away. However, the powers that be finally awarded the "Kill" to Staff Sgt. Richard L. Smith who was tail gunner for 1st Lt. Bob Moreman flying Low Lead in the 359th Squadron. I've never been able to figure out how the tail gunner on the lead plane could shoot down an enemy fighter coming in from the rear of the formation. Twenty or so other tail gunners were firing at the same plane from positions further to the rear and hundreds of feet closer to the action. But, he was on the lead plane.

After this action we got a little too close to Germany's northernmost city, Flensburg and flew within range of a battery of 88MM flak guns, and a battery of larger guns that was fairly accurate. This was after the target where the flak was fairly intense and accurate. Also at Eckernferde where a single battery of three guns peppered a few of us with fragments.

Of the thirty-nine B-17s that participated in this mission, seventeen had battle damage, with eight major and nine minor. We were lucky that none of us was shot down. Even the Me110 that we shot down had fired rockets at our group, but missed.

The Me110, 210 and 410 were all very similar but could be identified by close scrutiny of the tail, the 210 and 410 having a single
tail. No matter, they were all enemy planes. The 110 had a twin
rudder rather like a small version of the B-25 Mitchell Bomber, but
other than that, the resemblance was superficial. These twin engine
fighter-bombers were no match for our P-51s and they usually hung
back to wait for a gap in the fighter support, at which time they
flew behind the bombers and fired rockets into the formation from
behind. They had to get within a half mile of the formation to be effective, and this posed a dire threat to them as the forgoing narrative
reports.

Mission number 30. August 5th, 1944

The 303rd Bomb Group had been flying two missions per day for quite a while, and today each squadron planned to put up ten B-17s each. This would be forty B-17s

Beiser was leading our squadron for this rush job, and only six of us made formation with their assigned group. A few of the planes were so rushed that they were not fully loaded with bombs. We were to bomb six different targets in France in support of the ground troops. We were in the "E" squadron of the 41st Combat Wing, and we assembled over the Harrington Buncher at 3500 feet. Since we were late in taking off, we took a short cut to Splasher 10 and then directly to Beachy Head at 20,000 feet. As a result of this short cut, three of our planes couldn't catch up and tacked onto another squadron.

Our three-plane squadron's target was Crepieul, France where we did a ten-minute bomb run. Flak gunners did not fire on us as they did some of the other squadrons, and none of our squadron was damaged. The "A" squadron lead ship was hit by flak, which knocked out the manual aileron controls, and tumbled the gyros that operated the auto pilot, just forty five seconds before bombs away. The bombardier recovered in time to do a fair job in his bombing attempt.

The "D" squadron was twenty minutes late to their target when they had to circle to avoid a large formation of British Lancaster's in their path. At the target one plane was hit by flak which disabled two engines. That squadron flew a direct course to England so that the disabled plane could land at Ford, near the white cliffs of Dover.

We saw two of the German rocket planes, the Me-163 "Komet," but with their five to six minute fuel supplies none could reach the 303rd formations. P-51s shot down several German fighters that day. I think that this must have been the original intent of the mission, to lure up the German fighters so that our fighters could eliminate them.

Today was Beiser's last mission, as it was for most of our original crew. I had two more to go. I had the same co-pilot as yesterday's mission, but was flying a mixed crew of gunners who were making up missed missions. Why me, Lord?

My old favorite airplane, "Betty Jane," flown by another pilot, had to abort this mission when the pilot had to turn off both inverters due to an electrical short caused by a urine "spill." Many crewmen didn't like to use the relief tube that was located near the forward bulkhead of the bomb bay, and simply relieved themselves on the bombs or in the bomb bay. Usually nothing happened, but this time the amplifiers were shorted out and no boost could be obtained for the superchargers and as a result they could not get to altitude.

This practice was forbidden, but was often violated as in this case. The pilot brought the "Betty Jane" back to base with the wet bombs, and the culprit was disciplined by having to fly an extra mission. The official report was softened to indicate that a urine can was accidentally knocked over instead of what actually happened. Thus, the culprit might have lost rank as well as having to fly another mission if the whole truth had been revealed.

Mission 31. August 7th, 1944
Paris, France

Today's mission would target a large fuel storage area in an area inside the city limits of Paris. It was almost on the banks of the Seine
River, in the St. Ouen section of the city. My diary reads: "Paris,
France (St. Ouen). Flak really rough. They tracked us all the way. I
was luckier than most as I only got a few holes. Target CAVU except
for haze. Carried 38, 100 pound bombs. Over enemy territory two
hours and five minutes."

I was flying in the number two position on the right wing of
the lead plane. My new co-pilot for today was 2nd Lt. G.C. Lawrenson and we were flying A/C number 42-102569 which had no
nose art. Thirteen airplanes were able to bomb this target while the
rest went to Chartres, France to bomb the airfield there as a target
of opportunity. From our bombing altitude of 25,000 feet the visibility was fair, with the target being obscured for a time with a thin
layer of clouds. Another group from our wing turned in front of us
at our altitude, giving us some violent prop-wash. Even so, twelve
of our thirteen aircraft bombed the primary target, but with only fair
results. The new airplane being flown by Lt. Walker in the number
four position did not bomb, because the bombardier failed to turn
on the selector and salvo switches. They brought their thirty- eight
bombs back to base.

Of course there was a salvo switch at the bombardier's station
as well as one in the pilot's position. The bombs could be dropped
at any time from either location, armed or unarmed, but even a half-
second delay would cause that plane's bombs to overshoot the target
by several hundred feet and possibly kill a great many French civilians.

We were in a ticklish situation where we had to be extremely
careful not to bomb built up areas in occupied France. We knew that

we would occasionally kill non-combatants in occupied countries, but we always tried to avoid this.

The bombs that we dropped had no nose fuses and had a one fortieth second fuse in the tail to give them instantaneous ignition. We were carrying two thousand gallons of gas for this five hour and forty-five minute mission.

There was intense flak throughout our seven-minute bomb run, and just after bombs-away it became very accurate until we took evasive turns. The German gunners were slow in getting our range while on the bomb run, and by the time they got us in their sights the bombs dropped and we turned away to foil their two and a half kilometer sighting lead. Of the thirteen planes in our low group, only three escaped damage. We had five planes with major damage and five, including mine, with minor damage.

Most of my new crews had a very exciting start to their combat tours. We were reminded of Winston Churchill's words from his earlier time in the Boer war: "Nothing is quite so exhilarating as being shot at and missed."

Chapter 27

Mission number 32. August 8th, 1944
Supporting our troops
MY LAST MISSION!

Our mission for today would be to try a tactical attack on German ground troops in an area eleven miles south of Caen, France. Captain Bob Sheets was leading today's raid with a ten-man crew. This used to be standard for the Flying Fortress, but they had lately been reduced to a nine-man crew. Bob Sheets was in aircraft number 42-97311, "Shoo Shoo Baby" of our 427th Squadron. Tech. Sgt. Frank X. Neuner was in Bob Sheets' top turret. He was a good buddy and roommate of my regular ball turret gunner, Charles W. Latta. We knew Frank from his experience of swimming in the English Channel on the first of December 1943. His aircraft, piloted by Lt. Eckard, ran out of gas after a mission to Solingen, Germany. They had to ditch in the Channel, but all were saved by Air-Sea Rescue.

I was assigned to "Tail End Charlie" for this raid, which was also "Purple Heart Corner," since there was nobody behind me. I had the same crew as on yesterday's raid, but with two different gunners on make-up missions.

My erstwhile pilot, Theodore "Bud" Beiser was acting 427th Operations officer, while Bob Sheets flew the lead position. Beiser had just finished his tour of duty and was doing this office work while waiting transport to the States.

This 41st "B" Combat Wing, Lead Group with twelve B-17s did an assembly at 5,000 ft over the Harrington Buncher Beacon and departed the English coast at Portland Bill at 14,000 feet, which was to be our bombing altitude. The combat wing ahead of us didn't turn on the briefed IP and we had to follow them around to avoid flying a collision course. There were no clouds over the target, but the haze was so bad that we couldn't see the bright red and yellow markers that our ground troops had put out to identify the target that they wanted bombed. We made a bomb run, but the lead bombardier didn't drop because of this problem. The high group was the only one of our three groups to bomb the primary target, and they missed it by over a half-mile. Luckily their bombs still fell in German occupied territory, destroying a lot of apple trees where a lot of vehicle tracks were visible.

Our secondary target had a cloud bank over it at 12,000 feet, so we finally picked a railroad siding and made a five minute bomb run and dropped 446, 100 pound bombs on that target with fairly good results, cutting the rail lines and a highway.

According to the mission summary, flak was "Moderate and inaccurate at the Primary." Bob Sheets at the front of the formation wrote this, while I was a quarter mile back and 500 feet lower. My diary reads: "Caen, France. German front line defenses. Flak was really rough as we were at 14,000 ft. Didn't drop on primary and finally dropped on railway yard, but good. CAVU. I'd rather go to Berlin. Finis. DFC."

Only one B-17 of our group was damaged. Guess whose? At one time the flak was bursting all around our plane, but several hundred feet away most of the time. I could see the angry, red center of these explosions several times. I often wondered if I was overly sensitive because it was my last mission, and thought that they were determined to get me on this one last chance. I thought at the time that one of those bursts might actually have my name on it.

After we returned to Molesworth at fifteen minutes past three PM, I did the necessary paper work and came out of the airplane, only to find the crew lined up in front of the airplane by the nose art, "Miss Lace," to congratulate me. My co-pilot, 2nd Lt. George C. Lawrenson who just finished his second mission asked me,

"How does it feel to finish your missions and get the Distinguished Flying Cross?"

"Wait a minute and I'll show you." I replied.

With this, I took off my "Fifty Mission" hat, removed my "Flak Beanie," and handed them to Lt. Lawrenson.

"Hold these for me, will you?" I said, as I untied and dropped my flak suit, which I picked up and handed to Lt. John. P. Emmet, our navigator, who also acted as our bombardier. I removed my oxygen mask and throat mike and handed them to Tech Sgt. Leroy H.M. Foerster, our engineer-top turret. I unhooked and removed my parachute harness, which I gave to Sgt. Robert H. Hitchcock, our radioman. I lifted my "Mae West" life preserver over my head, and handed it to Staff Sgt. Myron M. Musyka, the other waist gunner. I removed my leather A-2 jacket, which I handed to our ball turret gunner, Sgt. Joseph A. Czerwonka who had shot down the Me-110 on the Peenemunde mission. My flight gloves I handed to Sgt. Darrell L. Garlick, waist gunner who had just finished his first mission. I took off my flight coveralls with its escape kit and handed them to Sgt. Wayne L. Rughe, our tail gunner, also on his first mission. This left me with my uniform pants, shirt and shoes. I walked to the middle of the line of crewmembers and faced them.

"How does it feel to finish my missions, you ask?" With this, I did a standing back flip and landed on my feet. The crew applauded as I took a bow like a ham actor, the same as I did in my High School plays. The standing back flip was a standard with me that I learned at McLeansboro, Illinois High School. I never told the crew how scared I was on this mission when the flak started bursting around us.

But now it was over, and I could actually look forward to going back home where instructors wouldn't yell at me and other people wouldn't shoot at me. Utopia, here I come! I was not yet twenty-two and a half years old, a combat instructor with thirty-two missions under my belt. They were giving me credit for three more missions, so that my official records would indicate that I actually flew thirty-five missions. I guess my job of flying new crews on their first missions made me earn it.

My last mission on August 8, 1944 lasted four hours and forty minutes with an hour and fifteen minutes over enemy territory. That was to be my last flight in Europe. Once a person's tour of duty was over, they got in a hurry to get rid of you in order to make room for the replacement crews that were coming every few days. Of course they would allow one to sign up for another thirty-five missions, but few ever did.

During my thirty-two missions, I flew twelve different B-17s in combat, plus two trips in the "Barber Pole," "Scarlet Harlot" weather plane of our 427th squadron.

I flew combat in the "Buzz Blonde" twelve times. "Betty Jane" five times, "Sweet Rosie O Grady" two times, "Tiny Angel" two times, "Miss Lace" two times, "Queenie" two times, "Jigger Rouche, Kraut Killer" one time, "Full House" one time. The other five had no nose art.

The first and third of my students that I took on their first missions were killed in action just four or five weeks after my tour was over. I took H.C. Clark on his first mission on July 17 and he and three other officers, and two enlisted men were killed in action on August 14 in the "Jigger Rouche" when German fighters shot them down over Wiesbaden. "Tiny Angel" that I flew on my 24th and 30th mission was shot down at the same time with the pilot, engineer, and one waist gunner killed. This was the time that the German FW 190's had installed the huge 30MM cannon under their wing. A single round from one of these cannon was enough to bring down a bomber in most cases.

On January 10, 1945, "Buzz Blonde" that I flew on 12 missions, collided with "Iza Vailable 2" over Bonn, Germany, destroying the tail gun position, killing the gunner, Sgt. M.M. Mooney. The nose of "Buzz Blonde" was badly damaged, causing the bombardier and navigator to bail out, thinking they were out of control. They had little choice, since the oxygen system in the nose was destroyed in the collision. They became prisoners of war, while the others regained control and made emergency landings at friendly airfields. The pilot and co-pilot of "Iza Vailable" received the Distinguished Flying Cross for keeping their aircraft from crashing, with much of the tail missing.

The "Betty Jane" that I flew five times, including the glide bomb attack on Cologne was shot down on September 13, 1944, with the pilot being the only one killed when his parachute failed to open.

"Full House," the only "new" B-17 that I flew in combat was in a mid-air collision with another 427th aircraft. Seventeen men were killed in the two aircraft, with only one survivor. The newer B-17's were unpainted except for group and squadron markings.

On November 21st 1944, my third "student" was killed, as was all but the radio operator. They were flying one of the "newer" planes built in 1943. This was one of the unpainted B-17s that were starting to show up during these months.

During a shuttle mission to Russia, "Miss Lace" which I flew on my last mission was hit by flak near the Russian lines and landed in Poland where it was abandoned. "Queenie" later made a crash landing in England, but was salvageable.

During my thirty-two missions, the 303rd Bomb Group lost twenty B-17s to enemy action. One of our B-17s made an emergency landing in Switzerland with sixty holes in the airplane, some disabling. I was able to see many B-17s of other groups shot down as well. Not one bomber from the 303rd ever went to Sweden, although one nearby Group had 8 bombers land there to sit out the war.

As a result of these twenty losses during my three plus months of combat, eighty crewmen lost their lives, some being murdered by German civilians. It appears that at least one was shot because he was a Jew. The pilot and co-pilot of one downed bomber were hung in small trees and pitchforked to death by German farmers. This had always presented a dilemma to combat crews who had heard rumors of such murders. I had carried my 45 pistol on my early missions, but later abandoned this practice. If caught by civilians, you might fend them off until a military man arrived, but on the other hand, this might give a military man an excuse to shoot you, claiming that he had been threatened. Catch 22.

During the course of the war, starting with their first mission on November 17, 1942, our "Hell's Angels," 303rd Bomb Group, flew three hundred and sixty four missions, ending at Pilsen, Czechoslovakia on April 25, 1945, just thirteen days before Germany surrendered. Unfortunately, German flak gunners got the last of the 181 B-17s lost from our group, killing three of the eight-man crew in our 427th Squadron's "new" B-17, 44-83447, that had no nose art. The 303rd Bomb Group flew more missions and dropped the second most bomb tonnage of any other Group in the European Theater. This was probably because we flew longer missions and thus more gas and fewer bombs. Our group had the first heavy bomber to fly 25 missions, and the first to fly 75 missions. Walter Cronkite flew with us on D-Day and Clark Gable flew as gunner on one of our missions.

One of the most disastrous missions flown by the 303rd Bomb Group was on September 28, 1944, just after I had finished my tour of duty and returned to the States. On that day, eleven of our twenty-eight B-17s were lost, mostly to German fighters. Ninety-nine of our men were missing and five were returned wounded in badly shot up Fortresses. German civilians murdered some of our men.

The latest version of the FW 190 had an added feature. Carried under one wing was a 30-MM cannon, which could bring down a bomber with one well directed hit. This was the main item of our losses that day.

I never could believe how lucky I was to survive the war when I saw so many others shot down. While quite potent, the 20MM cannon had less that one fourth the explosive force of a 30MM shell. The 50 caliber machine guns of the B-17s were also quite potent that day, destroying at least nine enemy fighters. And the B-17 crews saw many others go down.

I have acquired a letter written on May 6, 1945, just one day before the Germans surrendered. It is written by a crewmember of a bomber that was shot down on April 10 of that year. It is written to a close friend on another crew. I present a transcript here for the reader to think about the fortunes of war. The historian for the 303rd Bomb Group Association, Harry D. Gobrecht, did the necessary research to find more information on this ill-fated mission for me, and corrected the spelling of names.

May 6, 1945
Sunday
Germany

Dear Pappy,
    Since our crew exchanged general "sweating out" sessions with your crew, maybe you'd like to know just why

we didn't return to the base on the April 10th mission. Ten to one you guys think that we just scurried off to some nice soft neutral country, and settled down to quiet repose. No such thing, Pappy. Not old crew "14." Now, if it were crew "13"- well-

Seriously, Pappy, I'd like to let you know what happened; that is, as much as I was able to take note of. From what I'm about to relate, you'll gather that there are a few bits of story missing. Maybe you'll be able to fill it in for us.

We were hit by flak on the bomb run. The left wing---sorry, I've run out of ink, and there's none available. (pencil) Anyway, to continue, the left wing was pretty well peppered. The majority of hits were between the one and two engines. We began to lose gas like mad!! The bombs were dropped short of the target, and we were forced to leave the squadron. For protection Dolan stuck close to the bomber stream, though we were losing altitude.

I can't give you much information as to the mechanical flaws that the hit caused, but we never had more than two engines turning over at a time after we were hit. Naturally we were damned near out of gas.

Murphy made some quick calculations, and headed us towards the Magdeburg flak corridor. This was the closest route to our lines. We made the corridor perfectly, but we didn't make the lines.

Naturally, while Dolan and Lamar were keeping the ship in the air the rest of us were busy. Maxim was helping Murph and calling off to me to take pictures of various things. This I was doing between throwing out everything I could lay my hands on to lighten the load of the ship.

Dick Covert and DeMan were busy tossing out equipment too. At intervals Dolan would cut all switches to avoid fire- which didn't break out, by the way-; so Dick couldn't use the radio equip. And Jack Marks was doing his damndest to get what gas he could transferred to #4 engine.

Well, despite a valiant effort, Dolan finally had to tell us to prepare to bail out. We put on our chutes, and kept on working, trying to jettison the ball. We didn't have the tools for it, though. You might make a note of that Pappy! God, we sure could have used 'em. I even tried to use a gun barrel to no avail.

Finally Dolan gave three rings on the alarm bell and then a long ring. I was over by the ball, Dick and Shorty was nearer the door than I, but they didn't seem to want to go. Or else they didn't hear the bell. Anyway, I shouted at 'em to get out, and when they took no action I stepped to the escape hatch and looked down. Boy, we weren't very high. I glanced back at the tail, and Chuck Sarockas (*spelling?*) was still there. I whistled and shouted. Then I jumped.

Particulars on personal feelings and such I'll give you on request. Dick, Shorty and I landed quite close together. We were captured almost immediately. I counted five chutes besides my own before my view was impaired by the position of my landing.

Lt. Sell, a pilot from 487th, who was shot down the same day, is almost positive he saw us go down, and counted nine chutes. Dolan, Lamar, Murph, Marks, Chuck and Maxim haven't turned up in any of the places we've been held. By the way, we landed about ten kilometers from our lines.
I've tried my damndest to get some information as to what happened to the other six of the crew. The Germans didn't exactly take to our unexpected visit, though, so I had to be careful.

If you have any information Pappy, will you please write me at my home address,

Dave Nicolette
329 Auburn Ave.
Grand Rapids, 6
Michigan

There's a possibility that the others escaped.

Another thing, will you try to get the home addresses of the rest of the crew. I don't have any personal stuff with me.

What little I have the Jerries got me, and the stuff I left at the base- well I don't suppose I'll get much of it back.

Tell Lyster, Osborn, Connery, Hepp, Hartman, and the other guys I'm doing pretty good now and tell them to write me at home. I think that is where I'm going.

Thanks Pappy,

Dave Nick.

Lt. Kenneth Dolan (P)	POW	Rutledge, PA
2Lt. Kenneth E. Lamar (CP)	KIA	Iowa Falls, IA
2Lt John S. Murphy (N)	KIA	Delta PA
Sgt. Larry T, Maxim (Toggalier)	POW	Oxford, MA
S/Sgt. Jack K. Marks (TTEngineer)	KIA	Lakewood, OH
Sgt. Ralph R. Covert (Radio)	POW	Mount Pleasant, PA
Sgt. Oscar A. DeMan (Ball Turret)	POW	Depew NY
Sgt. David W. Nicholette (WG)	POW	Grand Rapids, MI
Sgt. Charles (NMI) Sarockas, Jr. (T)	KIA	Chicago, IL

The "Pappy" that this letter was sent to, is Robert (Bob) Burns who now lives on Maryland's eastern shore just over the bay bridge from Annapolis. Burns was a pilot with two duty tours to his credit and over thirty thousand hours flight time with his duty as a pilot with US airlines.

What David W. Nicholette didn't know at the time he wrote the letter was that four of his crewmates were killed in the bailout or crash of this B-17 of the 486th Bomb Group, 834th Squadron, 3rd Air Division. They were shot down on a mission to Brandenburg, Germany, crashing near Ziesar, Germany after being hit by flak and German fighters. This is the information that he could not disclose in his letter, and the Germans did not tell him that his four buddies had been killed. It is not known whether or not civilians murdered his buddies after they bailed out, or were killed by German fighter planes after most of the crew had bailed out.

All American aviators were volunteers, and many of us who are alive now had to live with the guilt of surviving when so many were lost. I always said that it was as if fate were throwing darts and if it missed you it sometimes got someone else. Such are the fortunes of war!

Much of the combat narrative here has been verified through the National Archives in Washington, DC. I spent nearly every Thursday for two years in the copying of the 303rd mission reports. All those 303rd veterans who live near the Archives participated in the copy work under the direction of the late George Stallings who was one of the premier pilots of the 303rd Bomb Group. We copied over ten thousand pages from the Archives in order to get our Historian, Harry Gobrecht the necessary records for his 920-page book, Might in Flight which is no longer in print. Harry graciously allowed me to verify my memory of my missions from his extra research.

Our 303rd Bomb Group Association has available a thousand-page CD that was initiated by veteran, Edgar Miller. It may be ordered on the Web at 303rdbga.com. This web site is the work of Gary Moncur: the son of one of our B-17 "Thunderbird" pilots and it has been awarded the top prize of all the web sites in the country.

Keith Ferris, the famous aviation artist is a member of our Group. He is the artist who painted the 70-foot wide 303rd B-17 mural in the aviation gallery in the Smithsonian Institution.

Chapter 28

Homeward

After I flew my last mission on August eighth, 1944, I was quickly processed to go home. I had to turn in my parachute, Mae West life preserver, and other items relating to combat. I kept the 45 automatic pistol that had been issued to me.

I was surprised to find that during the financial settlement that I owed the U.S. Army 31 dollars and 50 cents to pay for the 42 box lunches, at seventy five cents per lunch, that I carried on the airplane during combat missions. Since I only flew 32 missions, it shows that I had gone on ten other attempts that were scrubbed or aborted. I knew that officers had to pay all their own expenses, but I thought that they might overlook the lunch fees during combat. No such luck as they were deducted from my pay.

As we stood waiting for the bus to Liverpool on September third, we were to examine the baggage of the enlisted men in the group. I made a cursory examination of the ones that I was assigned to, and finding no contraband, I returned to my own baggage that consisted of a B-15 garment bag, a duffel bag and some smaller items. Hearing laughter nearby, I walked over to see what was going on.

One enlisted waist gunner had taken his fifty-caliber machine gun apart and was intending to smuggle it back to the States as a souvenir. He might have gotten away with it, but the barrel was too long to fit into his duffel bag, and he had wrapped the end with a shirt, hoping that it would pass. As it was taken away from him I hoped that he intended to disarm this weapon if he had managed to steal it.

We all took a bus to Liverpool and boarded the U.S.S. Wakefield, which was to sail the next day without escort. I didn't feel too secure about this as the German U-boats were still in plentiful supply at this stage of the war. We were assured that the Wakefield was faster than any U-boat, and that we would be perfectly safe. It occurred to me that an intercepting course might negate this superior speed.

The second day, September 3rd, 1944, aboard the Wakefield came and went without us leaving port. There was a rumor that there was a German submarine spotted thirty miles outside the harbor. On the third day as I was lolling about the upper deck I was brought up short by a series of explosions. I looked up to see seven or eight bursts of flak at about a thousand feet above the ship and out in the harbor a bit. They appeared to be from our vessel, and I judged them to be forty-millimeter. I had never heard so loud an explosion in combat since the B-17s were so loud that they drowned out all but the closest bursts. Just as it started getting dark, we pulled away from the harbor to take a direct route to Boston. I think the flak bursts were to alert the stragglers that it was time to board.

On our trip to Boston, I never saw so many airmen get seasick. Somehow the ship's motion is different from that of a bomber, but the sickness is identical. And contagious. I almost got sick myself at one time. The Wakefield had a gyrostabilizer and the continuous shuddering and grinding was very conducive to seasickness by any but seasoned sailors. I managed to get by without getting sick and for pastime a bunch of us would go forward and lean into the wind which was about thirty-five miles per hour. During the trip home I never saw another vessel until we were almost to Boston. During the voyage I had found myself in the chapel with only the Chaplain there. He gave me a Bible as he did anyone who wanted one. It is inscribed, "Presented to 1st Lt. Richard R. Johnson by USS Wakefield Chaplain A. L. Murray, September 5, 1944. I still have it.

When we arrived in Boston, the sea was very calm and the harbor seemed alive with small whales. Mostly all we could see was spray from their blowholes, but they were nearly everywhere.

After going ashore on September 8th, 1944 we were taken by bus to Camp Myles Standish where we were processed and sent to our next assignment. I asked to be returned to MacDill Field in Tampa where I had finished my B-17 combat training less than six months before, and where I was still a member of the MacDill Field Yacht Club.

The train going south took me to Norfolk for a few days leave with Mom and Dad. Then off to Miami Beach where I spent three weeks in the Good Hotel for an "R & R," or rest and rehabilitation. The military services had taken over all the hotels at Miami Beach for this purpose.

Things were pleasant at the Good Hotel and they had dances nearly every night. I mostly sat and listened to the music, since I had never learned to dance.

I did a lot of walking about the streets and beaches and gathered up a few coconuts and sent them home in a gunnysack (burlap bag). The city had not yet started cutting the coconuts before they fell off the trees and a dent could be seen in some of the occasional cars that parked under the trees. Later, the city undertook a big campaign to remove the nuts before they matured. One had recently fallen into a baby carriage, killing the infant inside. There was quite a bit of talk about it while I was there.

I soon found myself back at MacDill field where I was to be a combat instructor, training replacement crews still going to Europe to fly B-17s. I had no flight time for September and October 1944, due to change of station and leave times.

In early October Mom and Dad got a telegram from the War Department saying that my brother Harold became missing in action on September 29th from a battle in the Hurtgen Forest in western Germany. This was in the very early stages of the battle that the Germans launched in a futile attempt to retake Aachen from the American troops. As a result I was given a seven-day bereavement leave to go visit Mom and Dad in Norfolk.

In November I started instructing in various aspects of combat flying for the replacement crews. I instructed a little over ten hours in instruments and just over an hour of night landings for one pilot who was short on his records.

Since I was instructing in instrument flight, I had to take one hour of Link Trainer on November fourth to satisfy the check pilot. Some of the B-17s that I was instructing in were "G" models with the chin turret like those in combat. The "F" model used for most of the training was without the chin turret.

When I arrived at MacDill Field the previous January, there was still a number of Martin B-26s on the field. These Marauders were just then being phased out in favor of the B-17. Now, the B-17 was to be phased out in favor of the Superfortress, B-29. The runways had been in the process of being lengthened when I left to go overseas. There was quite a number of B-29s already on hand while I was instructing in B-17s.

I was informed that I could instruct in B-29s and receive a promotion to Captain with only a six-week transition course. I told the Operations Officer that I would let him know in a few days. I had already been recommended for Very Heavy Bombardment when I left Europe. This meant that I would probably be sent to the Pacific to bomb the Japanese if the war dragged on much longer. There were quite a few B-17 and B-24 pilots returning after having completed their combat tour in Europe and they were becoming instructors just as I had.

My dilemma was short lived. A B-29 from MacDill took off one morning and had an engine failure right after departure. The pilot tried to make the circuit of the pattern to make an emergency landing, but could not maintain altitude on three engines. It had lost so much altitude, that by the time it turned to final approach, the left wing clipped some pine trees and it crashed on the bomb storage bunkers, killing most of the crew, the only survivors being in the tail. The airplane burned after impact, but none of the ammunition was affected.

At this time, I was appointed Summary Courts Officer to take care of the effects of the pilot and co-pilot. The Pilot, a Major who had survived combat duty in Europe, was married and living in Tampa with his wife. This simplified my job in his case, taking a week or so. His wallet with thirty dollars inside was torn nearly in half. I took the money to the base bank and exchanged it for new money, at the same time returning his "B" gasoline ration stamps and exchanging the "A" stamps to give to his wife.

The Co-Pilot, being single, was another matter. I had the sad task of going through all his possessions and shipping them back to his parents. I had been told to not return any materials that would bring them additional pain.

There was a large stack of letters in his footlocker from his girlfriend that I had to read. They had been having a great deal of friction and were about to break up at the time of his death. I finally decided to destroy them, and took them to the base incinerator.

During a telephone conversation with the girl friend she asked if I had found any letters. I had to lie to her and tell her that he must have destroyed them. I had to go all over town collecting his cleaning and to check all tickets in the footlocker.

Finally I cleaned out the footlocker and started to take it to supply for re-issue. The footlocker had a cloth liner, and when I ran my hand around the inside I found a bulge that turned out to be three hundred and twenty dollars that he had secreted there. I turned it into a money order, which I sent to his mother. I elected not to accompany his body back home as it would have been tough for me to handle emotionally, so I sent another officer who lived not too far away from his home, arranging a few extra days off for him.

Before I got all this straightened out, another B-29 lost an engine just after take-off and crashed in an almost identical manner as the first, killing most of the crew.

I decided that the B-29, while resembling a larger B-17, it certainly was not the same. A B-17 could fly all day on three engines and even climb a little. The B-29 was fairly new and all the bugs had not been worked out of it yet.

I therefore decided that I didn't want to be an instructor in a B-29, and so I accepted the position of Assistant Provisional Group Commander. Thus I was able to check out a B-17 any time I wanted to fly or to make up flight time, the requirement being four hours per month in order to qualify for flight pay. My new job gave me an office and a 9 to 5 work day with occasional instructing jobs.

Part of my duties was to take the "Crew of the week" on a fishing trip to Mullet Key. This was a Sunday excursion, using one of the crash boats that wasn't being used for the "One A Day In Tampa Bay" duty that was left over from the Martin Marauders. The crash boats went forty-five miles per hour and made it to Mullet Key in less than an hour where we fished from a large ship pier in forty feet of water. This was a weekly thing with me, mothering a ten-man crew who had scored the best in gunnery or bookwork. We were still sending these crews to Europe on a regular basis and I was supposed to tell them what to expect. I didn't tell them everything.

I went on so many fishing trips that I was getting tired of it. On one trip a crewman snagged a large mullet that was hardly injured, so we strung it on a six-inch shark hook that was attached to a sixty-foot chain and tossed it overboard just as we were leaving. The next Sunday when we arrived, the chain was hanging slack, so we started to bring it in. Much to our surprise it held a three hundred-pound Jew Fish. We took it back to MacDill Field and gave it to the German prisoners of war that roamed parts of MacDill. They cleaned it, made steaks of it, and we had a big fish fry for all the combat crews. Another time the crews caught a dozen large flounders, which they gave to me at the end of the fishing day. I took them to the enlisted men's mess hall and had the prisoners clean them for me. Somehow I ended up with less than three pounds of fish from my dozen large flounders. At any rate, I decided to fry them myself with the Mess Sergeant's help. I quickly learned that the fish were so tender that they could not be turned over with a fork. They were quite delicious, and we enjoyed them very much.

Another of my duties as Assistant Provisional Group Commander was to be paymaster for the combat crews. On the morning of payday I would strap on my 45 automatic pistol and go to the base bank to draw out the funds which was all cash. A crew of enlisted men counted the money into envelopes, and took names and identified each man, who would proceed down the line, finally stopping in front of me, whereupon I would give him his envelope after he saluted and identified himself.

I was the responsible party to all this, and if any money was lost or missing, I would have to pay it back to the Government. At the end of six months I had handled several hundred thousand dollars, and only lost one dollar and thirty cents.

The German and Italian prisoners of war that were encamped at MacDill Field were required to salute all officers, who were not required to return the salute if they didn't want to. For several months, still being a little arrogant from being shot at by their countrymen, I didn't return their salutes, but finally relented as my combat experience got further into the past. It was easy to tell them from other folks on the base as they had the bold POW on their shirts, both front and back. They never had it so good.

I wasn't doing much flying at this time except to get my required four hours per month. On December 14, 1944, I made a two and a half-hour flight, and the next day I did two hours and forty minutes. Whenever I decided to check out a B-17, getting a crew was easy. As soon as I walked into the ready room, all the guys sitting around would jump up and ask to go along. The wings on my jacket always identified me as a pilot, and they all needed the same four hours per month that I did. I often took a twelve-man crew on these jaunts.

One day a B-17 from our field did not return from a training flight and we all went out to look for it. We flew over the entire southern half of Florida at about a five hundred-foot altitude, in a spread formation, but no sign of the missing bomber was ever found. I always suspected that it went down in the Gulf of Mexico.

In January 1945 I decided to take piano lessons, since there was a fine piano in the Officers Club where I could sneak in to practice before the barflies arrived. I took lessons for about six months, but every time I tried to practice, some wise guy would walk by and say,

"How ya doin' Maestro? It was rather intimidating, and all I learned from my fifty-cent lessons was how to run the scales.

Suddenly one day my parents got a card from my brother, Harold. He had been wounded and captured by the Germans. This was our first news that he was alive after being reported missing in action on Sept 29, 1944. Mom called the Adjutant General who later confirmed that Harold was indeed a prisoner of war. We learned that he had been caught in a firefight and having shot several German soldiers, was himself shot. Harold had fired his BAR (Browning Automatic Rifle) into a haystack, where he saw movement, with the bullet striking a German soldier in the chest below the breastbone. The bullet missed all the vitals, emerging through the soldier's back. And the soldier walked with Harold to the rear after Harold was captured! A German gunner had shot Harold from the side, with the bullet just grazing his lower jaw, across the chin. The bullet took off all the flesh just below his lip, exposing the roots of his lower teeth.

Harold was searched after his capture but he still had a German P-38 pistol in his belt that he had removed from a dead German Officer. While riding to the German compound he hid the pistol under the hay that they were riding on, knowing that he might be shot if he were caught with it. He later told me that he had to walk from Belgium to Poland in the winter of 1944-45 with only first aid supplied by the Germans. The German army was hard-pressed taking care of its own men by this time. Harold and the other prisoners walked in a loose gaggle with only two or three German guards. They were encamped in many places, staying just ahead of the advancing Allied Army. They finally made their way to Stalag 2-B where they remained until being liberated by the advancing Russian Army.

When captured, Harold was six foot, three inches tall, weighing one hundred ninety five pounds. When liberated, after nine months as a prisoner, he weighed one hundred five pounds. He said that when the Russian tank crashed through the barbed wire entanglement of their compound he thought that it was the happiest day of his life. Then he said that it was a minor preview of his feelings when he first saw the American flag of the advancing American troops.

Meanwhile during this time, the Officers Club at MacDill Field was planning to have a big party at the end of January, but the liquor supply was getting low, and none was available in Tampa because of rationing. So, it was decided that three B-17s with oversize crews would fly to Havana, Cuba to replenish our stores. Batista was a benevolent dictator that we got along with fairly well and Cuba was not involved in the war. I was to pilot one of the B-17s with a crew of twelve, as was the other two airplanes.

This gave us thirty-six people to buy two cases each of various spirits, which was the limit allowed. Seventy-two cases were deemed enough to last a few months. All the liquor that we bought in Havana had been shipped from Tampa to begin with, because we had treaty obligations with Cuba. Most of the officers, including myself, had their own bottle behind the bar at the Officers Club. We always allowed a few friends to share the bottle when we weren't there, but this was a large base with a lot of officers who liked to party, thus the need to go to Havana. And this was not the first trip. They were all listed as "Goodwill visits."

We left before noon on January 22nd, 1945, and were to return on January 25th. Our Base Commander, Col. James B. Carroll was on the lead plane, and we also had a few nurses flying as crewmembers. We treated the whole thing as a lark, flying loose formation all the way to Cuba on this three and a half-hour trip. Most of the crewmembers except flight engineers were officers on this particular "mission."

After we circled Havana we landed and took care of all the niceties, and went to our various hotels that had been pre-arranged. The officers and nurses from my crew decided to go shopping in Havana to buy trinkets to take home. I bought a pair of castanets for my mother, on one of which the vendor engraved "Dick," and "Mom" on the other. After it got dark we all went to Sloppy Joe's bar with its sawdust covered floors. Going to Sloppy Joe's was a required tradition. Of course there was the mandatory photograph, and it shows all the gang with a drink in their hand except me. I have a pair of castanets in my hand, me being the designated flyer.

Later that evening, after the nurses went to their quarters, one of our guys who could speak two or three words of Spanish, decided that the seven of us should go see an "Exhibition." We wanted to know what an exhibition was, but he merely said,

"You'll see. Give me two dollars each." So we all gave him two dollars each and he hailed a cab. He had a little trouble getting his message across, but finally the cabby said,

"Ah, Exhi-bish-she-on, Si, Si." So all seven of us piled into the cab and we drove into the Havana slums where the cab driver stopped at a house and our "Hero" knocked on the door. A lady came to the door and was harangued by our friend about "An exhibition," until she finally told him it would cost twenty-five dollars. He said that we only had fourteen dollars and that was it. She said no, and we started to return to the cab when she told us that she would accept the fourteen dollars.

She led us through the hall to a small bedroom with a dim, red bulb in the ceiling. She pointed to the chairs around the bed and we all sat down. Shortly, two young women and a young man came into the room. They had forgotten their clothes! What ensued for the next fourteen minutes on that bed was quite an education for me. After a dollar a minute of gyrations the three 'Entertainers' left as suddenly as they arrived.

Sloppy Joe's bar in Havana, Cuba on January 22, 1945
The author is on the left with castanets and no drink
(designated flier)

Half of these men were from the Ground Eschelon, being crew members for this Jaunt

After three days of sight seeing and having our portraits done in pencil, we returned to MacDill field. After landing late that evening, I was about to walk to the Bachelor Officers Quarters when Col. Carroll said that I could ride with him and his driver. I was flattered that the base commander would show an interest in me, a mere first lieutenant. But instead of letting me off at the BOQ he took me to his house which was about a block from my billet. He said that he would like to hear about my combat experiences since not many combat veterans had yet returned. We sat on the porch and he had his aide bring us a drink. And then another. And another. Finally he dismissed the aide and poured the drinks himself.

Shortly I found his hand on my knee. Then he placed my hand on his leg. I removed my hand and he started trying to unbutton my trousers. It finally dawned on me that our Commanding Officer was a life-long bachelor for good reason. He liked guys. As he was getting more and more aggressive, I sort of sobered up enough to say that I had to go to the bathroom, and the bushes would be fine. I literally tore myself away from him and headed for the bushes, but didn't stop until I got to the BOQ.

I was so angry about his attempted rape that I made no bones about the whole episode when I talked to fellow officers, even on the telephone. Evidently the word had gotten around about my seditious talk, because Col. Carroll suddenly retired right in the middle of a war. I had decided to face a General Court Martial if need be.

Things finally returned to normal and I fell into my regular routine. In June I needed twelve hours to make up back months, and found a way to do it almost in one day. A C-47 pilot was to fly to Washington, D. C. to pick up a Brigadier General and return him to MacDill Field. He needed a co-pilot, so I volunteered to go along. It couldn't be any harder to fly than a B-17, I reasoned.

We took off early on June 22nd, 1945, with a few other men who needed to make up flight time. It took us four hours and fifty-five minutes to fly from Tampa to Bolling Air Force Base in Washington with my flight listed as co-pilot. The General bought us lunch at the Officers Club and we headed back to Tampa. I got four hours and forty-five minutes of qualified dual with one hour of instrument time. That was my only flight in a C-47. This airplane was the same as the famed DC-3 that is still flying today. The main difference between a C-47 and a DC-3 is the paint job and paper work. C-47s loaded from the left side of the fuselage, like most military planes, but the DC-3 had the loading door on the right side. Also, most C-47s had a beefed up tail for the purpose of towing gliders and tow-targets.

Late in July I decided to get my four hours flying time so I went down to operations to pick up a B-17. As I walked into Operations I noticed a truck tarring the street. As soon as I walked into the outer office, Major Brown said,

"Lieutenant Johnson, will you please move my car around back as they are tarring the street." With this he tossed his keys on the desk and went into his back office. I looked out the window and saw that the tar truck was getting closer, so I picked up the keys and walked out to Major Brown's car. It was a 1937 Dodge Coupe. I got in and started the car, but killed the motor when I let out the clutch. I re-started the car and again killed the motor. After three times of this, with the tar truck coming ever closer, I finally left the car in low gear with the clutch out and started the motor with a "Hump, Hump, Hump" until It finally got moving enough to smooth out. Luckily it was already headed in the right direction, so I merely turned left around the corner and headed for the parking lot behind the office. As I got to the rear driveway, there were some GIs working on a pothole, so I stepped on the brake to stop, thus killing the engine again.

"You have plenty of room, sir, just go on past." So I re-started the motor and let out the clutch. I killed the motor. I re-started and killed it again. I finally started it in low gear as before, and promptly ran up over the six-inch curb and back down. I managed to get the car parked by the Major's back door, walked through the hall and placed his keys on his desk and went back to the BOQ and laid down. I was as nervous as I had ever been during my worst combat missions. I had never driven a car in my life!

I never quite lived this down. Here I was, almost 23 years old with 32 missions, and was a combat pilot instructor. I drove a sixty-thousand-pound bomber through thick and thin without once getting off the taxiway. But I didn't know how to drive a car!

Shortly after this episode I decided to buy a car, so I found a young officer who had a 1936 Pontiac touring car with the infamous "Knee Action." I paid him seven hundred dollars for the car and driving lessons. Three days after I got my Florida drivers license I got a warning ticket for going forty in a thirty zone. The combat ribbons may have helped.

Soon after I got the car and became an "expert" driver I met a young lady and we started dating. She was a year younger than I was, but she soon taught me what I had been missing for the past several years. I was not a very good student, but she was a very patient teacher. So, now I had a new "Medal" to wear. –Only in my sub-conscious mind, of course.

I made up my missing flight time in August. On the 20th I started out, but had a runaway turbo right after take off, so I feathered that engine to prevent engine damage and immediately returned to base. Except for the turbo failure that caused an abort on what was to be my sixteenth mission this was my first, ever, in-flight malfunction, even in combat. One circuit of the field, twenty minutes. On the 22nd I flew four hours and ten minutes to make up my lost time with the car-parking incident. The next day I made a four hour and twenty minute flight to bring me up to date. This was a check ride that I received periodically for my instructor's rating.

On September 5th, 1945 I flew as an instructor, giving another pilot four hours and five minutes of night instrument instruction. This was to be my last flight in a B-17 and my last flight in the Army Air Force. I thought that it was significant that my last flight was as an instructor, having given it up as a career less than a year earlier, but still having the rating.

At this point I had accumulated enough points to be separated from the service. A physical examination revealed that I had tonsil and adenoid problems. 1st Lt. Henrys Tripp who was the flight surgeon said that he could save me two hundred and fifty dollars by removing this problem for me, so I said to go ahead. I entered the base hospital to first have my nose operated on. I had a deviated septum caused by an errant baseball batted by Cousin Everett when I lived in Macedonia, Illinois. Lt. Tripp repaired this and the whole thing was quite tolerable. Three days later he removed my tonsils and this was a different story. My throat was so intensely inflamed that I could hardly swallow ice cream. But, on September twenty first I was returned to flying status. I never used it, however, since I was sent to Drew Field in St. Petersburg to be separated from the service.

Officers are never discharged from the service, but merely separated. This gives the Army an excuse to call you back in case of national emergency if you go on active reserves. I chose to go on the inactive reserves, which in effect closed the book on any future service.

In retrospect, I've often thought that I should have stayed on the active reserves, but I would have been sent to Korea in that case. Some few men took exams to go into the regular army but few succeeded due to the demobilization fever that was sweeping the country. I didn't look into this as I knew that it would be difficult since I only had a high school diploma. But now it was time to get into my 1936 Pontiac and go home, back to the civilian life that I had left a little over three years ago.

1945 at MacDill Field, Tampa, Florida.

Back at MacDill Field 1944-45 as a combat flight instructor shortly
before I learned to drive a car.

Chapter 29

Civilian again

The first part of my trip north was to go back to the McLeansboro area to visit my Grandfather and Grandmother Johnson. They had been living near Johnson's Corner since the fall of 1934 when they abandoned the Naylor, Missouri area. Grandpa had always been a carpenter, and so he built his house from salvaged lumber. He had bought three shacks from a nearby village and trucked them to Macedonia where he pulled all the nails and stacked the lumber according to size. My father's job was to straighten all the nails for re-use in the new house. He ended with over three kegs of used nails. Before Grandpa and Grandma moved in, Grandpa dug a cistern. This was merely a holding tank to catch rainwater from the roof of the house. The collected water was filtered through a charcoal filter of Grandpa's making.

When I arrived at Grandpa's house in Macedonia, there was only one room available to sleep in at that time, so I stayed with my father's cousin Everett Johnson, and his wife Pauline and their children Walter Holt and Mary Virginia. I hadn't had time or finances to buy civilian clothes, and was still on terminal leave from the Army Air Force until late October. Besides that, the uniform with all my medals was very impressive to the home folks.

After a few days of visiting the Johnson family, I headed northeast to Piqua, Ohio where I was born. I wanted to visit the Burt family, my Mother's folks. I stayed with Aunt Bernice Burt Williams for a few nights and Aunt Wanda Burt Warling for a few more. Mom had a bunch of brothers and sisters, and her father was still living there, so I had quite a visit.

After impressing them all with my combat stories, I went on to Norfolk, which was my current home with my parents. My brother was in and out of the army hospital at Valley Forge, Pennsylvania for plastic surgery on his chin. They also were treating him for pleurisy and TB that he had contracted while a prisoner of war, They hadn't allowed us to see him for several weeks because of his condition.

Eventually they allowed him to come home after he had gained back about a third of his lost weight. The livid, red scar on his chin was healed from his fourth operation, and they had scheduled one more operation to try to eliminate most of the scar, but he refused to go, saying that the little scar didn't bother him.

During Harold's walk from Belgium to Poland in the bitter winter of 1944-45 he had contracted tuberculosis and pleurisy. These conditions, along with his nicotine addiction did permanent damage to his lungs. The Germans often gave their prisoners the potato peelings and a slice of black bread as a daily ration, after giving their own troops the meager ration of potatoes.

I have Harold's diary in which he wrote:

"Today we got three potatoes and two slices of bread to last us for the next three days. I could eat it all right now."

He later told me that in April of 1945 they were all slowly walking along with their three guards when somebody spotted a pig wandering about. With a big whoop, they all took off after the pig while their three guards sat under a tree to wait. There was no place to escape to, so after they caught the pig, they had a big pork barbecue to which the guards were invited.

After they got to Stalag 2-B and were there for a few weeks, Harold said that on one day they could hear artillery exploding in the far distance. The next morning after they got up, they noticed that no guards were in sight. Harold and the other prisoners milled around for awhile wondering if they were to be shot during an "escape attempt," when suddenly they heard a tank crashing along through the underbrush. It was a Russian tank that merely ran through the barbed wire entanglement into the compound.

A Russian officer opened the hatch and stood up, saying something in Russian, which none of the prisoners understood. Finally the Russian waved his arms toward the hole in the fence and motioned for them all to leave in the direction of the advancing American troops. In just a few hours of walking toward the west, they came upon the American troops. Harold said that it was the most memorable day of his life. Finally he would get to see his wife Doris, and daughter, Diane, and the rest of us. The great trauma of World War Two was over for us. Mom was a Two Star Mother with the banner proudly displayed in the front window of our home at 1514 Granby Street in Norfolk.

Fortunately, she never had to endure the agony of becoming a Gold Star Mother, which would have meant that she had lost a child to the war. Harold lived on partial disability, which paid him a small pension from the Army. As his health deteriorated, the disability was gradually raised until he was at 100 percent. But, he never stopped smoking, even when he had to go on oxygen full time. He died on Pearl Harbor day, December 7, 1993, and my mother died on November 15, 1994 at the ripe old age of 94 and a half. This made me an orphan, since Dad had died on Christmas Eve in 1968, of emphysema, one month after his 70th birthday.

After I was back in Norfolk for a few days, I went out to the Prest-O-Lite plant to see the old gang that I had worked with less than three years ago. Mr. Van Osselar was glad to see me and so was the rest of the gang. But there was a small hitch. According to law, they had to hire me back after finishing my tour of duty. So, I had job security, but with a troubling aspect. All the defense plants were laying off people in large numbers and this meant that my job would put one of these family men out of work with few prospects for a new job. And the welding gas was not in hot demand any more.

I felt bad, but needed to work, so I told Mr. Van Osselar that I would get back to him. Meanwhile, Harold had finished his therapy and had gone to Washington, D. C. to work as a painter. He said that he had several jobs, and that he would like me to help him.

Meanwhile I had bought a thirty six-foot boat with a twelve-foot beam. It was a Chesapeake Bay CatBoat that had been converted to a motor boat in 1936. They had removed the sixty-foot wood mast and nine-foot lead fin and put some large chunks of concrete in the forward hold for ballast to offset the weight loss. I left the boat in the care of Mom and Dad and moved to 616 "D" Street, SE with Harold and his wife, and his wife's mother. Harold and I went to work and started making a bit of money. We had a slight advantage over many other painters, being fresh veterans. It looked good in the classified ads that Harold had placed in the Washington Times Herald and the Washington Evening Star. Both of these papers are long gone.

One day I decided to drive out to see how the Chesapeake Bay looked compared to the Norfolk area. So I drove my 1936 Pontiac sedan (with the infamous knee action) out Pennsylvania Avenue to its end. Its end was in Deale, Maryland which is a Waterman's town twenty miles south of Annapolis. My only good clothes were still my uniform which I was wearing. I stopped in the Post Office that was in Henry's Store, just across the street from the lookout tower that had been erected during the war as a civil defense aircraft-spotting tower.

The postmaster, Mr. Weems Nihiser was in the store and we struck up a conversation. He said that if I was looking for property in the Deale area, he had just sold his waterfront property on Mason's Beach to Mr. Earl Bryant, and that he might be willing to resell it. I had already tried to buy a six unit apartment building on "C" Street SE within sight of the Senate Office Building, but couldn't get a banker to give me a GI loan on it, because, as he said, "it was too much trouble." So that deal fell through. I had planned to pay two thousand dollars down and get a mortgage for the other four thousand. I had saved the two thousand dollars from my military pay.

Deale is in a part of Anne Arundel County known as The Great Swamp, and Colonial settlers had given names to some of the roads that are quite descriptive. There is Swamp Circle Road, and Muddy Creek Road. Further north is Fiddler's Hill Road that once connected Muddy Creek Road to Solomons Island Road, part of which was built over an old Indian trail known as The Old Ridge Path. Many of these roads were built over old Indian trails and the area is rich in Indian ruins at the ends of some of these roads, such as Cumberstone Road. The Smithsonian Institution now has a research center in that area.

After I got somewhat oriented in the areas I went to see Mr. Ruby Downs, the only Realtor in the Deale area to see if he had anything. What he showed me didn't satisfy me, so I got in touch with

Mr. Earl Bryant about the Nihiser property. It was three and a third acres next to land owned by Pete Mason, a descendent of the original Masons that developed Mason's Beach prior to 1924. Mr. Bryant said that he would sell me the place for nine thousand dollars with two thousand dollars down, and he would finance the rest at sixty-eight dollars per month. A little steep, but I thought I could swing it. So I called Mom and Dad in Norfolk and they drove up to Deale.

When they topped the last hill on Route 256, Mom said the sight of the Chesapeake Bay looked like it must be a little bit of Heaven. A lot of people still think that way. There were no trees in the fields above Saint Mark's Chapel because scrub timber was being cleared from the land by Mr. Ralph Leitch and his deaf brother, Joe, and Harvey Chew, their black tenant who lived in a house on Rockhold Creek on the farm.

It was May 2nd, 1946, when Mom and Dad moved into the old Mason Home place that I had bought. Then on May fifth, Mom got sick and I called Doctor Emily Wilson who said that Mom seemed to have indigestion, and that it would be all right by tomorrow. But Mom got so sick that afternoon that I put her in the Pontiac and took her to Prince George General Hospital. I had not yet been to Annapolis and didn't know how to get there, but I did know where there was a hospital in Washington. When we got to the emergency room she was diagnosed as having a ruptured appendix, so the famous Doctor, "Button Hole" Cox, operated on her that evening. He was known as "Button Hole Cox because he was so deft that he could remove and sew up an appendix through an incision that was barely big enough for two fingers to penetrate. He seemed to think that without penicillin my mother would not have survived.

A few days later I got a bill from Doctor Cox's office for the surgery. It said "Fifty dollars, Seventy five dollars or One hundred dollars." I asked the nurse what that meant, and she said to pay whichever one I felt that I could afford. I paid seventy-five dollars, which was the total cost of an appendectomy.

After a few more days of getting settled, Dad and I decided to go back to Norfolk to get the boat. So Harold drove us there and we loaded the boat with all our furniture and other belongings. We had stuff piled all over the decks. The boat had a Model "A" Ford engine for power, and would go six knots without straining, so we set out. I had charts for the trip except for the Norfolk Harbor area. But anyone could find the Chesapeake Bay, right? Wrong. I drove up Mobjack Bay until the water got so shallow that we couldn't proceed any further. I asked a crabber where the Chesapeake Bay could be located, and he laughed at me. But he finally told me how to get back on course.

It took us three days to get from Norfolk to Deale, driving almost day and night. We had no compass, so I navigated by whatever means presented itself. One night I picked a light that was on our course and followed it for an hour until I discovered that it was a large ship headed south. There was no moon that night, so I found myself going in a large circle for a while until I was clued by the stars moving erratically. It's a good thing I was not a navigator in the Great War. We finally arrived in Deale and tried to get into Parker Creek, but the tide was low and the opening could not be crossed. So we went back around to the community pier in Deale and tied up until the tide was high enough to get into Parker Creek. In a few days we had our boat and furniture tied up to the pier at our new residence.

Wages had gotten to about a dollar per hour, but work was scarce so, I finally decided that I should join the Fifty-Two Twenty Club. This was a twenty-dollar per week dole for unemployed veterans. I made one trip to Annapolis and applied for my stipend, but was given a hard time about looking for work. I had to give three references each week, whether real or imaginary. I found that the desire to help the returning servicemen was largely imaginary, so I never got the first check from them, or any after that.

I thought about the GI bill for going to college, so I went to see about that. On the form was a question about my schooling being interrupted by my service and I told them that it wasn't, because I went from a defense plant into the service. They said that a little white lie was acceptable, but I felt that the ethics would be against my upbringing. So I didn't follow through. In retrospect, I might have violated the ethics a bit and become one of the foremost neurosurgeons in the world and would have paid back in income tax, many times the cost of the schooling. So much for my ethics. Besides, I couldn't even afford the living expenses at that time.

People have asked me why I didn't get a job flying for an airline. I had less than a thousand hours flight time and those who flew transports in the Asian Theater had several times that. Not only that, over fifty thousand pilots were recently released from the Army Air Force alone. And me with only a high school diploma!

Chapter 30

Life in Deale, Maryland

After living in Deale for a while I met many nice people, including a few of the young bachelors that lived here. One of the first was Carl Nutwell and his older brother, Reggie. Then Lawrence Rogers and Douglas Howard. We were soon car-pooling to go to Wayson's corner or Upper Marlboro. We met Earl Tucker who was a good bowler and regularly beat the rest of us, except Carl who occasionally beat him. At that time, Duck- Pins was our game, while baseball was the week end games. The Methodist Church was Cedar Grove, like the town's original name before there was a post office. When the post office finally got to Cedar Grove before the turn of the century, there was already a Cedar Grove in western Maryland, so our Cedar Grove was named after a local family Named Deale. The first postmaster may have been a Deale relative.

The young bachelor group would car-pool, leaving most of the cars parked in Benny Weiner's parking lot. This store was diagonally across the street from Henry's store. One evening Carl Nutwell and I arrived at Weiner's store and found Lawrence Roger's car sitting alone while he rode with some one else. Carl said that he would fix the car to give Lawrence a thrill. He had one of those "Smoke and Squeal" bombs from Detroit's Johnson Smith & Co. that he fastened to the distributor. Days and months went by without Lawrence saying a word. Finally after two years he finally mentioned that some day he would find out who put the smoke bomb on his car. We still acted innocent, but that was our first clue that the device had worked. This was a payback for the time I came back from Wayson's Corner with Carl Nutwell. After he left I found that someone had jacked up a rear wheel on my car and I had to jack it up and remove the block before I could move.

In mid-summer of 1946 we had a mini-reunion of Mom's sisters and brothers. They all came to Deale to enjoy the Chesapeake Bay. We often took the CatBoat out of Parker's Creek during High tide and anchored it just outside the creek. I had built a small skiff and we would take it full of our folks out to the boat and go on an outing in the bay. There were plenty of fish in the Bay at that time.

It was on one of these skiff trips that I first met Jack McKibben. We had loaded the skiff with so many people that we only had about four inches of free board, but the creek was very shallow. Aunt Lois was sitting on the bow of the boat while I was operating the outboard motor on another skiff that I was using to tow them out of the creek. The tide had gone out, and when we tried to round the point by McKibben's house, the towed skiff touched the bottom and did a nose-dive, wetting Aunt Lois from the waist downward. Previous loud talk and laughing, had attracted Jack and his father to the yard, and when we went under, they practically rolled on the ground while the rest of us had a laughing fit trying to get the water out of the boat. We finally went on our way with everybody wet from the waist down. Jack was just ten years old at the time.

It was in early summer of 1948 that Mom and I had gone to pick blackberries on Virgil Howard's farm along Maryland Route 258. We had picked about a gallon of berries when I heard a whimpering puppy in the bushes. I told mom and evidently the puppy heard me and came to me. It whimpered with every step and when it came to me I was shocked to see that it was covered from head to toe with fleas.

It was a shorthaired mongrel and the fleas could be seen roiling on every hair, even in its ears and the edge of its eyes. There were tens of thousands of them. Since we were ready to go home I told Mom that I would take this poor abandoned puppy home and either get rid of the fleas or put it out of its misery.

Back at the house I couldn't find any insecticide in the garden shed except some rotenone powder that we had been using to kill flea beetles in our garden. I placed the puppy on some newspapers and powdered her from head to toe with this rotenone which is the same plant extract that was used to kill the northern Snakehead fish in the Southern Maryland pond in the fall of 2002. Soon the puppy fell asleep and in less than an hour there was a perfect outline on the paper of dead fleas from this puppy. They were two and three deep. I gently carried the puppy to our porch where she slept for 24 hours. When she woke up the next day she was the happiest puppy I had ever seen. I gave her a bath, fed her and named her "Mitzy."

We kept Mitzy for several months until a friend asked for her for her little girl. She said that girl dogs have a better personality than boy dogs. We gave her to the friend, but I will never forget this dog because of the agony I saved her from.

Not long after this, Mom's sister Lucille and her husband John Lynn moved to Deale from Piqua, Ohio with their three children, Dick, Lawrence (Butch), and Judy. Dick Lynn and Jack McKibben were in the same class at school and became friends. Before they were old enough to drive, I often took them roller skating in Annapolis.

And then I met Marjorie. Marjorie Moreland was in the same class with Dick and Jack and she also went roller-skating, but I didn't meet her there.

The Crotts brothers had built a barbecue restaurant across from Wheeler's Hardware where I would often come for a fine pork barbecue. I usually went in pretending to be starving and they would hurry to have a sandwich ready for me.

One day I went in for this purpose and noticed that there were two cute young girls working behind the counter. I soon learned that they were Iva Manifold and Marjorie Moreland. On a later day I went in to buy a sandwich and gave Marjorie a dollar bill to pay for one of their forty five-cent barbecue. When she put my change on the counter it landed in a puddle of water.

"Good for you," I said teasingly, "you have just passed the final exam to be a waitress. You have placed my change in the only wet spot on the bar." At this, Marjorie picked up a bar rag and wiped up the water and then tossed the wet rag in my face.

"This girl likes me." I said to myself. "Maybe I should ask her out." After a few more encounters at the restaurant she finally said that she would go for a ride with me in my newly acquired 1949

Ford, since I had gotten rid of my 1936 Pontiac (with the infamous knee action).

It was a hot July 7, 1952 that we drove down to the wide, sand beach at Fairhaven. The beach, now gone, was over two hundred feet wide at that time. Marjorie was wearing shorts and a terry-cloth top, which caused me to have an irrational desire to wash my hands and then look for a place to dry them. We didn't stay long at the beach since an angry, black cloud was approaching from the northwest. Before I got her back to the Ralph and Margaret Leitch household where she lived, it seemed that the whole bottom fell out of the cloud.

Marjorie's mother, Laura Woodfield Moreland had died when Marjorie was fourteen months old and the Leitch's took her to raise, Mrs. Leitch being a sister to Marjorie's father.

Eventually I would pick Marjorie up at the old Leitch store that was also their home, and we would go roller-skating in Annapolis, often taking Dick Lynn and Jack McKibben with us.

Marjorie and I soon became engaged, and on November 20, 1954 we were married at Cedar Grove Methodist Church while the rain fell in torrents. After the 4PM wedding we got into the 1949 Ford and drove to Sarasota, Florida. We spent our two-month honeymoon in a small house that Mom and Dad and I had bought the previous year with money from the sale of part of the Mason's Beach property.

Three years later our son, Carl was born on December 6, 1957, and our first daughter, Leslie was born ten and a half months later on October 25, 1958. We had planned to have them close to-gether so they could play together. As it turned out, they also fought together. We had decided to limit our family to these two children, so I went to see Dr. Davis, an urologist in Annapolis to get a vasec-tomy.

There is nothing very exciting about getting a vasectomy, but I neglected to go for the follow-up test to see if the operation was a success. Somehow I could just see the doctor give me a little cup and send me into a small room while he stood outside the door twid-dling his thumbs. At any rate Marjorie got pregnant again, and I started to tell her that I was like the meanest man in the world, who didn't tell his wife that he was sterile until after she got pregnant. I thought better of this corny joke and went for the follow-up test that I had delayed for almost a year.

Doctor Davis gave me the "Whoops" news that I was still just a wee bit virile and that he would do another vasectomy for free if I wanted. I wanted.

The first operation had cost seventy-five dollars, and so I got a "buy one and get one free" sale. Not many men can claim the distinction of having had two vasectomies.

Our last child, Brenda was born on April 15, 1960, and I always called her our little income tax deduction.

Chapter 31

Flying again

Flying was not a subject that I thought too much about in the early years of raising our family, but I often stopped by Lee Airport in Edgewater to look around. In those days of the mid forties to early nineteen fifties the Navy had a squadron of biplanes nick-named the "Yellow Perils" operating out of a large hangar that was located very close to Maryland Route 2 that ran near the airport. There was also a grass runway that ran alongside this highway where there is now a Giant Supermarket. Lee airport had been operating at this site since about 1930, and Kenny Lee was the manager after I started visiting there. He was later killed in a plane crash near Riva that is across Beard's Creek from the airport.

A few years after I started visiting the airport, the "Yellow Perils" were retired and the large hangar became a machine shop. There were no other buildings on the airport except a pilot's lounge next to Mom's Restaurant on route 2, so the planes all sat out in the open. Mom's Restaurant was exactly on the end of the runway as was the machine shop. Airplanes damaged both buildings several times by pilots landing long with not enough room to stop.

Then in 1959 I was coerced into joining the Civil Air Patrol. I helped build the CAP Quonset hut at Lee Airport and became a First Lieutenant in the Annapolis Senior Squadron, keeping my military rank, which was the custom. I later started the Deale Composite Squadron which had seniors and cadets. I was commander of the Deale squadron for a few years and then became Group three Commander.

In 1960, Turfield Miller started building a large hangar at Lee Airport after his business was moved from Harbor Field in Baltimore. He still called his business Baltimore Aero Service, and I became a regular visitor.

I also got to know Walter and Amy Neitzey who owned Deep Creek Airport in Churchton, Maryland. We went into a partnership to operate Deep Creek as a business, buying 80-octane aviation gas for twenty-five cents per gallon and selling it for forty cents. Sam Huntington and "Hank" Henry had airplanes at Deep Creek and were instrumental in getting me to fly again.

My first civilian flight was with "Hank" Henry who took me up in a Cessna 150. On our short trip to Easton Airport on the Eastern Shore of Maryland he gave the controls over to me and had me fly for a while and then make a turn. The last airplane I had flown was a B-17 and when I started my turn, Hank laid his hand on my arm and said rather casually,

"E-e-easy, Johnson, Its just like squeezing a titty. You do it gently." It had been fifteen years since I last piloted an airplane and the edges were pretty rough. Especially since the smallest airplane I had ever flown was a Stearman Biplane which is more than twice as big as a Cessna 150.

Sam Huntington and Hank Henry were pilots for Capitol Airlines, which later became part of United Airlines.

So here I was flying again and not being hollered at by instructors or being shot at for trespassing over the wrong area. It seemed that flying could actually be fun! One problem to be solved was my lack of a pilot's license since I had neglected to go for the paperwork in Tampa before getting out of the service. I had enough time to qualify for a commercial rating if I had taken the one-hour test. But at that time I never planned to fly again knowing that I couldn't afford it.

But now, I would spend seven dollars per hour for rental of a Piper Colt at Lee Airport for a little dual instruction. The Colt belonged to Mrs. Florence Parlett who was the owner of Annapolis flying service, operating out of Lee Airport. One of her instructors, Ed Sester took me up for a few hours until he decided that I was ready for the flight test. He had been charging me three dollars per hour for his time in the air with me. I don't know if I made him nervous, but he lit an awful lot of cigarettes while we flew together.

There was a joke about the two-place Colt and its four-place sister, the Tri-pacer concerning their respective glide ratios.

"If the engine quits, throw a brick out the window and follow it down, as that will be your glide angle." This was gross exaggeration, of course. Well, not very gross. The story goes that the owner of a Colt decided to carry a brick with him as he flew just in case he had an engine failure he could follow it down. Sure enough, one day he had an engine failure so he threw the brick out the window and tried to follow it down. He soon lost track of the brick but managed to get the plane on the ground without damage. Except that he no sooner got the plane stopped than the brick fell through his wing.

So, on December 15, 1963 I took the Colt over to Laurel, Delaware and came back the same afternoon with the rating of commercial pilot. I had about ten hours of dual and solo in the Colt at that time. The Colt was the first airplane I had ever flown that had the tail wheel up under the nose. Except for the one ride in the Cessna 150 that I didn't land that day.

I decided that flying could be fun under the right circumstances, so I got back with Walt Neitzey and we bought a 1941 Piper J-5 Cruiser as equal partners. We took up a few rides and did a little instructing of students, but the airplane was not paying for itself, so Walt sold me his half and I soon had a job with Dave Perko pulling aerial banners. I furnished the airplane and the gas and flew the banners over Washington and Baltimore for twenty-five dollars per hour, giving Neitzey ten percent off the top when I snatched banners from his field. The customer had to pay a thousand dollars for a minimum of ten hours flight time at the hundred dollars per hour rate in those days.

It took several hours to put a banner together with all the fiber glass rods between each letter and the little spring clips to hold the ribbons in their proper place. It was easy to have bleeding fingers when a banner was ready to fly. The weighted leader pole had to be fastened onto the forward end of the banner with a bridle of ropes leading to the hundred-foot leader line. The elongated drag and lift chute had to be mounted on the end of the banner to keep the banner flying high at the end and to keep it from snapping itself to pieces.

Then "Blackie" Blackwell heard about me. He wanted me to tow for him when I could, so I flew to Ocean City, Maryland one warm Saturday and thought that I would be towing banners with my J-5. But he wanted me to use his airplane instead. He had a Piper Cub, J-3 that he had been using part of the time as a spray plane. The normal J-3 has a 65 horsepower Continental engine, but this one had an 85 which looks very much the same as the 65. Also, the J-3 is supposed to be flown solo from the back seat because of weight and balance. This J-3 had a big empty spray tank in the back, and there was no seat, and so it had to be soloed from the front seat. Others had been flying it, so I supposed that I could do so by being very careful not to use the brakes, which would cause it to nose up easily on a landing roll. Brakes weren't needed on a J-3 anyhow, except for turning purposes, since it landed so slowly that it would run down by itself in three or four hundred feet after landing on grass.

A famous aerobatics pilot once said that 'the J-3 was a fine airplane and was so slow that it could just barely kill you.'

The banner was laid out along the edge of the runway at Ocean City Airport with a one hundred-foot leader that went back toward the tow plane. And the line was looped into a slipknot over two poles with the line hung loosely across them, held with clothespins. Just over the tail wheel was a hook that could be opened from the cockpit by yanking on a release line to drop the leader line and banner as a unit. Before takeoff a small, fifteen foot nylon rope with a three prong grab hook at the end was looped into the tail hook and the grab hook handed to the pilot through the side window of the cockpit.

Shortly after take-off, the pilot would toss the grab hook out the window, leaving it to dangle behind the tail on the end of this fifteen-foot rope. A low departure pattern was flown with a diving turn made to final to line up on the two poles containing the rope loop. This diving approach with wide open throttle was made to get all the speed possible, and just as the airplane crossed over the two upright poles with the rope, the pilot pulled up into a steep climb, trading airspeed for altitude. The banner was still lying ahead of the plane at a slight angle to prevent fouling. As the grab hook caught the pick-up loop a slight jolt let the pilot know that the banner had been captured.

He immediately leveled off and went on his way. The hundred miles per hour during pick up was reduced to eighty at level-off at about two hundred feet and the banner unrolled neatly and fell in behind the plane. The banner stayed upright because of a leader pole that had extra weight in the bottom end. It also had a small, elongated lift chute at the tail of the banner to prevent snapping and flutter and to keep the banner about level. Most banners pulled by small planes have five-foot letters. Larger planes can pull seven-foot letters and even "billboards."

On this day, I got into Blackie's J-3 and taxied out for my first banner. The little cub took off like a rocket with its larger engine, and I picked up the banner as usual. However, as I flew down the beach near Ocean City's famous boardwalk, I noticed that my visibility was fast disappearing due to oil slowly covering the windshield. The gas tank on a J-3 is just in front of the windshield and has a little wire on a float that bobs up and down on this wire in front of the pilot, which acts as a gas gauge. Soon the oil was so bad that I had to look out the side window to see properly. It is important to see properly when flying banners just barely above the water.

Finally I figured out a way to clean the windshield. I pulled the nose of the airplane up sharply and then pushed the nose down hard past the horizon to cause negative "G" forces, thus spraying gasoline out the little hole where the gas gauge wire emerged from the cowl. With a brief smell of gas, the windshield was clean for a while. Since the J-3 has no electrical system there is very little danger in this operation as all the heat from the engine is well forward of the gas fumes.

I towed seven banners for Blackie that day while cleaning the windshield about three or four times each trip, watching the oil pressure gauge very carefully. I later found that the culprit was a poor prop seal which allowed oil into the upper slipstream. Before I took my J-5 and went home, I told Blackie that I'd like to fly my own plane the next time.

Dave Perko had been towing banners out of College Park airport in Washington D.C for some time. Or, rather, he was having others tow them for him since he wasn't a pilot. Usually he would be there to signal if the approaching pick-up plane were too high or too low so that the pilot could adjust his altitude. Each miss was a go-around with loss of towing time and added gas and wear and tear on the plane.

At one time, College Park Airport inside the Washington DC Beltway had a cross-runway that extended almost to Arco airport next door. Arco was closed before I started towing there, and College Park's cross-runway was also closed, so we snatched the banners from that old runway and flew out over Arco, or in the opposite direction. We had to watch for traffic before we crossed over the active runway.

Finally, Mr. Brinkerhoff told us that we would have to snatch our banners off the edge of the active runway since our crossing pattern was un-nerving some of the other pilots doing an approach to landing. So we would have to take a place in the traffic pattern which was always busy on weekends when the Redskins were playing.

One Sunday Dave Perko sent me to tow a banner around the stadium while the Redskins were playing football. He couldn't go out there so he sent me alone. I was stationed at Deep Creek on the Chesapeake Bay, so we made up the banner there and I rolled it up and stuffed it into my J-5 with one end over my shoulder. I flew to College Park and unrolled the banner and set up my pick-up stakes and laced the rope over them. I put my grab hook on the tail and placed the grab end into the side window. I took off, tossed the grab hook out and got into a regular traffic pattern. None of this low stuff here. It came my turn and I approached the pick up point, yanked the plane up steeply, but felt nothing. I had missed the rope, so I got back into the pattern and tried again. I missed again.

"Damn, I'll be all day in the pattern and won't make any money at all." I thought One more time in the pattern and this time I know I'll get it because I'm a bit lower this time. Wham! I got it that time, but the airplane wallowed around like a beached whale. I looked out the window and saw that I had picked up the banner by the landing gear. Now I knew why I had missed. I was too low and the grab hook was bouncing on the ground and bounced over the rope, which is only about four or five feet off the ground. How it missed the prop I'll never know, but here I was headed toward the railroad tracks and the campus of the University of Maryland, barely climbing. I was going so slow that the air speed didn't register properly and I saw that I could not clear the trees next to the college, so I did a very shallow turn to the right and followed the low terrain behind the college.

Meanwhile I had reached out the window and was able to touch the polyester rope that was pulled up snugly around my landing gear. I reached into my pocket and took out my penknife, opened it and laid it on my lap. Since I couldn't drop the banner in the conventional manner, I was going to cut through the rope, airplane fabric and all if I found that I would not clear the trees. I was climbing so slightly that if the engine had hiccuped, I knew that I would be a BMOC. Not "Big Man on Campus," but "Big Mess on Campus."

Climbing ever so slowly, I finally got up to the thousand-foot altitude that four others and I were all towing from, and I went on flying and wallowing around the stadium for a half-hour. At the end of my allotted time I returned to College Park and landed on the hard surface runway, dragging the banner behind me. I noticed no ill effect during the landing, so I pulled off and removed the banner, rolled it up and went back to Deep Creek. It was not a good day.

Dave Perko had more confidence in our flying ability than we sometimes did. One day I was out of state at a Civil Air Patrol convention and Dave wanted a banner pulled, so Jack McKibben being a commercial pilot, took my J-5 and went to College Park to pull a banner that Perko had already set up. Jack looked at the banner and told Dave that this airplane only had an eighty-five horsepower engine, not a hundred and eighty five. Dave told him that they often pulled thirty-five letters in similar airplanes, so Jack gave it a try. They were using the cross-runway at that time so Jack snatched the banner and said that the airplane just seemed to stop in mid-air. He staggered out past the line of trees at the north edge of the field, but the banner didn't quite make it. He left three or four letters in the trees, but managed stay in the air. He towed the banner around the stadium minus four letters. "Your best banking is always done at

Subu...." (Suburban). Evidently the J-5 only wanted to pull 33 letters.

"Blackie" Blackwell often towed his own banners and one day he lost one over the edge of the stadium and it fell straight into the parking lot. The lead pole, which weighs about six pounds on the bottom end, stuck through the roof of a late model Cadillac. That's the kind of luck I would expect: don't hit anything cheap, hit a Cadillac.

When I bought the J-5, the wings were covered with "Razorback" fabric, which is a primed fiberglass. It is difficult to work with, so I covered the fuselage with "Eonnex", which is a polyester fabric coated with epoxy instead of the usual dope.

Late in the fall of 1968, when I thought banner towing season was over, a fellow offered me eighteen hundred dollars for my 1941 J-5 Cruiser, so I sold it to him. This was a premium price in 1968. At that time, Bob Orme from Mayo decided to sell his two airplanes. One was a 1946 Piper PA-12 Super Cruiser, which was parked at Lee Airport. He was asking twenty five hundred dollars and I told him that I had just sold my J-5 for eighteen hundred and I offered him that amount for it. He said,

"If Mrs. Parlett doesn't want any commission I will just take you up on that." So we went to see Mrs. Parlett and told her the problem. Her answer was simple.

"I have known both of you for a long time, and if this is a deal between the two of you, then I don't want anything from the sale. I wish the best for both of you." That was the end of her conversation and she went about her business. Dear Mrs. Parlett! And so I just endorsed my eighteen hundred-dollar check over to Bob and he signed the bill of sale.

There was no need for me to check out in the PA-12 since it is just a more modern version of the J-5. Both planes are three seaters, but the PA-12 has an electrical system and a starter, which the J-5 lacked. It also has a more powerful engine. Instead of the 85 horsepower Continental engine, It has a Lycoming engine that had been souped up to provide 115-horse power at take off.

A short time after I got the Super Cruiser I got a telephone call from "Blackie" Blackwell. He wanted me to tow a banner for one hundred hours in thirty days and I told him I would do it. But when I sold the J-5, I had neglected to keep the Gasser release hook that was on the tail, so I got busy that night and made one that looked exactly like the Gasser Hook that all the tow pilots were using. The next day I was at Deep Creek installing my new hook and release line when Blackie landed and brought the banner that he wanted towed. It read "DON'T BUY ESSO." He told me to tow it everywhere I could and to be sure to get the one hundred hours. He was to pay me twenty-five dollars per hour.

It seems that the "Don't Buy Esso" banner was being paid for by the union. Esso was buying gas pumps from a non-union factory in North Carolina and the union went on strike.

The banner was an old one that Blackie had made up from odds and ends of "rotten cotton," and used bamboo sticks instead of the usual fiber glass rods and nylon letters. It was so short that I didn't bother to snatch it off the ground, but merely laid it out ahead of the plane at an angle and dragged it off. The weather in December was brisk enough that the airplane fairly leaped off the ground and climbed steeply enough so that the banner didn't drag but just a little bit. I had decided to fly a four-hour flight on the first day and two three-hour flights on the next. Thus in twenty days I could fly the one hundred hours required. My range was under five hours, so I couldn't do a five-hour trip per day without getting dangerously low on fuel.

The weather was not good in December 1968 and I flew in the worst weather that I had ever flown in with a small airplane. One crystal clear morning with the wind blowing thirty-five miles per hour from the northwest, I took off with the banner and headed for Baltimore. I had planned to fly around Baltimore and then circle around to Washington and to Manassas, Virginia and back to Deep Creek. First I aimed toward Annapolis and on to Baltimore by way of Ritchey Highway. I flew along the highway and noticed a red Volkswagen coming up behind me. He soon passed me and went completely out of sight ahead of me. It took me an hour and a half to fly from Shady Side's Deep Creek airport to Baltimore, which is forty miles!

"Let's see," I thought. "If I go to Washington from here and then to Manassas, I will have this same head wind going home. That would take about an hour more than the gas would last." So I decided to stay up-wind, flew around Timonium and the Bowie-Belair area, until I figured that I had about an hour to go for my four-hour trip. It took twenty minutes to fly the fifty miles or so back to Deep Creek. My landing there, into a gusty 30 mile headwind, made my touch down groundspeed about 25 miles per hour.

One problem was the condition of the banner. It was so rotten that I had to fly at seventy miles per hour to keep from ripping it to shreds. I had to fly at nineteen hundred RPM instead of the usual twenty two hundred. Even then I had to spend two or three hours every evening just sewing patches on it. I got to be quite a seamster.

I had flown about fifty hours in December when I got a call from Mom who was living in Sarasota, Florida. Dad had been seriously disabled for some time with emphysema, and on December 23, 1968 he died. As I took my family to go to his funeral I left Walt Neitzey to tow the banner while I was gone. We were only gone a week since Marjorie had to get back to work at the Board of Education and I had to finish my banner towing. When I got back, Walt had only flown seven hours due to bad weather.

Horse races were going on every day at the Bowie Racetrack, which is only about twenty miles from home, so when I resumed the towing I circled that track every day. Finally the sports writer for the Washington Post wrote an article entitled, "Bowie fans get the Message." He tracked me down and called me on the phone one evening to find out what was going on.

One day I had started flying to Washington with the banner when I spotted a large Esso station. This was in the days before self serve and there were many employees. I made a tight circle around this station and on the second circle, one of the employees saw me. He called to the others and they all came out to see what was going on. Finally all the employees and a couple of customers were standing outside. I made another circle and went on my way leaving them to wonder why I was picking on them.

I wasn't as smart as Walt about the weather and one day while flying around Bowie there appeared some snow showers that got so intense that the engine started icing up and losing power. I had to add carburetor heat to get alternate air because the snow that was impacting the air scoop was choking off the filtered air. Also, since I was flying in IFR weather at times I would fly away from the race track until the weather cleared between snow showers so that any FAA man at the races wouldn't turn me in. I was following the horses around the track and since they made a smaller circle than I did, they always beat me. I was flying at seven or eight hundred feet.

Meanwhile, the Esso Company (now Exxon) complained to Blackie, asking why he was flying this banner when he already had a contract with them. Blackie told them a half-truth that he wasn't flying the banner but said that he could fly a counter-banner. They told him to go ahead, so he hired another pilot to follow me with a banner that said "Buy Esso Extra." Then the union complained that it looked like we were saying, "Don't buy Esso," "Buy Esso Extra." So Blackie said that he would counter that one too. He hired a third pilot to tow a banner that said, "The Tiger is a Scab." Talk about working both ends against the middle! At any rate the three of us would take turns leading or trailing, but usually taking off from different airports.

Eventually NBC sent a camera crew out to Deep Creek Airport to interview me and film a banner lift off. They also interviewed the union folks that were there for the publicity. During my interview the newsman asked me if I would use Esso gas in my airplane and I told them that if I had to I certainly would. This didn't set too well with the union when channel 4 used that statement to overshadow the message that the union was trying to get across. I had just about flown my hundred hours by then, and had been paid twenty five hundred dollars by Blackie. I made enough profit in that month to pay for my eighteen hundred-dollar airplane.

During election campaigning that year I was asked to tow a banner for Larry Hogan who was running for congress. I towed the banner for a few days and went on to other things. Then I had the bright idea that a simpler banner could be custom made instead of all the rods and pins and very expensive nylon letters.

So I got a sheet of polyethylene about fifty feet long and six feet wide. On my garage floor I painted a large figure 8 with space marks. I then laid the plastic sheet over the figure and started painting letters. Any letter can be made following various lines on the figure 8. With the help of my son, Carl who was 12 years old at that time, we painted, "VOTE LARRY HOGAN FOR CONGRESS." It was a short banner, but it was mostly for a test, so I attached the leader pole using duct tape and did the same with the tail chute. I had painted the sign with a fast drying black lacquer that adhered to the plastic well enough. So, one sunny day my whole family went to Deep Creek to see it fly.

The plastic banner was so short and light that I decided to save time and just fly it off the ground. So I laid it out ahead of the airplane as far as the leader line would allow and attached it to the tail hook of my plane. The take off went well and the banner flew well, and so light that I couldn't tell it was back there. Marjorie reported that it was easy to read and was quite stable. Of course I could look out the side window and see it also. I was very pleased with my invention. I could paint a letter a lot faster than pinning nylon letters in a series, and save a bundle on material at the same time.

And then the duct tape let go at the tail chute, which fell off, and the end of the banner started snapping like a flag in a gale. Soon pieces of poly were coming off the end of the banner. I slowed the plane down but it didn't help much. By the time I got back on the ground the banner read: "VOTE LARRY HOGAN FOR CON---"

I enlisted my family to help pick up scraps of poly plastic off the runway. Fortunately I had stayed over the field and didn't foul the environment. It just fouled my mood and Carl's, and I never did try it again, although with a better fastening system I might just---

Dave Perko brought three banners to Deep Creek one day and I was to fly one from there to the stadium where the Red Skins were playing again. I hooked my grab hook to the tail and took off. As soon as I was airborne I tossed the grab hook out the side window, but instead of dangling below the airplane like it is supposed to it just fell off onto the runway. My release hook had come open for some reason, so I immediately came around and landed. Dave came running up with another hook that was attached to a small steel cable and handed the grab hook in to me. I again took off and tossed it out the window and came around and made a high speed pass at the banner while Marjorie and the kids watched.

I hooked the pick up loop on the first pass and immediately pulled up steeply to trade speed for altitude. But when the banner took up slack, my rudder went to the full right position and the small cable locked it against the stop. This threw the plane into a violent skid to the right and the only way I could go straight ahead was in a full forward slip with the nose high. A very dangerous situation! Dave had handed me the hook and allowed the cable to go over the rudder horn instead of under it. When I tossed the grab hook out the window, the cable fell over the rudder horn and back. This meant that the weight of the banner would cause the rudder to lock so tight that I couldn't budge it with pressure on the rudder pedal. And the steel cable would not stretch to allow any slack.

I yanked the release cable until I actually tore a hole in the liner of the cockpit, but of course the banner would not release because the cable was aimed forward in the hook, over the rudder horn and then straight back.

As I tried to go straight ahead with wide-open throttle, the plane would shudder in a partial stall and start losing altitude, and I was only at a hundred feet at that time. The banner was starting to drag the ground and slid over a fence and a small cedar tree in Dr. Dent's yard. I could see out the side of the airplane and finally saw what the trouble was, and knew that I couldn't do any thing about it. I found my arm beginning to quiver as I pushed the throttle, and I was breathing audibly through my mouth. Finally, I said aloud, "Easy, Johnson, or you'll hyperventilate." Finally I discovered that a small push on the stick to the right would gain me about ten feet of altitude before the shuddering started again. Since the banner already applied full rudder, I could get a small gain during that brief moment of stick pressure. At one point I noticed that the air speed was reading an impossible twenty miles per hour. The plane would stall at 45 mph with full throttle.

Meanwhile, I was able to do my small increments so that I got the plane up to about a hundred and fifty feet and the banner no longer dragged the trees. I did a short right turn to final and landed on the right wheel holding full left aileron. With the banner dragging in the grass the landing roll was only about two hundred feet.

I taxied back and got out of the airplane.

"Dave Perko, you son of a bitch," I said, "are you trying to kill me right in front of my family?" Dave made no reply, getting busy laying out the banner again, and I got busy taping a small wrench across the rudder horn at an angle so that any future mishap of this sort would cause the cable to slip off the rudder horn. Of course, it was my own fault for not looking out the side window after throwing out the grab hook. I could easily see the rudder horn if I stuck my head out far enough, but I guess I didn't like the slipstream in my face. But I never towed another banner without looking at that rudder horn.

After this half-hour delay I went ahead and towed the banner after Dave strung it out again. Six weeks after this incident another pilot wasn't so lucky at Deep Creek. The same thing happened to him that happened to me, except he was flying a Citabria and it doesn't have the high lift wing of the Cub, and so he went down in the marsh off the end of the runway and flipped his plane upside down. Fortunately for him, the marsh was soft and not much damage was done to his plane. However it put him out of the banner towing business for a few weeks.

I have known of several pilots who were killed while doing banner work. Most of these were during the banner pick up phase of the operation. To do a neat pick up without too much stress on the banner, it is necessary to pull up quite steeply to trade speed for altitude. Unfortunately, those pilots who were killed or seriously injured either pulled up too steeply, or didn't push over quick enough. Air speed will bleed off at a high rate on the pull up and must be carefully monitored. Most of these banner-pulling planes have gravity feed gasoline systems with the gas tanks above the engine. On a hard push over, the negative "G" forces cause the gas to leave the carburetor, thus stopping the engine.

With only two hundred feet or less of altitude, it is impossible to get the nose down quickly enough to regain flying speed, and so the airplane will stall and fall to the ground when the engine quits.

Many of the young pilots who take up banner towing are low time pilots trying to get bigger numbers in their log books and get paid a few dollars at the same time. Two of these young pilots who barely had their commercial pilot's licenses were killed at Ocean City during my banner towing days. One young pilot did the steep climbout and pushed over too fast and being gravity fed, the gas left the carburetor and the engine quit and the plane fell straight down, breaking off both wings and destroying the airplane. The pilot survived this incident with a broken back. Done properly, banner towing can be fairly safe, but requires a great deal of skill and caution. It is not particularly hard on the airplane if not pushed too hard.

Airplane engines are a tough lot and will work surprisingly hard. Auto engines have been tried in airplanes, but usually their crankshafts aren't strong enough for the constant load. A modern limousine can normally go along at sixty miles per hour idling along using only about 35-horse power since it has its main workload on the road surface. This is in contrast to an airplane engine, which must work constantly to carry the weight of the airplane through the air.

Chapter 32

"GIs die, Mr. Nixon"

During the talking phase of the Vietnam War there were a lot of protesters, many of whom seemed to wish for the United States to lose this war. Many others merely wanted the United States to extricate itself from an unpleasant and unpopular war. The poor soldiers fighting this war were not receiving the proper support from the home folks, and many of America's fighting men had been dying for some obscure reason. Quite a few traitors did all they could to give aid and comfort to the enemy. These traitors became rich after the war, instead of the punishment that was meted out to the traitors of World War Two.

Mildred Gillers, a.k.a. "Axis Sally," was an American citizen during our war with the Axis powers. She was captured by American troops and went on trial for treason. She served a sentence of twelve years in prison for her activities, and has been living in the U.S. anonymously since her release from prison.

William Joyce, a.k.a. "Lord Haw-Haw," was a British citizen who also broadcast propaganda over German Radio, aimed at British and American troops. After his capture after D-Day he was tried by a British Court and found guilty of treason. He was sentenced to death and was later hanged.

During these Vietnam talks, money was raised by so-called Peace-niks for demonstrations against the war. These demonstrations took many forms, but one unusual form was the towing of a banner around the White House in Washington, DC.

One day, Dave Perko called me and said that he wanted me to tow a banner, so I went over to Deep Creek Airport to get ready.

I was there ahead of Dave and was fueling my plane when he unrolled the banner that I was to tow. He said that he wanted me to

tow it around the White House for half an hour. I read the banner:
GIs DIE WHILE TALKS GO ON, MR. NIXON. I told Dave that I
would not tow a banner for a bunch of Hippies to protest the war.
Dave said that it wasn't Hippies that asked for the banner, it was for
the philanthropist, Mrs. Cafritz. In that case I decided to pull the
banner, as I knew her to be a patriotic American.

There was, and is, a small forbidden zone over the White House
where, for security reasons, no one is allowed to fly. Also, just a few
blocks away, the Naval Observatory where the VP lives is also a
forbidden zone.

I approached the White House from the east and started a turn
around the outside of the observatory. This took me too close to the
Potomac River that was congested by airplanes going into National
Airport, so I counted the streets between the White House and the
Observatory. Since there was four city blocks between the forbidden zones, I decided to fly my subsequent circuits through that clear
area, and flew very carefully between them on all my subsequent
trips. I'm sure that if it had not been a protest banner, I probably
would have had a call from the Secret Service. Or perhaps a missile.
On one circuit I heard the air traffic controller talking to an airliner
coming down the Potomac and telling him that he had traffic near
the White House, which of course was me. The airline pilot told the
Controller,

"I have him in sight. It's a plane pulling a banner."

"What does it say?"

"It's a protest banner."

"Roger, continue your approach."

I made it a point to never say anything on the radio unless I was
in trouble. I didn't wish to be identified, as I was flying at an altitude
that might be interpreted as being below the minimum allowed. I
was indicating about a thousand feet, so that Mr. Nixon could be
sure to read the banner. An engine failure at that altitude would have
found me on the Ellipse. The Mall was still full of streets that were
full of traffic at that time.

After I made ten circles around the White House I returned to
Deep Creek Airport and dropped the banner. A photographer with

the Washington Post had taken a telephoto picture of the banner for their next edition.

I believe that I am the only pilot who ever towed a banner around the White House. The others are probably too smart.

On one banner-towing trip to Washington pulling a bank sign, I found the weather going so sour that I could barely make out the streets in Washington. My compass was not acting quite right, so in order to find my way back to Deep Creek, I lined up on the streets of Washington and set the Directional Gyro on 90 degrees and headed for home. My DG precessed at about three degrees in fifteen minutes, so that wasn't a problem. The problem was the weather. A huge thunderstorm had built up between Washington and home while I was busy over RFK stadium. I was not able to penetrate the backside of this storm and it was getting late in the day. As I tried several places, I finally gave up and headed toward Freeway Airport near Bowie.

By then, the rain was coming down in torrents, and lightening was blinding. I crossed over John Cohen's private strip and almost landed there because of the darkness and lowering ceilings, but I could see Freeway not too far ahead, so I elected to go there. I flew into the wind and dropped the banner alongside the runway and decided to land down wind since it was so dark I was afraid to make another circuit of the field. So I landed down wind, down hill, and used every inch of the runway. It was raining so hard that the tires would hydroplane when I touched the brakes.

As I taxied up to the gas pump, Stanley Rodenhauser was sitting in the lounge. I got out of the plane and walked over to greet him. He said that he thought that he would have to scrape me off the end of the runway. I called Marjorie and told her where I was and she agreed to bring the children and come get me. We had always flown there and neither of us had ever driven to Freeway Airport and didn't know how to find it by road.

I told Marjorie that I would walk out to Route 50 which goes along the north end of the airport, and she could pick me up from under the nearby overpass.

I stood under the overpass for over an hour, being driven up to the very narrowest part of the structure by cells of driving rain. Meanwhile, Marjorie was having her problems.

On State Route 468, a low lying field had water over the top of fence posts and many roads were flooded. She had to make a few detours to even get to route 50, and at times it rained so hard that she had to pull off the road. But she finally found me, wet and cold, crouched up as high as I could get to avoid getting any wetter. We made our way back home and the next day she drove me back to retrieve the airplane. I picked up the banner that I had dropped along the runway, and flew back to Deep Creek. I really earned that fifty-dollar banner-towing job.

As I mentioned in my early life experiences, thunderstorms have not been too friendly to me because, exactly ten days after the first thunderstorm, I was caught in an almost identical situation. I had flown a banner around RFK stadium in Washington and while I was there another big storm developed all along the Patuxent River and I could not penetrate the backside of it.

So I decided to fly to Lee Airport in Edgewater, since the day was getting late and the clouds made it even darker. I was driven down to five hundred feet by scud and torrents of rain until I decided to fly into a small opening in the backside of the storm. As I flew into this "sucker hole" as they are known, it closed in on me so quickly that I went IFR for a short while, being driven down to two hundred fifty feet. Fortunately I knew the territory well enough to know that there were no towers in that area, so when I got turned around again, I found the edge of South River. I flew along the edge of the river until I came to Beard's Creek. Dropping down to two hundred feet I flew along until I spotted a large number 12 on the ground.

I knew this to be the runway, so I dropped the soggy banner alongside, and, decided to land on the grass. I made this stupid decision in order to protect the airplane somewhat in case I nosed over with all the water over the runway. When I touched down it looked like a speedboat throwing a great plume of water. I had to add a little power to keep from nosing up. The water was at least four inches deep, and as I taxied up to the hanger door I stepped into water over my shoe tops.

Then I did another stupid thing. After I tied the airplane down, I decided that the banner might be partly on the runway and create a hazard the next morning, so I started walking down the runway to retrieve it.

Lightening was striking all around as I walked down the runway, and it's a wonder that I wasn't struck, being the highest object in that area. I suppose the rain was falling so hard that the lightening couldn't see me. I gathered up the banner with the metal clips and headed back to the flying service office that was still open. As I walked in, soaked so thoroughly that even my credit cards in my wallet were wet, a man asked me,

"Was that you who landed a short while ago?"

"Yes, that was me, and as you can see I am wet all the way through."

"Wow, I have never seen anyone land like that before. With all that spray I thought it was a speedboat." He said.

"And it is going to be my last such landing." I replied. "I think I just used up eight of my nine lives."

Two category 6 thunderstorms in ten days were enough for anyone. (Thunderstorms are rated from one to six. The weather service reported that both of these storms topped sixty five thousand feet!).

Chapter 33

Rev. Harold L. May

Harold May came to Deale to be the pastor at Cedar Grove Methodist Church in 1961. He was interested in aviation and wanted to learn to fly, so he looked me up. I gave him a few lessons in my J-5 Piper Cub until he got ready to solo. Walt Neitzey gave him a check ride and sent him out on his own.

Soon after solo, Harold bought an Aeronca Champ from near Gettysburg, Pennsylvania, and I was elected to go get it for him. Frank Miller had a late model Cessna 172 that he flew Marjorie and I to get it. But first we flew to the Civil War Battlefield to take a short air tour. After a few passes between the various monuments, we found the grass airstrip where the Champ was located. After a thorough pre-flight, I pronounced the plane sound enough, so Frank gave the prop a spin and I was off to Deep Creek airport. The Champ is much like the Piper J-3 with tandem seating for two. The student would sit in the front with the instructor in the back. Unlike the J-3, which was soloed from the back seat, the Champ was soloed from the front. It flew much like the J-3 except it was a bit heavier and landed a few miles per hour faster.

I had helped Harold set up a print shop in Deale after he acquired an old letter- press and a few dozen fonts of lead type. We printed posters and letterheads, business cards and such, setting the type piece by piece from the small bins that are now popular with antique dealers. The printing business didn't do very well, except on one occasion when a vandal desecrated St. Marks Episcopal Chapel. The damage was discovered at eight in the morning and by ten I had a poster on the door offering a five hundred-dollar reward for the arrest of the culprit. I had gotten that much telephone pledges before I started printing the many posters. We never had to collect the pledges, since the vandal was not arrested, even though many people thought they knew who he was.

After Harold gave up the print shop, he decided to fly to Duke University to further his education. Every week he flew the trip to Durham, North Carolina; went to school for the week and returned to Deale for the weekend. He found that the airplane didn't have enough range for the trip, so he landed in a farmer's pasture next to a gas station on the highway where he took a five gallon can to buy auto gas for the rest of the trip. This was before there was an STC (supplemental type certificate) for auto gas that could be used in various planes.

On one trip the weather turned a little bad and he got lost. So he picked out a nice big pasture and landed. The farmer who owned the farm was a devout Methodist and with Harold landing there was like a message from Heaven. Harold spent the night, ate with them, and made many return trips.

Without further incident, Harold finally graduated from Duke and we all went to his graduation.

Back in Deale, things returned to normal and we took turns flying the Champ, or my J-5. Harold didn't get his private pilot's license until he was transferred to Hillcrest Heights, Maryland where he took additional flight training. While he was still living in Deale I recruited him to be chaplain of the Deale Civil Air Patrol Squadron that I had started just a short time earlier. Most of his daughters became Civil Air Patrol Cadets.

Harold and Helen had five daughters, Gracie, Pamela, Beth, April, and Christy. Mrs. Helen May didn't much care for flying, but all the girls loved it and Gracie insisted that I fly aerobatics with her, so I did the limited aerobatics that the Champ is capable of.

One day, with Gracie in the front seat we were flying around the edge of the Chesapeake Bay and I was doing an occasional aerobatics maneuver. Loops were easy enough, and spins were OK but her favorite was the hammerhead turn. This is accomplished by flying into a slight dive to gain airspeed, adding power and pulling the nose straight up, using the wing as reference. As soon as the wing tip was vertical to the horizon, I would apply full rudder in the direction I wanted to go. As soon as the nose dropped straight down and backpressure added to the stick, the throttle was closed to idle. Upon pull out, the track over the ground was reversed from the starting maneuver.

On this particular day, we had done several hammerhead turns and I decided to do just one more to please Gracie. I pulled the airplane into its vertical climb and decided to turn to the left. But no, I had already done several to the left and at the last sec I decided to do this one to the right.

Too late! The airplane stopped in midair with the nose pointed straight up. It then did a tail slide, falling about a hundred feet backwards. Instinct had me pull the stick back, thus causing the airplane to change ends, well past the vertical, going straight down. As it gained airspeed it was as if a giant sledgehammer had struck the bottom of the fuselage. With a resounding "Whump" the cockpit was filled with dust, debris, pencils, paper clips, charts, coins, and anything ever lost in the airplane.

And the engine stopped. We were at fifteen hundred feet and not close enough to Deep Creek to glide there on a dead engine. I started looking for a place to put down "an arrival" short of the airport, but none seemed particularly good. It was very quiet.

Finally I leaned up and pointed to the instrument panel.

"Gracie, do you see that little round thing? Twist it to the left and pull it out." She figured out that the primer was what I was pointing to and did as I requested. Although the engine had quit, the propeller was still turning. Thank Goodness for a metal prop.

"Now push it in with the heel of your hand, rather quickly."

When she did so, the engine caught for a few seconds, and the plane surged ahead a few dozen feet.

"Do the same thing over and over," I said, "while I aim for the field." After about fifteen of these maneuvers we managed to stretch our glide enough to make the field with room to spare. Of course when we landed the propeller stopped turning and our friends at the airstrip had to come push the plane the rest of the way.

Upon taking the carburetor apart, it was found that trash had stirred up into the float valve, thus cutting off the fuel to the engine. The primer works independently of the carburetor, thus our ability to feed two cylinders of the engine with "an eye dropper."

I do not recommend a tail slide in any light plane not specifically designed to do so. It is very stressful on the airframe. And, the pilot. But Gracie thought it was all just great until I did the tailslide. She wasn't too happy about that, but didn't get perturbed.

Don Parks had a Cessna 140 at Deep Creek and he was also a good friend of Harold May. One day an L-16 belonging to the Maryland Civil Air Patrol got away from the driver, who was hand propping it alone. It got away from him and chewed the right wing off Don's 140, so he and Harold decided to go partners and buy a Taylorcraft that was for sale in Pennsylvania. It was a BC-12D model that had a side by side configuration. Rev. May was elected to fly it home, so they drove up to get it.

The airplane was out of license, but what the heck, it seemed OK, so Harold hopped in and took off for Deep Creek. He got lost again. Seeing a highway under construction with workmen on a portion of it, he decided to land to find out where he was. The Taylorcraft flies much like the Aeronca Champ, but will land much slower. As Harold flared to land, the "T-craft" as it is called, floated and floated, until he saw that he couldn't make it. So he added power to give it another try. But he didn't quite clear a bulldozer that was parked on his "runway." At about 30 mph his left landing gear caught the bulldozer and dumped him straight down, destroying the airplane and breaking two ribs on our errant pilot. So his total time in a Taylorcraft was one take-off and one "arrival."

Harold didn't want anyone to know that he was flying illegally, so he cut the numbers off the side of the airplane before the newspaper took a picture. After he got back to Deale he didn't tell anyone except Don and me about the mishap, even concealing his injury from the parishioners. His wife Helen then told me that he even hid the injury from her. Her first knowledge of it was the preliminary reading of this account.

But somebody in Pennsylvania knew somebody in Deale and sent a copy of the newspaper article to him or her, and the word was out. There were no repercussions, except a lot of kidding.

Poor Don Parks didn't have much luck with airplanes, and eventually gave up flying.

After seven years as pastor of Cedar Grove Methodist Church, Harold was transferred to a church in Indian Head, Maryland where he finished his flight training. He then flew weekly to Duke University to finish his Seminary work. Upon his graduation there, the Deale area was well represented by his many friends, including Marjorie and me.

After being transferred to Hillcrest Heights, Maryland in the early 70s he developed leukemia and his doctors decided to try blood platelets to be donated by his daughter Beth who was in Navy Boot Camp in Florida. The navy was reluctant to release Beth for this purpose until the Red Cross "went to bat" for them.

The platelet infusion worked for only a shot time and he died on March 7, 1978. And so I lost another good buddy.

Harold's wife, Helen died on June 29, 1997 from complications of diabetes and kidney failure. Their oldest daughter Gracie who loved the aerobatics is now a grandmother.

Chapter 34

Crash of a Vickers Viscount

Just two years after I joined the Civil Air Patrol, a Vickers Viscount crashed near Ellicott City, Maryland after striking a flock of Whistler Swans. The Maryland Wing of the CAP was immediately called out to the crash site to search for clues and airplane parts of this Capital Airlines commuter plane.

In just a few hours we had found all the parts of the doomed plane and a part of the swan that brought it down. The CAP stood guard on the site until the FAA had removed the black box and other such items. Maryland State Police and coroners deputies gathered up the parts of the seventeen people who perished in the crash.

Incredibly, the black box revealed that the airplane had struck the swans at the unbelievable altitude of seventeen thousand feet. The main impact was near the root of the right horizontal stabilizer where a six-inch diameter hole was driven through the main spar, spraying the entire inside of the stabilizer with swan parts. The body of the swan passed through the forward spar and bent the rear spar, jamming the elevator hinge in a slightly up position. This caused the plane to nose up into an uncontrolled climb. The pilot quickly reduced power to the four turbo-prop engines so that the plane mushed along in a nose high attitude. He immediately declared an emergency for a landing at Friendship International Airport and was cleared straight in. As the flight progressed, the pilot had managed to get the airplane down to six thousand feet at which time the stabilizer broke off at the hole that was caused by the impact with the swan.

This immediately put a double load on the left stabilizer and the airplane pitched nose down steeply. The pilot had no option but to pull back on the yoke to try to bring the nose up.

When flying, all aircraft have a sizable download on the horizontal stabilizer in order to maintain stability, and to compensate for weight and balance differential. In the case of a large airplane the download may at times be hundreds of pounds pressure. With one side of the horizontal stabilizer lost, the other side had to double this download in order to maintain controlled flight.

At six thousand feet the left stabilizer broke off due to this increased load. The nose immediately pitched down into a dive past the vertical until it struck the ground in an eighty-degree inverted position. With the loss of the tail, any plane will seek its best streamline flight, which is almost always in an eighty degree inverted dive.

The destruction was complete, and of course there was an explosion. Fortunately, no one on the ground was killed in this freak accident.

One of the strange incidents of this accident was that Jack McKibben and Sam Huntington, my good friends, were at the site. I flew with Sam that day, but I never knew that Jack was flying one of the search helicopters at that time. Sam and I directed a ground crew to parts of the swan while another crew found the severed right stabilizer more than a mile from the other.

Chapter 35

Crash of a B-52 carrying 2 Hydrogen Bombs

On January 13, 1964 a B-52 carrying two hydrogen bombs crashed on Big Savage Mountain near Cumberland, Maryland and the Civil Air Patrol was called out to look for it and the crew members that had bailed out of it. During a bitterly cold blizzard in the middle of the night, the huge bomber had encountered violent turbulence at high altitude and the tail of the craft was wrung off. The bomber immediately nosed over, out of control in a steep dive. Most of the crew was in summer flight clothing when they bailed out, but the bailout kit contained protective clothing and a tent of silver Mylar. Also in the kit were some food rations, a first aid kit, and a small thirty-caliber carbine.

The next day we found where the bomber had crashed and burned, but the bailed out crewmen were nowhere to be found. It was later determined that the radar bombardier, Major Robert J. Towney had gone down with the plane. His body was found at the crash site. The blizzard prevented effective search, and the National Guard arrived, as well as a ranger team and units of the Air Force and Navy. Inter-service rivalry was still in full effect and so the Civil Air Patrol was eventually charged with coordinating the entire mission, assigning ground and air teams to look for the downed airmen. Heavy equipment was needed to bring out the wrecked bomber and the two damaged hydrogen bombs. This was all done by the Air Force while the search for the missing crewmen was going on. Examination of the wreckage indicated that four men had managed to get out of the doomed plane.

The pilot of the plane, Major Thomas W. McCormick, had landed near a roadway and was getting his gear laid out when he saw cars on this road, plowing through the snow, so he simply walked up the embankment and caught a ride to the village.

Due to the weather, it was two days before another man was found, frozen to death. One of our search planes directed a ground team to where a parachute tent was seen with tracks in the snow leading up the mountain. When the search team reached the survival tent they found it empty, so they followed the tracks in the snow which led them through drifts that reached their armpits at times. Up the side of the mountain was a barn that the tracks seemed to be headed towards, but the team found provisions that had been thrown away by the man that they had determined to be the navigator, Major Robert L. Payne. Major Payne's tracks led to the barn, which was open on both ends. By the time he had reached the barn he was so numb with cold that he had lost his reasoning powers.

He had walked through the barn and gone on about a hundred feet where the rescue team found his frozen body. He still had matches in his pocket that he could have used to burn the barn if his mind had not been so impaired by the cold.

That same afternoon another survival tent was spotted and as the search plane circled, a man stepped out and waved at them. It was the co-pilot, Captain Parker C. Peedin, who had landed in a clearing. He had set up his tent and gotten inside and stayed "cozy warm" until he saw the rescue team coming to get him. He said that it was when he stepped outside to get back into his flight gear that he got cold for the first time. He had gotten so warm in the tent that he had taken off his outer garments. And the temperature had stayed at ten below zero all during the three day search, with winds blowing from the northwest at twenty to thirty miles per hour, making the wind-chill factor about forty degrees below zero.

Four days after the crash, on January 17th, the third and last survival tent was found near West Salisbury, Pennsylvania in an open field, but it was only laid out and was not erected. The Civil Air Patrol plane that spotted it reported that there were tracks leading away from the orange parachute toward the small village. I personally went with the rescue team that was to find the last man, tail gunner, Tech. Sgt. Melvin Wooten. As we got to the site we noticed that the village of West Salisbury was only about five hundred feet from his landing site. Sgt. Wooten had laid his gear out in preparation to set up the Mylar tent when he evidently heard noise from the village and decided to walk there. What he didn't know in the darkness was that a small creek lay between him and the town.

He had broken a leg during his blind landing and was trying to get help at the village. After he struggled through the deep snow for several hundred feet, he came to the creek. His tracks showed that he had stopped there for a few minutes, perhaps calling for help, but of course no one was out in the middle of the night in a blinding blizzard.

At last he turned to his right and started walking along the edge of the small creek. After about two hundred feet he tripped over a tree root and fell partly into the creek, which was not frozen at that time. This is where we found him, frozen in the ice. We had to use axes to cut through the ice that was about six inches thick by that time. We took his body to a house in the village that he had been trying to reach. It was there that the medical examiner found that he had suffered the broken leg.

Before we were able to leave Cumberland and clear up the paper work, a flat bed tractor-trailer arrived with the two hydrogen bombs that had burned in the crash. They were covered with a tarp somewhat, but I could see that they were about the size of a Volkswagen "Bug." A technician told me that the case of these bombs was over six inches thick of tool steel and could be dropped from any height on bedrock without rupturing the skin to release any radioactive material. Even burning in the crash had no effect on them, but merely stripped off the fixtures, such as the parachute shroud that would lower them to the ground should they ever be dropped in anger.

Also, the danger of accidental triggering was practically impossible. Even the officers on the plane that might drop them could not activate the fuses by themselves. One officer had to go to the bombs and perform a series of functions. Then the other officer went to them and did another function. Neither officer had any idea what the other officer was doing. I believe that this system is still in effect to this day.

An Air Force C-124 Globemaster was brought to Cumberland to

carry the bombs and some secret electronics back to their base for repair or disposal.

General Curtis E. LeMay, Air Force Chief of Staff extended his "grateful thanks" to the Civil Air Patrol personnel for their dedication to the job at hand despite severe weather during the operation. This search and rescue mission was probably the highlight in the history of the Maryland Civil Air Patrol's activities, before or since.

The next year after the B-52 crash, a Cessna 210 crashed near Hagerstown, Maryland, The Cessna, a light twin engine craft, had disappeared after canceling an Instrument Flight Plan while still on approach to Hagerstown. Evidently the pilot was able to see the airport from some distance and thought to save time with procedural turns. Unfortunately there were clouds in the area and as he let down in a line to the airport, he missed the gap between two mountains and crashed while in the cloud.

The Civil Air Patrol was called to look for the crash site and after many fruitless sorties we flew into the edge of Pennsylvania and found the crash site. We immediately called the CAP Pennsylvania Wing and asked them if they would like to finish the mission since it was in their area. Their operations officer said that since we had found the crash, we could finish the mission and they gave us permission to go into their territory.

Since the crash was on a steep mountainside, we called in an Army helicopter to take us as near as possible to the site. A huge, twin rotor H-21 "Flying Banana" arrived and we all piled in. We landed at the base of the mountain and started climbing a sixty-degree slope covered with loose stone. It was so bad in places that one had to cling to small trees and bushes to proceed. We finally reached the scene of the crash and of course there were no survivors. The customer had arranged with the pilot for a flight to visit their son who was graduating from a nearby school. Lost in the crash was the pilot, the man and wife and ten-year-old daughter.

Again we called in a Ranger team who went to the top of the mountain and cleared a patch of woods big enough to get a helicopter in. They then carried the bodies to that clearing and a helicopter brought them out.

The Civil Air Patrol held many training sessions for the Seniors and Cadets, including simulated air rescues, or SARCAPs. On one appointed day, Billy Franklin and I flew an L-16, Aeronca Champ to Lee airport in Edgewater, only to find that Mrs. Parlett had canceled flights that day because of high winds. So Bill and I decided to fly back to Deep Creek before it got any worse. Bill had his pilot's license so I was sitting in the back seat with my arms folded. Just at flare, a sudden downdraft dropped the plane about ten feet onto the ground with a resounding crash, breaking the right landing gear which then hung by one pin down below the door,

"You take it," he said, since I had been instructing him earlier. He was quite upset. The plane had bounced back into the air, and with the added throttle, continued to fly.

"Thanks a lot." I said, as I kept the airplane near the ground in case anything was seriously broken. I shook the controls to give added stress to the airframe just to be sure that it would continue to stay in one piece. I finally landed the airplane on the left gear and right wing tip. No further damage was done, not even to the wing tip. It cost fifteen dollars to repair the plane.

Billy was later killed when his Cessna Cardinal crashed on a take-off from a New York airport while he was en route to Alaska. So I lost another friend.

In 1972, after serving in many positions in the Civil Air Patrol, including Wing Operations Officer for a time and Aircraft Maintenance Officer for a longer time, I finally retired from the CAP at the rank of Lt. Colonel which I had held for a few years.

Chapter 36

Drugs

In May 1977, the Archeological Society of Maryland, Inc. conducted a dig for their annual Field Session, a hands-on teaching tool for archeological enthusiasts and professionals. I was president of the Anne Arundel Chapter and we sponsored the dig at a large Indian village site on the Sansbury farm near Rose Haven. The Indian site was in a large field where corn was just about knee high. In the course of the dig we found many artifacts while digging in only two hundred seventy five square feet of a site that is a quarter mile long and five hundred feet wide. We had over eighty volunteers and professional archeologists participating in the dig for ten days.

But that is not what this story is about. Before the dig started, I had to make several trips to the site to clear brush and find spaces for people to park.

On a fine Thursday, May 26, a week before the dig was scheduled to start my wife Marjorie and I went to the site only to find an airplane sitting in the cornfield. It was a rather large, single engine plane that looked a bit like an overgrown Cessna 182. Along the road were several pick-up trucks and cars, all with Virginia license plates. Several guards were posted around the field, which was about a thousand feet long. Something didn't look right to me so I started walking toward the airplane with Marjorie, but was stopped by the guard before I got within a hundred feet of him.

"Get back," he yelled, "we are about ready to take off."

"I have permission to be here." I yelled, and continued to walk toward the plane. "Do you have permission to be here?"

"Yes we have permission, and I'm telling you to get back, and I mean it." Meanwhile the pilot started the engine and the plane began to taxi to the end of the field away from the road that was about six feet above the level of the cornfield.

"Come back Dick," Marjorie said. "Don't get involved with them. Something doesn't look right about this." Not being too bright, I continued my harangue.

"Did you tell the FAA or the farmer about this?" I yelled.

"Yes, we called the FAA and the farmer." He yelled back as the plane turned toward the long direction of the field.

"Did you call the police to block traffic on the road?" I insisted, as the airplane started its take off run.

"Yes we called the police," he yelled, "What do you think we are, a bunch of amateurs?" About then the pilot of the plane realized that he couldn't get enough speed and suddenly chopped the throttle, whereupon the plane stopped and gas continued through the engine and ran out through the exhaust pipe to the ground and caught fire.

"You look like a bunch of amateurs to me," I yelled with my hands cupped to my lips, "Ha! Ha! Ha!"

"Oh, buddy, you don't know what you're talking about." the guard yelled as he ran to the plane. Before he got there the fire went out by itself after scorching the bottom of the cowl and a small patch of corn.

"Come on, let's get out of here." Marjorie insisted, so I finally realized that I could only get in more trouble if I persisted in my inappropriate behavior, so Marjorie and I left, deciding to come back the next day, Friday May 27th.

In our archeological chapter was an Anne Arundel County Police officer who wanted to attend the dig, so I took him with me on this Friday mission, expecting the airplane to be gone. At first I didn't see it behind a small stand of underbrush but it had been hidden from the road and could only be seen from the dig site, so the officer and I walked over to take a look at it. There was not a soul around and the plane was empty. It had large cargo doors on each side and a large flat floor. From the data plate that I could see inside the airplane I could see that it was a Lockheed 60, a plane that I was not familiar with. As it turned out, only a few had been built.

After walking around the plane a couple of times the officer said that something was fishy and not to touch it. We then went about the business of preparing the archeological site and then left for home.

The next day, Saturday May 28, 1977, Marjorie and I went to the wedding of Bob and Shirley Dunlap's daughter Bobbi, which was held in the morning, with the reception in the early afternoon. As soon as that was over, we returned to the dig site as people were arriving in their campers. The police officer had already brought a drug-sniffing dog to the airplane and taped it off. He said that the dog "went crazy" around the airplane.

Meanwhile the dig went on and the airplane remained on the field during that time, and the poor police officer never got to participate in the dig during his vacation. A few days after the dig was over, I happened to be on Maryland Route 2 when I met a truck carrying the dismantled plane down the highway.

The plane belonged to a fixed base operator at Eastern Airport near Baltimore who had leased it to a group transporting Washington Evening Star newspapers from Washington to Salisbury. What the group didn't tell the owner was that they weren't coming back empty, but were hauling drugs on the return trip. On this trip the plane broke an oil line and made an emergency landing in Sansbury's cornfield. After they had fixed the oil problem, they off-loaded their cargo, and tried to take off across the rows of the knee-high corn and soft dirt. Even though they had removed all of the cargo, the plane still was not able to make it out. Mr. Sansbury, who owned the farm, never did know about the airplane in his field or what had damaged his corn.

I later learned that the Drug Enforcement Agency sold the airplane and kept the money because of its clandestine activities, even though the owner didn't know that it was being used for a criminal purpose. I could never quite understand that system.

Airmen, and especially pilots, are special breeds. Facing death or serious injury, they sometimes shake off the adrenaline rush and make some of the most outlandish statements after a near disaster.

In 1952 an Air Force Pilot in a P-80, shooting star had a flameout over Venice Florida while I was there. Instead of jumping out and leaving it up there, he decided to dead-stick it into Venice Municipal airport which is an old Army airfield from World War Two days. It lies very near Florida State route 41. He slightly misjudged his approach and landed halfway down the runway going off the end and plowing up an eighth of a mile of palmetto brush before stopping a hundred feet from Rt. 41.

A motorist on the road scrambled through the palmetto brush and found the pilot standing on the wing.

"Hey, buddy," the pilot said, "where can you get a cup of coffee around here?"

In a more recent incident, My friend Jack McKibben tells of an F-14 Tomcat that was shooting landings on an aircraft carrier when his plane hopped the hook and went off the end of the carrier. It disappeared over the edge and men started running forward, only to see the plane reappear, going straight up with afterburners blasting away, and water pouring off the tailpipe where he had touched the water while rotating.

Gaining speed in a vertical climb the plane passed through five thousand feet when the Landing Signal Officer spoke on the radio.

"Sir, I remind you that the pattern altitude is fifteen hundred feet." There was no answer, and the plane continued its vertical climb until it was near fifteen thousand feet. Again the LSO spoke on the radio.

"Sir, I remind you that the pattern altitude is fifteen hundred feet, do you read me?"

Finally the pilot answered,

"Lieutenant Smith, do I ever bother you while you're taking a crap?"

During the early days of 1998 a Cobra Helicopter pilot had a flameout at night and had to do an autorotation at his airport. He misjudged his flare and landed tail first, breaking off the entire tail. Of course, without torque control, the rotors caused the machine to slide and spin down the runway. Seeing all the sparks in the darkness, the tower asked the pilot,

"Sir, do you need assistance?"

"Not yet," the pilot replied, "we haven't finished crashing."

Airmen also protect each other to a degree. At Lee Airport in Edgewater, Maryland, Turfield Miller was the fixed base operator for many years. Being rather outspoken, he was constantly being harangued by the FAA for little nit-picking things that they perceived to be a violation of regulations. Most of these FAA guys were young, wet-behind-the ear types, while Turfield was repairing airplanes since before WW 2.

Many years ago, Jack McKibben kept a Pitts Special at Lee Airport, and used it as a base while he did air shows. During one of his take-off routines he rolled the small biplane on its back for the climbout. It just happened that one of these FAA guys was at the airport talking to Turfield, when Turfield happened to notice Jack's illegal maneuver. Putting his arm around the shoulders of the Fed, Turfield aimed him toward the open hangar door until McKibben was out of sight. It happened that Jack stayed inverted all the way around the pattern and the Fed saw him roll upright before the approach. Thinking that Jack had just rolled inverted for a steep carrier-type landing he chewed Jack out when he got back to the field. He hadn't seen the inverted take-off and climb-out because of Turfield's help. Had the Fed seen this he probably would have written Jack up for not having an air show permit.

One Saturday the gang at Lee Airport decided to have a contest and I participated in the spot-landing contest. In this event a stripe is placed on the runway, and the fliers tried to do a full stall landing as close as possible to this stripe. The closest won a six-pack of beer to be consumed at Turfield's Saturday Crab feast at the hangar. I did pretty well with my Piper cub, J-5, landing three-point about fifty feet past the stripe. This was very much like my "Hurdles" at primary flight school in which I was required to land three-point within two hundred feet past a ribbon held twenty feet high by a couple of instructors holding long poles aloft with the ribbon across the top.

Turfield was always very good at airspeed control and said,

"Hell, I'll show you guys how to land right on the stripe." So he borrowed a friend's J-5 Cub (not mine) and flew around the pattern, controlling his airspeed to just a few miles per hour above stall speed. As he approached the stripe, he slowed down even more and landed exactly on the stripe. Except it wasn't a landing, it was "an arrival." He had dropped the airplane a few feet higher than it was designed to land, and the landing gear collapsed, leaving Turfield in an aero-sled, which only slid about fifty feet after the "arrival."

The airplane wasn't seriously damaged, but Turfield paid for all the beer at the crab feast that day. During his free repairs to the airplane he found that someone had installed J-3 landing gear on this much heavier Cub, and it couldn't take the 3-foot drop.

I regret to report that Turfield suddenly died on Sunday, May 24. 1998 shortly after working in his flower garden. This aviation pioneer was a premier mechanic even before the Second World War. He served in the Army in that capacity. I was his friend for thirty-nine years. He was 85 years old when he died.

When the McDonald-Douglas F-15 fighter was being developed, one of the early models with its tandem seating was out doing electronic tests. The test pilot sitting in the front could not be seen by the electronic control officer in the back seat because of test equipment. The tower kept a steady conversation with the pilot, telling him what maneuvers to do while the electronic control officer made notes on a large pad.

Suddenly it occurred to the electronic control officer that the tower was speaking to him directly.

"Were you calling me? If so please say again."

"Yes, Mr. Anderson, we believe that you should bail out now."

"Why should I do that?"

"Because you are alone."

"What?"

"Repeat: you are alone. The pilot accidentally activated the ejection system, and you are now alone."

After a long pause, Mr. Anderson said that he was qualified in the F-15 and that he would try to land it from the back seat.

"But you can't possibly see straight ahead from the back seat." the tower reminded him.

"I'm willing to try it." Mr. Anderson answered.

"Stand by while we get crash equipment in place."

"Thanks for the confidence."

Mr. Anderson made a perfect landing, thus saving McDonald Douglas about twenty million dollars.

Frank Pleasant who owns Wheeler's Hardware store in Deale, Maryland has told me about his experience in the Army that caused him to not re-enlist. In retrospect it is rather amusing.

During his brief Army career, Frank was assigned to the Mess Hall as a server. The Mess Sergeant was a large, gruff individual that reminded Frank of the football player "Mean" Joe Green. He had stripes on his arm from shoulder to almost his wrist. Frank thought that the sergeant must have been in the Army since day one.

One day during lunch at the Officer's Mess the servers were adding corn to the plates as it was ordered, but soon ran out. So they substituted lima beans when corn was ordered.

All went well until Lt. Reich (his real name) asked Frank where was the corn that he had ordered. Frank explained that they had run out of corn and had to substitute the beans, whereupon Lt. Reich said,

"I ordered corn and I expect corn. Take this plate back to the kitchen and get me some corn."

Frank took the plate back and told the Mess Sgt. what Lt. Reich had told him.

"We're out of corn and he will have to make do with beans." Said 'Mean," Take it back to him." So Frank returned to Lt. Reich's table.

" Sir," Frank explained, " Sergeant Mean says that we are out of corn, and beans will have to do."

" Now, you hear this, Private Pleasant." Lt. Reich said as he stood up, exposing the side arm that he carried. "I gave you an order, and it was a direct order, and you will follow that order. Do you understand? "

" Yes sir, I will give Sgt. Mean your order." Frank said as he left with the plate a second time. As he re-entered the Mess Hall and gave Sgt. Mean the message, Sgt. Mean exploded in rage.

"You go out there and tell that arrogant, shavetail son of a bitch that there ain't no more corn, and he ain't going to get no corn with this damn meal." So poor private Frank returned once more to Lt. Reich's table.

" Sir, Sgt. Mean says to tell you that there is no more corn, and Lima beans will have to do." At this, Lt. Reich slowly stood up, letting his hand slide across his pistol holster and patted it twice for emphasis.

"Private Pleasant, an officer has given you a direct order, and you have deliberately disobeyed that order. You have one more chance to return to the Mess Hall and when you come back there will be corn on this plate. Do you understand me?"

"Yes sir." Frank responded as he returned for the third time to the Mess Hall.

Near the entrance to the Mess Hall were three large GI garbage cans that the soldiers scraped their plates into. Frank dragged one can into the Mess Hall out of sight of the diners and when he returned to the dining area, the smug Lt. Reich had his corn.

Chapter 37

Afterthoughts

In my life I have always been interested in Archeology, Astronomy and Aviation. In the numerous talks that I give annually I mention that my hobbies all start with the letter A. I haven't gotten into the Booze, Brawls or Bimbos yet.

In 1975 our Anne Arundel Chapter of the Archeological Society of Maryland hosted the annual meeting of that society. We used the fellowship hall of St. James Church at Tracy's Landing, just three miles up the hill from Deale. Marjorie and I did most of the local arrangements, and since I was president of the chapter, I decided to try my hand at another poem for the occasion. It took me an hour or so, and I managed to write what I thought was a decent tribute to archeologists. It has been well received, but I submit it here for the readers to form their own opinion.

THE ARCHEOLOGIST

I walk the fields, I search the streams
To seek the Ancient's hopes and dreams.
An odd shaped stone: a telltale clue,
Bits of charcoal, I pursue.

He left no sign, no written word,
The voice is gone the woodland heard,
This Ancient One who left behind,
These meager clues for me to find.

But never shall I see his face,
I'll never know his noble race.
But still I seek to find his way,
While seeking mine from day to day.

Not knowing what fate to him befell,
The mists of time hide all too well.
But meaning from this life unknown
May add meaning to my own.

In the past few years I have received the County's highest award for preservation activities, and have received the State's highest award for archeological preservation.

I am proud of these awards that were presented by my peers.

In December 1997, I wrote another poem, which I called "The Cruise From Hell."

Jack McKibben and Gina Rankins offered to deliver a yacht from Deale to Ft. Lauderdale, Florida. They started out on November 29th and immediately started having trouble. In the Norfolk area they had such vibrations that it shook the pictures off the walls, so Jack jumped overboard to check the props and shafts. Nothing was in disorder, but that night a freezing rain covered the decks and the wind made navigating very difficult. In North Carolina they stopped and had the boat hauled to check the props and shafts. Finding nothing wrong, they continued on, only to run into a terrific fog bank. Before the fog gave out they ran into horizontal rain which inundated them with three inches of rain every day for four days. One day they couldn't start the port engine.

We were getting daily reports of the latest fiascoes, so I took a couple of hours and wrote the poem which can be sung to the tune Oh! Susanna. I framed and hung in his kitchen so they would see it when they got back. Jack is a retired pilot with United Airlines. Here is that poem called:

THE CRUISE FROM HELL The odyssey of Gina and Jack

AHOY, AHOY! THE MIZZENMAST: AVAST THE POOPDECK
    ICE,
BELAY THOSE TURNING WHEELS, AND CAST THOSE
    FATEFUL DICE.

OH, SEE THE FOG BANK COMING, OH, HEAR THE WARN-
    ING BELL
WE'RE ON OUR WAY TO SOUTHLAND ON THE WINTER
    CRUISE FROM HELL.

WE DON'T KNOW WHERE WE'RE HEADED, NOR EVEN
    WHERE WE'VE BEEN,
THAR SHE BLOWS, PORT ENGINE FAILS, THE SUN WE
    HAVEN'T SEEN.

OH, SEE THE SHOALS A-COMING, OH, SEE THE BILLOWS
    SWELL,
WE'RE ON OUR WAY TO SOUTHLAND ON THE WINTER
    CRUISE FROM HELL.

VIBRATION IN THE GALLEY, WITH HORIZONTAL RAIN,
WITH SCUPPERS OVER-FLOWING, WE'RE ON THE BOUND-
    ING MAIN.

OH, SEE THE SKIPPER OVERBOARD, OH, HEAR THE FIRST
    MATE YELL,
WE'RE ON OUR WAY TO SOUTHLAND ON THE WINTER
    CRUISE FROM HELL.

THE MARKERS ARE MISTAKEN, THE CHANNEL ISN'T
    THERE,
HELP IS NOT FORTHCOMING, AND WE'RE GETTING MAL-
    DE-MER.

OH, SEE THE TIDE AGAINST US, OH, HEAR THE WINDS
PELL-MELL,
WE'RE ON OUR WAY TO SOUTHLAND ON THE WINTER
CRUISE FROM HELL.

On June 18, 1998 The Federal Aviation Administration presented me with their Wright Brothers Memorial Master Aviator Award.
It is given to those who soloed more than fifty years ago and who remained active in aviation all those years. Since I had a current flight
physical and biennial flight review, Jack McKibben decided that I
should have the award. The award included a plaque and a golden
eagle pin. The award was given to me fifty-five years and one day
after my solo.

All forms of science fascinate me, but as far as astronomy is
concerned, I guess that I'm a sort of maverick. I have never claimed
to be a scientist, but not even for an instant did I ever believe in the
Big Bang theory of evolution of the universe. I dismiss it as just an
expansion of the old, discredited, Geocentric theory of ancient times.
In the first place, it doesn't make sense that all matter in the cosmos
could evolve from a singularity, or a pinpoint. The entire concept of
a "Big Bang" is based solely on the "Red Shift" to indicate speeds of
expansion of the Universe. I believe that this is merely a misreading
of the red shift, which might indicate distance to a particular galaxy,
not its speed away from our galaxy

The scientists who can't even tell me what gravity is, expects
me to believe that there was a beginning, and will be an end. This
is probably because the human mind cannot conceive of: Forever;
Endless; Nothing; or Emptiness.

Place your imagination into the farthest galaxy that can be seen
by the Hubble telescope. Then in a straight line, do this over and
over from one galaxy to the next. After a billion times, I believe that
you are no closer to the end of the universe than when you started
your journey. There will still be old, spiral galaxies doing their own
thing, just as our own Milky Way galaxy is doing.

I contend that the universe has always been here and will always
be here, and is endless. It's rather like Moses said when asked by

the Israelites, "Where did God come from?" and Moses replied that
God has always been here and will be here forever. Ask some of
these scientists to tell you what gravity is, and they can only de-
scribe gravitation.

It takes a galaxy billions of years to form into a spiral configuration, yet the Hubble telescope still sees spiral galaxies even to the
"edge" of the universe. If the big bang theory held water, the outer
limits of space should show galaxies in a diffuse pattern, just starting to acquire their spiral shape, which they do not. It would be
ironic if the Hubble telescope should disprove the big bang theory,
since the man that the telescope was named after was one of the
first proponents of the "Big Bang" theory. The world has been so
inundated in Big Bang theory that it is almost dogma, and no other
theories are tolerated.

I also don't believe in "Black Holes" or "Worm Holes" even
though they have been "Proven" by astro-scientists. I believe that
the nearest thing to a black hole would occur at the center of a spiral
galaxy or in the core of an atom. However, it is more likely, in my
view, that there is a giant pinwheel effect of unimaginable speed and
temperature at the center of spiral galaxies. As star orbits decay this
"Pin-Wheel" would be gobbling up stars at a fairly rapid rate and
spewing them out as gas and rubble along the galactic plane where
second generation stars, such as our sun, are born. This scenario is
a simplistic description of the "Steady-state" theory that I subscribe
to.

Distances are so vast, even in our own galaxy, that mankind will
never visit another solar system, at least not in the next thousand
years or more. Such a voyage would require several hundred years
to go from earth to the nearest sun-like star, which is about seven
light years distant. Exceeding the speed of light is the stuff of Star
Trek so what would be the purpose of sending a message to that star
if the answer came after fourteen years even if answered promptly?

Do I believe in UFOs? Yes. From outer space? No. I keep an
open mind about such things, but a Being from another planet has
never approached me that I know of. I believe that there is life on
other planets in every galaxy, but I doubt that we will ever have
physical contact with any of them. These "happenings" make good

reading or movie watching but must be treated as the fantasy they presently are.

As far as gravity is concerned, I believe it to be a particle rather than a wave, or ray. These energy particles pack the universe, and are being pulled into atoms that convert their slight mass into heat. As these particles are fed into the 'black-hole' nucleus of the atom, which spins at six or more billion revolutions per second, the lost mass carries everything with it, like flowing water, thus creating gravity. These particles, like electrons, act as a wave, and are the cause of speed limits in the universe. Just as a jet plane meets extra resistance when exceeding the speed of sound, these particles limit all speeds to the speed of light, which is the maximum speed that the particles can be pushed aside. At the speed of light, any mass becomes infinite as Einstein has hypothesized, and the atoms (mass) themselves are destroyed and converted to heat. It would take immeasurable numbers of atoms to create any measurable heat, but without this process of converting mass to energy, the temperature throughout the universe would be absolute zero. The planet Jupiter emits more heat than it receives from the sun because of this process, and probably the Earth's molten core is a result of the same process.

Perhaps the theory of the ether that was proposed in early times but later abandoned, should be re-examined.

Even though I keep an open mind, I don't believe in ghosts, since I have never encountered one. I have never seen any convincing evidence for the pseudo-sciences of telepathy, numerology, astrology, fortune telling, or precognition. When a fortuneteller gives me tomorrow's lottery number, then I will start to believe. It's a bit like long-range weather forecasting in an Almanac. We tend to remember the hits and forget the misses, which makes the forecaster look good.

Numbers are a handy invention of man and the universe knows nothing of them. Man is the only entity in the universe that has a need for numbers as far as we know. Thus the bad luck associated with Friday the 13th is a myth invented by superstitious people. The world will never come to an end because of a number.

As the reader can see, I have a rather complex mind, which I exercise quite a bit. At those rare times that I have insomnia, I lie awake and solve all the problems of the universe, but worry very little.

I believe that despite its flaws, the United States of America is the greatest country the Earth has ever known.

In 1997 I passed my second class (Commercial) flight physical with no restrictions, even for eyesight. I did the same on January 4th 2000, and again on February 2nd 2002. I did the same in February, 2004. I remain in good health, play a mean game of Ping-Pong, fly once in awhile, travel whenever we can, work on and fly my PA 12 Super Cruiser Cub, and still work a bit.

Marjorie and I celebrate our 50th wedding anniversary on November 20, 2004, We still live in the same house we moved into after our wedding in 1954. We are proud of our three children that we raised here, as they have never been in trouble with the law, don't smoke, and all have good jobs.

On May 22, 2000, Marjorie and I flew to Zurich Switzerland to visit a friend who showed us the sights for four days and then drove us to Liechtenstein for lunch. We then drove to Salzburg, Austria and saw all the sights for four more days after which we flew to London via Frankfort, Germany. In London we met with the tour group that we had preceded. It was a nostalgia tour for the 303rd Bomb group. We stayed in Cambridge for a few days and then drove in two busses to our old air base. When we passed through the gates there were about two hundred American military personnel in full dress uniform saluting as we drove slowly past. Our old air base is now the JAC or Joint Analysis Center that does satellite imaging for NATO and is always commanded by an American Military colonel or equivalent rank. We were to attend a hangar dance on that Saturday and when we arrived, they let us off the busses near the hangar. We milled around for a short while and then a bagpiper escorted us inside. Inside, we did not realize that there were fifteen hundred British citizens. As we entered, they all applauded constantly for twenty minutes until we were all seated. I doubt if there was a dry eye in the place. About a hundred or so were in forties costumes to pay us homage. There were about one hundred seventy in our group that included about seventy of us veterans. The British will never forget our effort in the war. Nothing could top this reception, but some of us continued our tour by going to the Normandy Beaches near Caen where we spent three nights and four days. (Caen was the site of my last mission on August 8, 1944).

After this we went on to Paris for four more days staying in the Hilton Hotel almost under the Eiffel Tower before returning to the U.S. on June 14.

I was elected President of the 303rd Bomb Group Association for he year 2001. We have several thousand members worldwide including veterans and families and friends of the 303rd. Under the direction of Gary Moncur we have a web site of over two thousand pages at {303rdbga.com} that the reader is invited to visit and comment.

The nostalgia for the "Good Old Days" is enjoyable when meeting old war buddies, but that was then, and we have to live in our own time. Perhaps we subconsciously know that our future is not nearly as long as our past, and so we sometimes try to bring back the glory days of our youth. "Therein lies the rub," as Shakespeare wrote.

About the only good thing about the "Good Old Days" is, we were much younger then.

The End (almost)

ISBN 141202501-X